The Problem of the Picts

THE PROBLEM OF THE PICTS

F.T. Wainwright (editor)
R.W. Feachem
K.H. Jackson
S. Piggott
R.B.K. Stevenson

MELVEN
M
PRESS

PERTH 1980

First published by Thomas Nelson 1955

ISBN 0 906664 07 1

This edition published by The Melven Press,
176 High Street, Perth, Scotland.

The publisher wishes to acknowledge R. Young of Inverness for allowing them use of his copy.

PREFACE

THIS is a composite work, and my first duty is to thank my fellow authors. Without their initial co-operation the idea behind it would have been stillborn, but even they do not know how deep I have fallen in their debt during the past three or four years.

We set out to examine the Pictish problem from different angles, in the belief that a team of scholars might advance further than a single scholar. We have tried to bring together the archaeological, historical and linguistic evidence, and that has made us more than usually careful about terminology. We use the name *Picti*, for example, in its historical sense as it was applied to certain peoples in northern Britain from A.D. 297 onwards. This is a technical limitation, perhaps, and it may appear pedantic, but we have thought it wise to distinguish between the historical Picts and those peoples who, though they may be the same in race and culture, belong to the period before the name *Picti* appears in the historical record. Peoples who are or may be ancestral to the historical Picts, as so defined, we describe as "proto-Picts". We believe we cannot be too careful at this stage.

Who were the Picts? And where did they come from? These questions lie at the heart of the Pictish problem, and we have not set ourselves to answer them. We have not shied away from them when they impinge upon our theme, as they do, but as a general rule we have kept our eyes on the historical Picts, and we have tried to isolate the various features characteristic of them and of the area occupied by them in the period A.D. 300–850. That has been our aim—not to write a volume which might be entitled *The Origin of the Picts*, though we hope we have brought a little nearer the day when such a volume can be written.

There is no chapter on ecclesiastical developments in Pictland, not because the subject is controversial but because it does not directly concern our theme. And we have not attempted to revise the work of Skene or to write a coherent history of the Picts. Our survey of the historical Picts and historical Pictland is designed simply to clear the ground for some future attempt to deal with fundamental questions which must be settled before a history of the Picts can be written.

Our several chapters were written independently of each other, and they were in typescript early in 1953. Students of the Picts seldom find themselves in agreement, and it is worth recording that in our informal discussions we were surprised, again and again, to find that our different approaches were leading to the same conclusions. A few minor divergences of opinion remain, but they are quite overshadowed by the overwhelming weight of our agreement. This is a new thing among students of the Picts, and we are encouraged by it to hope that our approaches are soundly based.

When the typescript of this book went to the compositor in 1953, its bibliography contained a dozen items which had not at that time appeared in print. Despite the fact that our publishers have spared neither trouble nor expense, the difficulties which inevitably attend the production of the first volume in a new series have delayed its appearance. We do not think, however, that it is yet out of date.

The compilation of the index presented exceptional problems, and my wife took this burden from me. It is her only formal contribution to the volume, but all who write will know how much more important are the informal contributions of wives.

F. T. W.

31 May 1954

CONTENTS

LIST OF PLATES

LIST OF ILLUSTRATIONS IN TEXT

LIST OF MAPS

Chapter I

THE PICTS AND THE PROBLEM

F.T. Wainwright

AN extreme form of an extreme argument declares that the Picts never existed outside the imagination of Roman panegyrists. If that were so, there would be no Pictish problem, and one writer joyfully seizes the opportunity to dispose of "an insuperable difficulty" by stating simply that "the Pictish story is a myth". Unfortunately, we cannot escape so easily as that. A similar argument would deny the existence of the Welsh peoples because they do not call themselves Welshmen—their preference for their own name, *Cymry*, is understandable, especially as "Welsh" is an English word (OE. *Wealas*) which means "foreigners" or "strangers". The argument is absurd and may be ignored.

Much more reasonable is the view that there is no Pictish problem in archaeology because archaeology knows nothing of the Picts. It is true that the people known to historians as Picts have not yet been recognised or satisfactorily identified in archaeology, and it follows that words like "Pict" and "Pictish" sit awkwardly in an archaeological context. Or, to put the same point in another form, archaeologists who value their reputation are reluctant to introduce the Picts into archaeological discussions. But a people or group of peoples widely known as the Picts undoubtedly existed, and there are at least archaeological aspects to the problems that have so long surrounded them.

The problem of their name is primarily philological, and it is raised here in its simplest form. Is the name *Picti* no more than the Romans' descriptive term for a "painted people"? Or does it represent a Latinised version of a native name, perhaps the Picts' own name for themselves? Isidore of Seville, writing soon after A.D. 600, tells us that the Picts take their name from the fact that their bodies bear designs pricked into their skins by needles. It is true that Isidore, inventing and retailing many a dubious story, is not a reliable guide in these matters, but in this instance he seems to have hit upon a reasonable explanation. It is a fairly obvious explanation, of course, even if it is no more than an unsupported guess. But it is not an unsupported guess. There was a tradition, over six hundred years old, that the inhabitants of Britain specialised in the practice of applying pigments to their skins. Julius Caesar had written: "All the *Britanni* paint themselves with woad which produces a bluish colouring."[1] And after Caesar there is no break in the series of writers—Ovid, Martial, Solinus, Herodian, Claudian, Jordanes—who mention this colourful practice. It may be significant that the later writers in this series refer specifically to tattooing, puncturing as distinct from painting, and that they refer specifically to the inhabitants of the northern parts of Britain.[2] Isidore's explanation of *Picti* is probably that which was widely believed in his own day; to all who understood Latin the word would immediately call to mind a "painted people". This would remain true even if it could be proved that *Picti* originally represented a native name which, when Latinised, bore a fortuitous resemblance to the Latin adjective *pictus*. W. J. Watson has argued that a native name does indeed lie behind the Latin *Picti*,[3] but philologists are not agreed and the whole question must be regarded as *sub judice*.[4]

The name of the Picts may be in doubt, but their existence as a people or group of peoples is not. We know what they were called in Latin, Old English, Old Norse, Old Irish and Old Welsh. The fact that we do not know their own name for themselves is tantalising, but it does not destroy or even impair their claim to a historical existence.

The Picts are a historical people in the sense that they appear in historical sources[5] and are recognised by historians. They are first mentioned by name in a panegyric by Eumenius (A.D. 297)[6] who associates the *Picti* with the *Hiberni* as enemies of the *Britanni*. A few years later, in another panegyric, occurs a reference to "the woods and marshes of the *Caledones* and other Picts".[7] From A.D. 360 onwards references increase in number, and the *Picti* are usually associated with the *Scotti* and the *Saxones* as hostile forces attacking the Roman province of Britain. Ammianus Marcellinus,[8] for example, tells us that the Scots and the Picts ravaged the districts near the Roman wall (*loca limitibus vicina*), and a little later he speaks of the

[1] BG V.14. (For a full list of abbreviations, authorities and references see below, under References and Abbreviations.)

[2] The literary sources referred to in this paragraph may be consulted in MHB xxxii (Julius Caesar), lxxxix (Ovid), x (Solinus), xci (Martial), lxiv (Herodian), xcviii (Claudian), lxxxiii (Jordanes). Isidore (Origines XIX.23) is most easily consulted in Holder II.995, or Chronicles 395.

[3] W. J. Watson (1926), 67–8.

[4] T. F. O'Rahilly (1946), 532–3. See also K. H. Jackson below, pp. 159–60.

[5] Conveniently brought together in Holder II.993–9, and in MHB i–cxlv.

[6] Holder II.993–4; MHB lxvii.

[7] *Caledonum, Pictorum aliorumque silvas et paludes* (Holder II.994); *Caledonum, aliorumque Pictorum silvas et paludes* (MHB lxix). The former reading could be translated, e.g. W. J. Watson (1926), 9, as "the *Caledones*, the Picts, and others"; but the latter reading seems to be the better.

[8] Holder II.994; MHB lxxiii.

Pecti, the *Saxones*, the *Scotti*, and the *Attacotti* as harassing the *Britanni* without intermission. He also informs us that the Picts were divided into two groups, to which he gives the names *Dicalydones* and *Verturiones*.[1] Other references, many of which are later in date than the departure of the Romans from Britain, may be consulted in Alfred Holder's *Alt-Celtischer Sprachschatz*. Gildas, Nennius, Adamnan, Bede and several Irish annalists join the growing list of writers interested in the Pictish north. All these writers were not chasing a myth. However obscure their origins and however complex their racial development, the Picts themselves are a genuine historical people.

To see them in some kind of historical context it is most convenient to consider the political situation in Britain as it was in the early years of the eighth century. By that time the Picts, a Christian people, had achieved a recognisable political unity and possessed kings, customs, and even traditions, of their own. Bede, who died in 735, recognised four peoples in Britain—the Britons, the Picts, the Scots and the Angles.[2]

The Britons were Celtic-speaking peoples who reached this island in a series of archaeologically recognisable invasions during the centuries before the arrival of the Romans. It has been suggested [3] that the last of these invaders, the *Belgae*, arrived only a few years before—some of them even a few years after—Julius Caesar's expeditions of 55–54 B.C. The Romans found the Britons organised under their rulers in a number of native states or tribal groups (e.g. *Atrebates*, *Brigantes*, *Iceni* and *Silures*) which covered what is now England and Wales and stretched northwards into Scotland. When the Roman armies withdrew, in the fifth century, the native kingdoms reappeared but quickly proved themselves quite unable to hold their own with the barbarians —Picts, Scots, Anglo-Saxons and others—whose incursions had contributed to the collapse of Roman power in Britain. During the fifth and sixth centuries the whole of north Britain up to the Forth-Clyde line seems to have been dominated by native British kingdoms. Their names and the names of their ruling families are preserved in genealogical compilations and early Welsh poems, and their peoples were known collectively to their southern kinsfolk as *Gwyr y Gogledd*, "The Men of the North". But we have little precise information about these

[1] *Picti in duas gentes divisi, Dicalydonas et Verturiones.*

[2] Bede (III.6) writes of "*omnes nationes et prouincias Brittaniae, quae in* IIII *linguas, id est Brettonum, Pictorum, Scottorum, et Anglorum, diuisae sunt*". He writes of language groups, but no doubt he was thinking also of political groups, and, rightly or wrongly, of racial groups. In another place (I.1) he adds a fifth language, Latin, but he makes it quite clear that he includes it only as an ecclesiastical language "made common to all the others by the study of the Scriptures".

[3] C. F. C. Hawkes and G. C. Dunning (1930), 150–335.

northern Britons, and we certainly cannot indicate on a map the boundaries of their various and probably varying kingdoms.[1]

There was, for example, a British kingdom centred on Edinburgh. Its people were known as *Gododdin*, a name which ties them firmly to the **Votadini* (Ptolemy's 'Ωταδινοί) who had occupied the whole area from the Newcastle Tyne to the Forth. Their last appearance in history occurs in the poem *Y Gododdin*,[2] which celebrates a gloriously suicidal attack against the Angles in what must be the first half of the reign of Æthelfrith (592–616), the Anglian ruler who first united the two Northumbrian kingdoms of Bernicia and Deira. The shattered remnant of another British kingdom, Elmet, held out a few years longer in the fastnesses of the central Pennines until it was finally destroyed by Æthelfrith's successor, Edwin. From 600 onwards the Angles thrust continually forward, westwards and northwards, pushing back the Britons and obliterating their kingdoms. All shared the fate of Gododdin and Elmet except what became the kingdom of Strathclyde. The Britons of Strathclyde, alone of British communities outside Wales, survived the consolidation of the Anglo-Saxon settlements in Britain. They were ruled from their ancient fortress at Dumbarton, "the fortress of the Britons". Dumbarton stands on the north bank of the Clyde, from which it is clear that the Britons also controlled the area immediately north of that river. For three hundred years after the reign of Æthelfrith they played a minor role in northern affairs, but they managed to retain their identity, if not always their independence. In the tenth century they enjoyed a brief revival of military ambition which saw the temporary extension of their power to the south of the Solway. And then they were absorbed into the Anglo-Picto-Scottish kingdom of Scotland.

The Picts in the age of Bede lived north of the Forth-Clyde line, and so far as we can see that line represents their traditional frontier throughout the whole of their historical existence, or at least from the departure of the Romans in the fifth century to the disappearance of their kingdom as a separate political entity in the ninth. There is a general presumption that they, like the Britons, were a Celtic or at least a Celticised people in the sense that they spoke a Celtic language. But this presumption has been attacked from more than one quarter, and for the moment the question of their language, like the question of their origins and archaeological affinities, must be left on one side.

[1] See, for example, W. J. Watson (1926), 127–9, 339–45; H. M. Chadwick (1949), 142–52; and references.

[2] *Canu Aneirin*, ed. Ifor Williams, Cardiff 1938. For English summaries see K. H. Jackson (1939), 25–34; and C. A. Gresham (1942), 237–57. For archaeological evidence of the **Votadini* see A. H. A. Hogg (1943), 136–47; and (1951), 200–20.

By the time of Bede it is clear that the Picts were a single people and that they "formed a definite kingdom, not a mere congeries of tribes".[1] Politically they were strong enough to hold their own against the Northumbrian Angles whom they had already thrown back to the Forth, their traditional boundary to the south.

The third northern people were the Scots, Celtic incomers from Ireland. They are first mentioned by Ammianus Marcellinus as barbarians who, with the Picts and others, were raiding Roman Britain shortly after the middle of the fourth century; but this is not their first appearance in this role, for it is clear that the *Scotti* of Ammianus are the same people as the *Hiberni* of Eumenius.[2] There are traditions, badly preserved but not contemptible, which have been held to support the view that some of these Irish marauders were already settling in east-central Scotland while the Romans were still in Britain.[3] But we are not immediately concerned with sporadic Scottish settlement in the fourth century or with the traces of it that may or may not be found in place-names and archaeology as well as in history and legend. Far more important was the foundation in the fifth century of the Scottish kingdom of Dalriada. It was a small kingdom, concentrated in Argyll and the adjacent islands, lying north of the British kingdom of Strathclyde and in what seems to have been Pictish territory. Dunadd was one of its military centres, and Dunollie was another. Its religious centre was Iona, from which Columba, founder and first abbot, carried Christianity to the northern Pictish peoples in the sixth century. The ecclesiastical supremacy of Iona gave to the Scots of Dalriada a prestige which extended far beyond the immediate confines of their tiny kingdom and helps to explain the cultural and linguistic influence which they later exercised in north Britain.

For some time after their arrival in Britain the Scots of Dalriada, owing some kind of allegiance to the parent kingdom in Ireland, seem not to have greatly alarmed their neighbours. Suddenly they appear as an aggressive and formidable people under Aedan mac Gabrain, who became their king in 574. Aedan fought a campaign in the Orkneys,[4] and his forces undoubtedly penetrated eastwards along the valley of the Forth.[5] He also fought a disastrous battle of "Circind",[6] an area usually identified with Angus and the Mearns. Adamnan tells of a

[1] F. M. Stenton (1943), 87.
[2] See above, p. 2.
[3] Cf. W. J. Watson (1926), 213–25; T. F. O'Rahilly (1946), 370–1; H. M. Chadwick (1949), 120–3.
[4] AU *s.a.* 579.
[5] W. J. Watson (1926), 129–30, 225; T. F. O'Rahilly (1946), 503–5; H. M. Chadwick (1949), 124–6.
[6] ATig (RC XVII.160): *i cath Chirchind.*

battle against the "*Miathi*",[1] which may well be the battle of Circind. The *Miathi*, who seem to represent the *Maeatae* of Dio Cassius,[2] may be commemorated in place-names (Dumyat and Myot Hill) near Stirling. They were apparently a Pictish people, occupying part, possibly all, of the area between the Forth and the Dee.[3] The details of Aedan's military adventures are necessarily obscure, but it is clear that he was a mighty king, aggressive if not invincible, a figure to inspire dread in his enemies. At the end of the sixth century it looked as if the Scots might become the politically dominant people in north Britain. But Aedan met more than his match in Æthelfrith who in 603 inflicted a crushing defeat on the Scots at "Degsastan",[4] dubiously identified with Dawston in Liddisdale.[5] With the defeat of Aedan the Scots lost the initiative; their strength was dissipated in local and dynastic feuds, and never again do they seem likely to dominate the political scene in north Britain. It was a king of Dalriada, nevertheless, who in the ninth century united the Pictish and Scottish peoples, and so ensured that north Britain should be called Scotland.

The Anglo-Saxons, the fourth people in Britain, spoke a Germanic not a Celtic language. Classical authors list them with the Picts and Scots as raiders of Roman Britain in the fourth century, and like the Scots they turned from raiding to permanent settlement in the fifth century. Like the Scots they came from across the sea, but direct from the Continent, not from Ireland. They pushed westwards, driving the Britons before them into Cornwall and Wales, and established such southern English kingdoms as Kent, Sussex, East Anglia and Wessex. We are concerned only with the northern half of the island and with the two Anglian kingdoms of Bernicia and Deira, which were united by Æthelfrith to form the single kingdom of Northumbria.[6] Bamburgh was the ancient Bernician "capital", another rock-girt stronghold like Dumbarton in Strathclyde and Dunadd in Dalriada. From coastal positions the Northumbrian Angles, like their kinsmen in the south, pushed westwards, destroying Gododdin, Elmet and other British kingdoms which existed in a twilight of post-Roman independence. They reached the western sea in Lancashire and Cumberland, and so isolated the Britons of Strathclyde from the Britons of Wales. Aedan mac Gabrain, flushed with northern victories, tried to halt the Anglian advance, but he was decisively defeated in 603 at Degsastan, and by

[1] Adamnan I.8: *De Bello Miathorum.*

[2] Preserved as Μαιάται by Xiphilinus. Cf. Holder II.388–9; MHB lx–lxi.

[3] See below, pp. 51–3.

[4] Bede I.34.

[5] Max Förster (1941), 796–811, has perhaps resolved the obvious philological objection to this identification, but the positive evidence in its favour remains slight.

[6] For the early history of the English kingdoms see F. M. Stenton (1943), R. G. Collingwood and J. N. L. Myres (1936), and R. H. Hodgkin (1935).

the middle of the century the kingdom of Northumbria stretched without a break from the Humber to the Forth.

The seventh century was "the age of Northumbrian supremacy". Æthelfrith's successors, Edwin (616–33), Oswald (633–42), Oswiu (642–70) and Ecgfrith (670–85), each in turn ranked as the strongest ruler in Britain. Bede tells us that Edwin was more powerful than any Anglo-Saxon king before him.[1] To Oswald he assigns an overlordship similar to that of Edwin, except that it seems to embrace the Picts and the Scots as well as the English and the Britons.[2] Oswiu, like all Northumbrian kings, had to contend with rivals south of the Humber, but in the north he was able to transform Oswald's vague overlordship into a political reality. "To a very great extent he subjugated and made tributary the Pictish and the Scottish peoples who possess the northern parts of Britain."[3] That this involved annexation as distinct from overlordship is strongly suggested by the description of Wilfrid as Bishop "of the Church of York, not only of all the Northumbrians but also of the Picts as far as King Oswiu was able to extend his authority".[4] Ecgfrith maintained his control over the newly acquired territory and no doubt tried to increase it. Early in his reign he crushed a revolt of the Picts, who "were threatening to cast off the yoke of slavery", an incident recorded by Eddius Stephanus in language which shows that the Northumbrian campaign was directed against what was regarded as a rebellion of subject peoples.[5] An oblique reference to the political situation may be seen in the establishment of a separate Northumbrian bishopric for the Picts: in 681 Trumwine became bishop "of the province of the Picts which was at that time subject to the authority of the Angles".[6] That Trumwine's ecclesiastical jurisdiction extended beyond the Forth is proved by the events of 685.[7] It is quite clear that during the second half of the seventh century Oswiu and Ecgfrith, not content with the vague overlordship exercised by their predecessors, had pushed northwards to annex Pictish territory beyond the Forth.

The aggressions of Oswiu and Ecgfrith mark the peak of Northumbrian ascendancy in north Britain. The Picts, the Scots and the Britons were all reduced to a state of formal subjection, and the Picts had suffered further by the annexation of part of their territory. But the Northumbrians had overstepped more than the traditional boundary of the Picts. They had overstepped also the limits of their own resources,

[1] Bede II.5, 9.
[2] Bede II.5, and III.6.
[3] Bede II.5. Bede also (III.24) says: [*Osuiu*] *etiam gentem Pictorum maxima ex parte regno Anglorum subiecit.*
[4] Bede IV.3.
[5] Eddius XIX.
[6] Bede IV.12.
[7] See next paragraph.

and they were unable to maintain the position won by Ecgfrith. On 20 May 685 Ecgfrith was slain and the Northumbrian army was destroyed in a battle fought against the Picts at "Nechtanesmere" in Angus.[1] Bede summarises the result: the Picts recovered that part of their land which the Angles had occupied, the Scots and some of the Britons recovered their liberty, the new Pictish bishopric came to an end, and Trumwine fled south with his followers.[2]

As an incident in the development of a Northumbrian hegemony in northern Britain the battle of Nechtanesmere was an unparalleled and irretrievable disaster. But it did not break Northumbria; the line of the Forth remained the Anglo-Pictish frontier, however insecure it may have been for a few years. Bede says only that the Picts recovered their lost lands in 685. He also says that Aldfrith, Ecgfrith's successor, nobly restored the ruined kingdom, though its limits were narrower than they had been before 685.[3] It is easy to overestimate the political significance of Nechtanesmere.[4] It did not, for example, inaugurate a period of Pictish ascendancy in northern Britain. The Northumbrians seem to have been worsted again in 698,[5] but in 711 they inflicted a decisive defeat on the Picts.[6] In 740 Eadbeorht "was engaged with his army against the Picts" when the Mercians seized the opportunity to invade Northumbria.[7] In 750 he conquered Kyle and other districts (unspecified) from the Britons of Strathclyde,[8] and six years later, in alliance with the Picts, he invaded Strathclyde and received the surrender of the Britons at Dumbarton, their ancient capital on the Clyde.[9] The Northumbrians were still a power in the north. They were strong enough to hold the line of the Forth, but Nechtanesmere had proved that they could not advance beyond it without courting disaster. That is the true significance of Nechtanesmere.

The most serious menace to Northumbria came not from the Picts, or from any other northern people, but from the Anglian kingdom of Mercia. A king of Northumbria might have been able to control the far north, at least superficially, if he had not been compelled to face more powerful enemies in the south. The rivalry of Mercia, aggravated by an almost unbroken series of dynastic disturbances, sapped the strength of the Northumbrians in the eighth and ninth centuries, but they were still maintaining their grip on the lowlands of Scotland when their kingdom succumbed to Danish attacks in 867. The traditional boundary out-

[1] For details of the battle and the site see F. T. Wainwright (1948*a*), 82–97.
[2] Bede IV.24.
[3] Ibid.
[4] F. T. Wainwright (1948*a*), 96–7.
[5] Bede V.24; ATig (RC XVII.216).
[6] Bede V.24; AU *s.a.* 710; ATig (RC XVII.222); ASC *s.a.* 710.
[7] Baedae Continuatio *s.a.* 740.
[8] Baedae Continuatio *s.a.* 750.
[9] SD II.40.

lived both the kingdom of Northumbria and the kingdom of the Picts.

The independent kingdom of Northumbria came to an end in 867, by which date the kingdom of the Picts had already disappeared as a separate political entity. In or about 843 Kenneth mac Alpin, king of the Scots, became also king of the Picts, and thereafter there was only one kingdom north of the Forth-Clyde line. We are not concerned with developments after that date, but it may be remarked that the kingdom of Scotland assumed its final shape only when the ruler of the Picto-Scottish peoples became the ruler also of the Strathclyde Britons and the Northumbrian Angles, that is when the traditional Forth-Clyde boundary gave place to the Tweed-Solway "border". The acquisition of the Northumbrian lands between the Forth and the Tweed determined to a great extent the racial, cultural, linguistic and political future of Scotland. But we are concerned with the Picts; and their independent existence as a nation came to an end with the accession of Kenneth son of Alpin.

We know considerably more about the Picts than the above outline might suggest. We have lists of their kings, we know something of their political divisions, their religious movements, their dynastic rivalries and their wars against their neighbours, and we possess more than a little evidence from archaeological and linguistic survivals as well as from historical material proper. There is plenty of evidence, incomplete and intractable though it is. Wherever we turn problems confront us: sometimes the evidence is missing, sometimes it is untrustworthy, and frequently it is beyond our comprehension. The Pictish language has vanished, but if its distinguishing characteristics can be determined from the few surviving fragments, that will represent a notable advance, for a study of its linguistic affinities will undoubtedly help to answer many questions about the Picts themselves. We should like, too, fuller and more reliable information about their kings, their curious custom of matrilinear succession, their wars, internal and external, the extent of their kingdom and the main centres of their power, their political and constitutional arrangements, their economy, their social structure, their cultural achievements, their paganism and their Christianity, and above all we should like to know who they were, where they came from, and how they were related to the various peoples who lived in Scotland before the name *Picti* is mentioned by classical authors.

Who were the Picts? This is the most difficult question of all. The "simple and obvious" reply, as given by Fraser, is that they were a people who inhabited part of Scotland from the third to the ninth century and were known to foreigners as *Picti*.[1] We may accept this as a definition of the historical Picts, but it is not an answer to the question. What we want to know is whether the Picts were a homogeneous or a heterogeneous people and where they or their constituent elements came from. Or, to put the point in another way, who were the Picts before they became known as the Picts? The question is fundamentally one of race and origin, and many answers, too many answers, have been offered. Bede tells us that the Picts are said (*ut perhibent*) to have come from Scythia, that they landed first in northern Ireland, where they obtained wives from the Scots, and that they then settled in the northern parts of Britain, the southern parts being already occupied by the Britons.[2] Bede's conception of historical accuracy and method is higher than that of many modern writers, and he is careful to indicate that the attribution of a Scythian origin to the Picts is based upon a report or tradition. He seems to have got the story ultimately from an Irish source, and his version of it in turn influenced later Irish scribes. At best it represents a tradition current among the Irish, and perhaps also among the Picts; but no concrete evidence has yet been produced to support the suggestion that the Picts came from Scythia, and the story must be dismissed as legend or literary invention.

In modern times other answers have been given. The Picts have been described as "Goedels", as "Brythons", as Celts who spoke a Gallo-Brittonic dialect allied to but distinct from both Gaulish and Brittonic, and as a pre-Celtic people of non-Indo-European origin. They have been brought to Britain in the Early Bronze Age, the Middle Bronze Age, the Late Bronze Age, and in various phases of the Early Iron Age. They have been associated with the beaker-folk, the broch-builders, the souterrain-dwellers, and the men who threw up the vitrified forts; and affinities have been found for them among the Eskimoes, the Finns, and the Illyrians.[3] There is apparently no limit to the theories that may be devised by those who delight in making bricks without straw. Often the Pictish question has been "settled", but seldom to the satisfaction of more than one person at a time. Adolf Mahr claimed to be able "to settle the archaeological background of the Pictish question, with all that it implies also for the ethnography of Great Britain": he identified the Picts with what he called the "River-ford People" whom he described as "epi-mesolithic" and whom he brought to Ireland from Scotland and to Scotland from the "Forest

[1] J. Fraser (1927), 173.
[2] Bede I.I.
[3] See, for example, the works of H. M. Chadwick, V. G. Childe, T. Rice Holmes, Henri Hubert, Joseph Loth, R. A. S. Macalister, Eoin MacNeill, Adolf Mahr, T. F. O'Rahilly, Julius Pokorny, Joseph Raftery and W. J. Watson.

Cultures".[1] Joseph Raftery professes to admire Mahr's "brilliant exposition of the Riverford People", but he silently telescopes the centuries and suggests that the Picts were invaders from England who about 175 B.C. introduced into Ireland what he calls an Irish "Iron Age II culture".[2] As another Irishman scathingly says, "You pay your money, and you take your choice".[3] Here, fortunately, we are not compelled to examine these and other opinions on the origin of the Picts. There is a great deal of truth in some of them, but in others the element of fiction, even fantasy, is so pronounced that Bede's story of Scythia appears (by comparison only) to be a model of scientific sobriety. They have been castigated with a severity no less entertaining than the ingenuity of the inventors who sponsored them; O'Rahilly's searing strictures, for example, are not altogether undeserved.[4]

Fundamental to this broad question of race and origin is the separate and narrower question of the Pictish language, around which has grown up a vast and not infrequently acrimonious literature. The problem of what languages or dialects were spoken in Pictland between A.D. 300 and A.D. 850 is immediately germane to our subject, and it is discussed at length below.[5] But firm conclusions on the race and origin of the Picts are at present beyond the horizon of attainment, and that is why, as explained above,[6] a solution of the problem is not attempted in this volume. The urgent requirement at this stage is to isolate the cultural and linguistic characteristics of the historical Picts and Pictland, so that in the future scholars may advance towards problems of race and origin from positions strengthened by a positive knowledge of what are or may be significant features in the terrain of available material.

It should be borne in mind that the evidence, from Julius Caesar onwards, is against the view that the Picts as known to history were a single homogeneous people. It is true that Bede and most writers after him refer to the Picts as though they arrived in Britain by a migratory movement comparable to those which brought the Scots and the Anglo-Saxons, but this is mere inference, apparently an argument from the known to the unknown, depending upon a parallel for which there seems to be no basis of fact. Dr W. Douglas Simpson, following T. Rice Holmes and others, neatly summarised modern opinion when he said that "Pict is a name without racial content".[7] Today philologists, archaeologists and historians, differing among themselves at many points, would probably all agree that the historical Picts were a hetero-

[1] A. Mahr (1937), 327–31.
[2] J. Raftery (1940), 275–81.
[3] T. F. O'Rahilly (1946), 434.
[4] T. F. O'Rahilly (1946), 353–84, 419–43, 529–38.
[5] Chapter VI.
[6] See above, Preface.
[7] W. D. Simpson (1943), 83. Cf. also W. D. Simpson (1935), 40–1.

geneous people and that the antecedents of Pictland should not be sought in a single race or culture.[1] The difficulty inherent in any attempt to identify the Ptolemaic tribes with later peoples who lived in north Britain is only one of the many pieces of evidence which all point in the same direction. Without at this stage promulgating theories of Celtic "military overlords" or intrusive "warrior aristocracies", theories which are themselves based largely on inference, we may fairly conclude that the historical Picts represent a number of racial and cultural groups which impinged or were superimposed on one another in the area which we recognise as Pictland.

Similar racial complexities no doubt form the background to other historical peoples, but in England by comparison there is at least a superficial appearance of cultural unity which finds no parallel in Pictland. It would be unwise to argue that seventh-century Pictland contained more cultural groups than, say, seventh-century Sussex, and it would be absurd to imagine that Sussex possessed a material culture uniformly and ubiquitously Saxon. It seems safe to assume, nevertheless, that racial amalgamation and cultural assimilation had not proceeded so far in Pictland as in England, and to assume that the individual racial and cultural elements in the population were more evenly balanced and nearer the surface in Pictland. The Picts had achieved political unity by the seventh century, but the integration of once separate peoples and cultures seems to have been both recent and superficial. The peoples to whom Eumenius applied the collective name *Picti* at the end of the third century probably regarded themselves as separate and distinct communities bound together, if at all, only in loose confederacies summoned into existence by the menace of the Roman legions.[2] Therefore we should not despair if the archaeological and linguistic features of Pictland refuse to be forced into a single mould. We should rather expect a heterogeneous people to be represented by a heterogeneous culture. It is by isolating its various features that we may hope ultimately to answer those questions of race and origin which have been raised only to be shelved. They had to be raised, however, for they dominate the background of our approach to the historical Picts.

The evidence available for the solution of our problems falls into one or other of three main categories. There are the written records of history (such as chronicles, lives of saints, topographical surveys and

[1] See, for example, T. Rice Holmes (1907), W. J. Watson (1926), J. Fraser (1927), V. G. Childe (1935, 1940, 1946).

[2] Daniel Wilson (1851), 471–2, W. F. Skene (1876), I.121, W. D. Simpson (1935), 39, and others, have made the reasonable suggestion that the pressure of Roman arms effected a consolidation of native peoples in the north.

lists of kings), the material remains of archaeology (fortresses, burials, dwellings, pottery, ornaments and the like), and the linguistic survivals of philology (names and forms embedded in historical sources, the wide field of current place-nomenclature, and a few inscriptions carved on stone). Inevitably the categories are not mutually exclusive. The inscriptions which provide evidence for the philologist are preserved on archaeological monuments just as their written equivalents are preserved in historical sources. And the linguistic evidence which is crystallised in the historical record is controlled by and at the same time throws light upon the circumstances under which the record was compiled. The divisions are not rigid, but they are real : the three different kinds of evidence demand the application of three different sets of specialised techniques and equipment. It is this fact that gives rise to great problems when an attempt is made to co-ordinate the results and researches of archaeologists, historians and philologists.[1] It is unwise for a scholar to stray too far from fields with which he is familiar, and no problem is at once so seductive and so treacherous as that of the Picts. So many reputations have been shattered that only the confident and the careless will today venture into this graveyard of rejected theories.

But it is here, as in no other period, that the need for co-operation and co-ordination is most urgent. The archaeologist may feel himself competent to deal alone with the remote ages of prehistory, and the historian may affect to disdain assistance in the study of a modern period, but in the gloomiest shadows of the Dark Ages no single scholar would claim to be self-sufficient. Specialists of different disciplines, bringing different methods to the varied assortment of evidence, must pool their resources and tackle together the problems that none of them alone can solve.

Terminology becomes doubly important when the attempt is made to co-ordinate the results of separate lines of study. The historian writes of Picts, Scots, Romans and Normans without caring greatly about the racial composition of what he has recognised as historical and political groupings. The archaeologist is compelled, by his material and by his method no less than by his training in prehistory, to refer to past peoples under such names as beaker-folk, urn-folk, sword-bearers, broch-builders and souterrain-dwellers. He is usually aware that he is merely describing culture complexes, and the use of such labels, which add nothing to the discussion, is both convenient and unobjectionable. Confusion sets in when he or another scholar rashly

[1] For a fuller discussion of the difficulties of co-ordination see F. T. Wainwright (1949), 76–82.

equates historical and archaeological conceptions, or is tempted to read racial or political implications into what are no more than cultural labels. To enliven the dry bones of the past by investing them with political intentions or a racial background is a hazardous proceeding the attractions of which are not always sufficiently resisted.

Terms like Celtic, Gallo-Brittonic, Gaulish, Brittonic and Goedelic are used by the philologist to describe languages and dialects. A Goedel is a man who speaks a Goedelic form of Celtic—no more and no less. It is not permissible to apply linguistic terms to human beings except in respect of the language which they speak. Archaeologists and historians are not precluded from describing a people as Celtic so long as they mean to imply only that the people in question is Celtic-speaking. It is misleading to use the term in a political sense, and it is always unwise to draw racial conclusions from the evidence of language alone. Strictly, a brooch cannot be Celtic—the man who made it may be a Celt, which means—again strictly—that he spoke a Celtic dialect, not that he belonged to a certain political or racial group. But by common usage many such words have passed into general currency, and others (e.g. "British", "Scandinavian", etc.) have more than one connotation. At this late date it is probably too pedantic to insist upon a formal and technical accuracy in terminology, but if one uses technical terms one should not so far forget their original or intended connotation as to build a theory upon an equation which is unintended or unproved. It is notoriously difficult to establish equations between archaeological and historical conceptions.

It is of paramount importance to remember that political groups as recognised by the historian do not in themselves imply racial groups as recognised by the ethnologist, and that neither political groups nor racial groups necessarily coincide with the cultural and linguistic divisions of the archaeologist and the philologist. The Picts are fundamentally a historical conception. They achieved a political unity, represented by the Pictish kingdom, but apparently they were never a single race. The various racial elements in Pictland may be reflected by cultural and linguistic divisions, but they need not and probably do not coincide exactly with them. If, as seems likely, the Picts were a heterogeneous people, we cannot assume that they possessed a common culture or spoke a common language. If the language (or languages) spoken by the Picts can be determined, it (or they) may be described as Pictish—unless philologists decide that it would be less confusing to coin an unambiguously linguistic term. Likewise if a certain structure or implement can be isolated as characteristic of or peculiar to the historical Picts, that too may be with propriety described as Pictish, unless archaeologists consider the term inadequate or insufficiently distinctive for the purpose. But neither linguistic nor archaeological features ought to be labelled Pictish until their association with the historical Picts in the historical Pictish period (A.D. 300–850) has been firmly established. It would be reasonable, perhaps, to extend the term to cover features firmly associated with, say, a second-century people which can be proved to have become part of the Pictish people proper, but in this context it might be less confusing to use some such term as "proto-Pictish".

It may seem that problems of terminology are unduly emphasised, but they lie at the heart of any attempt to throw light on the Picts. Our aim is to isolate cultural and linguistic features characteristic of the Picts and so to prepare the way for the co-ordination of our separate results. To speak of brochs as "Pictish Towers" or of souterrains as "Picts' Houses", both once honoured terms, is to apply misleading labels which suggest equations that are not established. It may be that broch-builders and souterrain-dwellers can be related in some way to the Picts or to the proto-Picts, but labels alone will not achieve this. It is our task to examine all possible relationships, and it would be unhelpful if a guess or an assumption were to impede a legitimate inquiry. Only the ignorant or the unwary will be misled by assumed or faulty equations such as lie behind expressions like "Pictish Towers" and "Goedelic Beaker-Folk", but other labels, misleadingly applied or carelessly interpreted, could easily obscure issues even from the practised eye. Since our object is to establish, if possible, equations between archaeological, historical and philological conceptions, it is of fundamental importance that no equation should be merely assumed.

It might be expected that historical sources would provide full information about political, constitutional and ecclesiastical developments among the Picts, and at least a few comments on their social and economic arrangements. But everything depends upon the sources, and these are both fragmentary and singularly difficult to handle. Bede's *Historia Ecclesiastica* and Adamnan's *Vita Sancti Columbae* are admirable within their limits, and Bede's limits are so wide that he provides the only satisfactory framework for a historical reconstruction of events in the period before A.D. 731. His notices of the Picts, only a few of which have been referred to above, are of inestimable value. But neither Bede nor Adamnan wrote from a Pictish viewpoint, and both were primarily interested in ecclesiastical affairs.

Important notices of the Picts are preserved in such Irish compilations as the *Annals of Ulster*, the *Annals of Tigernach*, the *Annals of Inisfallen* and the *Annals of Clonmacnoise*. The *Annals of Ulster* are especially reliable; they assumed their present form only late in the fifteenth century, but they follow with remarkable fidelity the earlier, often contemporary, material upon which they and other Irish compilations are based. It is not surprising that Irish annalists should incorporate information about the Picts; Iona offered a first-class line of intellectual communication between Pictland and Ireland, and there is some reason to believe that Irish scribes had access to a chronicle compiled in Iona and now lost. Unfortunately, Irish references to Pictish affairs are usually brief: there are curt entries announcing the deaths of Pictish kings, and cryptic notes on battles, burnings and sieges, which cannot always be related to their historical context. Fragmentary though they are, however, these notices will occupy a prominent place in any attempt to produce a consecutive history of the Picts.

Northern English writers after Bede continued to refer to the Picts when they impinged upon the troubled course of Northumbrian history. One series of northern annals forms a "continuation" of the chronological summary in Bede's *Historia Ecclesiastica.* Others, now lost, were used by later English chroniclers such as Symeon of Durham. Comments on early northern history by chroniclers of the twelfth and thirteenth centuries are seldom of value—many spring from a misinterpretation or a distorting expansion of statements made by Bede—but occasionally later chronicles are based upon older sources which have themselves vanished. Among the more important of these lost sources is the series of Northumbrian annals which is most fully preserved by Symeon of Durham. These deserve careful analysis. They also serve to illustrate the fact that, until all the major English and Irish chronicles have been subjected to examination by editors supported by all the resources of modern scholarship, the nature and reliability of their underlying sources will not be fully apparent.

The only historical source that might claim in any sense to represent a Pictish version of events is the so-called "*Pictish Chronicle*". As a national historical record it compares lamentably with the *Annals of Ulster* and the *Anglo-Saxon Chronicle*, for it is little more than a list of kings, to which lengths of reigns have been attached. Occasional and dubious historical notices, such as those which refer to the foundation of the church at Abernethy and to the baptism of King Brude by Columba, are not sufficient to justify its time-honoured description as a "chronicle".[1] The list of Pictish kings, which is all that we mean

[1] The name "Pictish Chronicle" has been used to cover varying amounts of material, more or less according to its arrangement in the manuscripts. Here it is used to describe the lists of kings which begin with Cruithne and end with the accession of Kenneth mac Alpin.

by "*Pictish Chronicle*", survives in several manuscripts, most of which have been edited by W. F. Skene.[1] They fall into two distinct groups, which we may call I and II. Group I consists of seven or eight manuscripts of which three have been labelled A, B and C; Group II consists of manuscripts labelled D, F, I and K.[2] The list of kings that underlies manuscripts of Group I, though it is not preserved completely in all of them, begins with Cruithne, the eponymous ancestor of the Picts (*Cruithni*), who is followed by his seven sons, also eponyms, and then by five or six other apocryphal rulers. We may call this Section 1 of the list. Section 2 (in Group I manuscripts only) consists of the "thirty Brudes", thirty kings all bearing the same name, who are supposed to have ruled "Hibernia" and "Albania" for 150 years. That they do not now add up to thirty in the manuscripts is a detail. A third section (following the "thirty Brudes" in Group I manuscripts, and following Cruithne in Group II manuscripts) contains some sixty[3] kings who bring the list down to the middle of the ninth century and to the accession of Kenneth mac Alpin.

A rough calculation of reign-lengths, several of which are improbably long and some of which are incredibly long, is enough to discredit the list as it stands. If we include the "thirty Brudes", it would appear that Cruithne lived somewhere about 1000 B.C.—with a wide range of possibilities, depending upon which manuscript we use and upon whether or not we allow his sons to reign concurrently. All of which is quite fantastic. Apart from other evidence, both historical and linguistic, it is clear that we must for the present regard Sections 1 and 2 of the *Pictish Chronicle* as fictitious or legendary. Section 3 seems to be historical in respect of the last thirty or so of its sixty kings, that is from about Brude mac Maelchon whose name appears half-way down this section of the list. If we take 843 as the date of Kenneth mac Alpin's accession and if we base a calculation on the reign-lengths in MS A, the accession of Brude mac Maelchon is placed about 553 or 554. This may not be quite accurate, but it falls into line remarkably well with the notice of his death in the *Annals of Ulster* (*s.a.* 583, *recte* 584)—according to the *Pictish Chronicle* he ruled for thirty years—and with the statement that he was baptised by Columba in the eighth year of his reign.[4] And Brude's successors, like himself,

[1] Chronicles 4–8, 24–7, 27–9, 323–5, 396–400, 149–51, 172–4, 285–7, 200–2.

[2] These distinguishing letters were given to the manuscripts by A. O. Anderson (1922), I.xlvi–xlvii. For manuscripts not listed by Dr Anderson see Chronicles 24–7, 323–5, and T. F. O'Rahilly (1946), 358.

[3] The number varies from manuscript to manuscript.

[4] Bede (III.4) places Columba's mission in 565 and Brude's conversion in the ninth year of his reign. The *Annals of Ulster* place Columba's mission in 563 (*s.a.* 562).

are mentioned from time to time in the Irish chronicles,[1] which puts their historicity beyond doubt. There is good reason, therefore, to accept as historical the second half of Section 3, that is the *Pictish Chronicle* from the middle of the sixth century onwards.

The earlier part of Section 3 (i.e. before *c.*550) may contain a few names derived from a good tradition, but as a list it seems to belong with Cruithne and the "thirty Brudes" to the mists of legend and antiquarian invention. Reign-lengths are again extended and, ignoring the "thirty Brudes", they would carry back the first Pictish king to the second, third, fourth or fifth century before Christ. This we cannot accept. We require more than the evidence of these lists to convince us that some or all of the peoples of north Britain had come to be called *Picti* and had achieved an advanced form of political unity so many centuries before they are mentioned by Eumenius. H. M. Chadwick thought the list might represent a genuine historical sequence, and he proposed to modify the reign-lengths so that the series would begin about A.D. 250.[2] But before we make any such attempt to bring this part of the list into the orbit of history proper we need better evidence of its historicity than we possess at present. It would be important if it could be demonstrated that the historical Picts existed and had achieved a certain political unity even half a century before they are mentioned by Eumenius, which is what Professor Chadwick implied, but we have no evidence that the various peoples who later appear as *Picti* had gone so far towards political amalgamation at such an early date. And the *Pictish Chronicle* alone cannot be regarded as evidence of such a political development. The plain fact is that historians at present cannot place any trust in or draw any conclusions from that part of the *Pictish Chronicle* which claims to cover the period before about A.D. 550.

None of the manuscripts of the *Pictish Chronicle* are early, and none are free from errors and discrepancies. The relationship of the manuscripts to each other and to a possible common original poses one of the most urgent problems in a historical study of the Picts. It has been suggested that all the surviving manuscripts incorporate or are derived from a compilation which was in existence during the early part of the eighth century. And it has been suggested that a manuscript which underlies one or both of the two groups was compiled or at least kept for a time at Abernethy. It has also been suggested, on rather weaker evidence, that one group of manuscripts (D, F, I, K) is derived from a copy which was kept at St Andrews or Dunkeld. But all these

[1] Examples are listed by H. M. Chadwick (1949), 14–20.
[2] H. M. Chadwick (1949), 6.

suggestions, some of which are more probable than others, are based upon inferences from internal evidence only, and internal evidence cannot be interpreted with any confidence until more is known about the composition and development of the lists as we have them today. We do not know, for example, by whom or at what stage (or stages) the various historical notices were added, though it is a fair assumption that the Abernethy notice, being common to all manuscripts in one form or another, is comparatively early. Recent surveys of and contributions to the problem have been made by H. M. Chadwick [1] and Mrs A. O. Anderson.[2] But much remains to be done, and the work will require specialised philological equipment, for a great deal of the evidence is embedded in the names themselves, their forms, and their variations. We need a facsimile edition of all the manuscripts.

It will be obvious that a whole series of historical problems arise from the paucity and the intractability of the sources. Their intractability is a greater obstacle than their paucity; indeed, when all the scraps of historical information are brought together their quantity is not inconsiderable. They may be consulted most conveniently in *Scottish Annals from English Chroniclers* and *Early Sources of Scottish History*, two collections of translations compiled by A. O. Anderson. Translations alone will not suffice for serious study, but Dr Anderson has provided the fullest conspectus of the relevant historical material, the clearest guide to the sources themselves, and a collection of notes and comments which are of permanent value to all who follow him in this field. The only large-scale attempt to weld the scattered fragments into a coherent historical account is that of W. F. Skene. His *Celtic Scotland* is a monumental work which today seldom receives the praise to which it is entitled. Critics have said that it contains too many unsound inferences and too many unsupported guesses, that it displays serious faults of historical judgment and a serious lack of specialised knowledge, and that it has exercised an unfortunate influence on the study of early Scottish history. There is truth in all these criticisms, and it must be admitted that Skene failed in his primary aim, which was "to lay a sound foundation" by divesting the early annals of Scotland of "the spurious matter of supposititious authors, the fictitious narratives of our early historians, and the rash assumptions of later writers".[3] Indeed, one of the charges against Skene is that he has increased the body of historical literature by too many rash assumptions of his own. But *Celtic Scotland* was written seventy-five years

[1] H. M. Chadwick (1949), 1–34.
[2] Marjorie O. Anderson (1949), 31–42; (1949–50), 108–18, 13–22.
[3] W. F. Skene (1876), 1.Preface.

ago, and it was a single-handed achievement which no modern scholar has attempted to emulate. Anyone who tried to produce on the same scale a detailed and coherent history from the fragmentary evidence available would certainly fall, though perhaps less heavily, into many of the faults condemned in Skene. Modern scholars are no doubt wise in their reluctance to attempt the impossible. Today the need is for more editions of sources, more analyses, more special studies. The consecutive history of early Scotland, like the consecutive history of the Picts, must wait until more spade-work has been done.

It may not be possible yet to wrest from historical sources a detailed and coherent history of the Picts, but it is possible to draw broad general conclusions which may throw light on our problems. From about 550 we have a list of kings which, derived from the trustworthy section of the *Pictish Chronicle* and corroborated at many points by Irish and English chroniclers, may be accepted as fundamentally sound and historical. Irish annals [1] record the deaths of Brude mac Maelchon; Gartnait mac Domelch; Nechtan mac Canonn; Kenneth mac Lugtren; Gartnait, Brude and Talorc, all sons of Foith; Talorcan mac Eanfrith; and, indeed, of most of the kings whose names appear in the *Pictish Chronicle* after 550. Brude mac Maelchon is also vouched for by Adamnan and Bede, and Brude mac Bile caught the attention of several writers by his victory at Nechtanesmere. Angus son of Fergus (Oengus mac Ferguso) and Kenneth son of Feradach are mentioned by the scribe who compiled the continuation of Bede's chronological summary and by the northern writer whose work was used by Symeon of Durham.[2] There is no need to multiply examples further, and there is no need to reproduce here the list as it has been worked out by Dr Anderson [3] and Professor Chadwick.[4] In many cases precise regnal dates cannot be given, and there are occasional breaks, discrepancies and other difficulties, but we may accept as satisfactorily established the series of Pictish kings which stretches backwards from 843 to the middle of the sixth century.

More important to our study, perhaps, than the date from which kings are found among the Picts is the date at which a single Pictish kingdom developed. If we knew when all the Picts came to recognise one king we should know when they achieved at least a nominal political unity. It might have happened as early as 550, or even earlier, but the evidence is against such a view. Historical sources suggest, though they do not prove, that the Picts were regarded as falling into two

[1] Especially the *Annals of Ulster* and the *Annals of Tigernach*. References will be found in A. O. Anderson (1922), I.86–275 *passim*.

[2] Baedae Continuatio *s.a.* 761; SD II.42, 45, 46.

[3] A. O. Anderson (1922), I.cxiii.

[4] H. M. Chadwick (1949), 14–22.

separate groups when Columba arrived in the seventh decade of the sixth century. Brude mac Maelchon (*d.* 584) had a fortress (*munitio*) or royal dwelling (*domus regia*), which may have been his capital, near Inverness,[1] and his dominion seems to have extended to the Orkneys.[2] Bede describes his people as the "northern Picts"; he distinguishes clearly between the "northern Picts", a pagan people converted by the labours of Columba, and the "southern Picts" who, according to his information, had received Christianity long before from St Ninian.[3] A powerful ruler such as Brude would certainly exercise an influence outside his own immediate territories, but there is no good evidence to support A. O. Anderson's suggestion[4] that he was probably king of Fortrinn.[5] His power may have been recognised among the southern Pictish peoples, for all we know to the contrary, but on the evidence at our disposal we should assume that he was regarded as king of the northern Picts.

The existence of another Pictish kingdom at this date might perhaps be inferred from the recorded death in 580 of "Cennalath, king of the Picts".[6] In what relation, if any, did Cennalath stand to Brude, who reigned for thirty years and died in 584? It is possible that he was a co-ruler—this seems to be the solution offered by MSS A, B and C of the *Pictish Chronicle* where it is stated that a certain Galam Cennaleph ruled for one year "with Brude". It is also possible that he was a sub-king who owed allegiance to Brude—a parallel might be provided by the Orkney king who was at Brude's court when Columba arrived.[7] And Professor Chadwick has suggested that he was a king among the southern Picts.[8] There are other possibilities, dynastic feuds and the like, and there is nothing to guide us to the correct one. Professor Chadwick may be wrong, but it still remains most probable that Bede's division of the Pictish peoples into northern and southern groups reflects a political reality which still obtained or was a very recent memory in the last decades of the sixth century.

By 685 Pictland formed a single kingdom. Or, to be more accurate, there is no reason to doubt that Brude mac Bile was recognised as king by all the Picts. Some of them had lately been subject to Northumbrian authority, but neither Bede nor any other writer hints that there was

[1] Adamnan I.37; II.33, 35.

[2] Adamnan II.42.

[3] Bede III.4.

[4] A. O. Anderson (1948), 35.

[5] On the name of the province, *Fortrinn*, possibly *Fortriu*, see T. F. O'Rahilly (1946), 26, 463–4. It occurs most commonly in the genitive as *Fortrenn* (sing. and plur.), but it also occurs as *Fortrinn* (dat. sing.), *Fortrind* (acc. sing.), and *Fortrennaibh* (dat. plur.). The nominative forms, **Fortriu* (sing.) and **Fortrinn* (plur.), are not found in extant texts.

[6] AU *s.a.* 579. See also ATig (RC XVII.153).

[7] Adamnan II.42.

[8] H. M. Chadwick (1949), 14.

more than one Pictish kingdom at the time of the battle of Nechtanesmere. There are obscure references to a siege of Dunnottar (681) [1] and to a devastation of the Orkneys (682),[2] which suggest that Brude, if not engaged in extending his territories, was finding it difficult to control all parts of his kingdom. It would be surprising if it were otherwise, for no king until modern times was able to enforce his will on the whole of Scotland. Brude, at any rate, was able to subjugate the Orkneys and to throw the Northumbrians back to the line of the Forth. And Irish annalists describe him significantly as king of Fortrinn.[3] It seems clear that he ruled Pictland from the far north to the Northumbrian boundary. Bede obviously regarded Pictland as a single political unit in his own day: he believed, for example, that *c.*710 the kingdom (*regnum*) of Nechtan mac Derile embraced all the provinces of the Picts (*uniuersae Pictorum prouinciae*).[4] And, indeed, his references to events of the seventh century, even before the reign of Brude mac Bile, never employ terms which suggest that he regarded the Picts as anything but a single political unit.

The century which follows the death of Bede provides many problems for the student of Pictish dynasties. Variations and discrepancies increase in the manuscripts of the *Pictish Chronicle*; we find rulers and co-rulers in some versions and not in others. In the Irish sources appear such figures as "Talorcan mac Drostain, king of Atholl" (739) [5] and "Dubthalorc, king of the Picts on this side of the Mounth" (782).[6] It might seem that Pictland was breaking down into a number of separate kingdoms. But this was not the case. Dubthalorc perhaps appears in the *Pictish Chronicle* as Talorc or Talorcan.[7] And Talorcan "king of Atholl" seems to have been a *subregulus*, not the ruler of an independent kingdom; he was drowned in 739 by Angus son of Fergus, and it has been suggested [8] that he was succeeded as "king of Atholl" by a brother of Angus, another Talorcan. This is not the place to pursue such problems; the point is that such examples probably reflect local government arrangements rather than separate kingdoms. Talorcan "king of Atholl" would probably have been described as a *mormaer* in the post-Pictish period or as an *ealdorman* by an Anglo-Saxon writer. We know little or nothing about local divisions and the maintenance of law and order among the Picts, and the subject deserves attention. The present point is merely that the appearance of local "kings" should not

[1] AU *s.a.* 680.
[2] AU *s.a.* 681; ATig (RC XVII.207).
[3] AU *s.a.* 692; ATig (RC XVII.212).
[4] Bede V.21.
[5] AU *s.a.* 738: *Talorggan mac Drostain rex Athfoithle.* See also ATig (RC XVII.243).
[6] AU *s.a.* 781: *Dubtholargg rex Pictorum citra Monoth.*
[7] A. O. Anderson (1922), I.253.
[8] Ibid. 214, 236, 239.

be taken to imply that the Pictish kingdom was disintegrating. The confusion in the sources is magnified by our own ignorance of internal arrangements. And to it must be added the real confusion which no doubt attended the appearance of the Scandinavian raiders at the end of the eighth century.

A summary of the development of political unity among the Picts cannot be more than a tentative and cautious expression of opinion. One gets the impression that the Picts, probably an agglomeration of independent or loosely federate peoples in the third century, were still in the sixth century groping towards a political unity which is clearly evidenced in the seventh. Their kingdom was never a close-knit, strongly centralised unit ; facts of geography, divergent elements in the population and dynastic weaknesses probably combined to ensure that political unity remained largely superficial and always precarious. But it was a real unity, and on occasions the Picts demonstrated that they could act as members of a single state. There is no reason to think that the kingdom disintegrated in the last century of its independent existence : the appearance of "subsidiary kingdoms" reflects no more than an obscure system of local government or, perhaps, the shifting centres of royal power. At best political unity among the Picts was a precarious thing, strong enough in times of national crisis, but usually weak and often temporarily destroyed by dynastic rivalries. With all its weaknesses, however, the Pictish kingdom continued as a single and separate political entity until the middle of the ninth century when Kenneth mac Alpin became king under circumstances which remain obscure.

Dynastic rivalries and external wars fall outside the scope of this volume. One day the historian may be able to co-ordinate the many obscure references and produce a consecutive historical narrative, but at present he requires the philologist's help in problems of identification no less than in the disentangling of his sources. There is, for example, the battle of *Monad Croib*,[1] fought in 728 between Angus and Alpin, a battle of high significance in a dynastic struggle for control of the Pictish kingdom. Will the philologist confirm that *Monad Croib* (*Monad Craebi*) is today Moncreiffe Hill near Perth ? And what about the equally important battle fought in 729 between Angus and Drust at *Druim Derg Blathuug* ? [2] Can we place any trust in the old suggestion that *Druim Derg Blathuug* survives as a name in Kinblethmont near Arbroath ? And are the *Maeatae* (*Miathi*) commemorated today

[1] AU *s.a.* 727, *Bellum Monid chroibh* ; ATig (RC xvii. 234), *Cath Monaigh Craebi.*
[2] AU *s.a.* 728, *Bellum Dromo dergg blathuug* ; ATig (RC xvii.235), *Cath Droma Deirg Blathuug.*

in Dumyat and Myot Hill? Moncreiffe, Dumyat and Myot Hill were all accepted as identifications by W. J. Watson,[1] and on these three hills there are native fortresses. Two of them, those on Moncreiffe and Dumyat, possess features which mark them distinctively as belonging to the Dark Ages. The third, that on Myot Hill, was first noticed by O. G. S. Crawford, who described it simply as "a native fort, hitherto unrecorded".[2] At this point we require the archaeologist's comments on the date and nature of these three structures, for there is a distinct possibility that the spade may bring them into closer and firmer association with known historical events and peoples. In the good old days the association would be assumed: "memorials of the battle" or some such phrase would gloss an assumption for which we require positive evidence.

Dumyat and Myot Hill, if they preserve the name of the *Maeatae*, may help to fix the territorial limits of that people. It is highly improbable that as names they were given to these places by the *Maeatae* themselves, if only because peoples do not usually give their own names to their own fortresses, however important they may be. We should assume that the name Dumyat, "fortress of the *Maeatae*", arose first in the speech of a neighbouring people to whom it was familiar as a landmark or by report. If the name *Maeatae* occurs in the names Dumyat and Myot Hill, therefore, the conclusion should be, not that these places were especially important (though they might have been), but that they were near the boundary which separated the *Maeatae* from the neighbours in whose speech the two names arose. In point of fact, there is good reason to believe that Dumyat and Myot Hill stood within a few miles of the southern boundary of the *Maeatae*.[3]

No modern philologist has expressed an opinion on the possible identification of *Druim Derg Blathuug* ("the red ridge of *Blathuug*" or perhaps "the ridge of *Dergblathuug*") with Kinblethmont, which seems to mean "the head (*ceann*) of the smooth (or flowery) mount (*bláthmhonadh*)". In May 1952 a Pictish symbol stone was discovered at Kinblethmont,[4] on the only high ground in that area, a low rounded mound of vivid red sandstone, which is almost certainly the "head of Blathmont" and may also be "the red ridge of *Blathuug*". In the good old days again it would have been assumed at once that the symbol stone was erected to the memory of Drust who was slain in the battle of *Druim Derg Blathuug*. What a fascinating series of conclusions could be drawn from such an association! And what a pity that the odds at present are so heavily and so heartlessly against it! There are many

[1] W. J. Watson (1926), 401, 59.
[2] O. G. S. Crawford (1939), 287.
[3] See below, pp. 40, 51.
[4] F. T. Wainwright (1951), 180–2.

problems of identification and association, but the validity of proposed equations depends upon the application of specialised techniques to positive evidence, not upon their attractiveness or upon the lack of contradictory evidence.

Similar problems obscure the details of Pictish relations with Scots, Britons and Northumbrians. We must rest content with an outline of historical events and with a general picture of Pictish power and civilisation. It is quite clear that the Picts were not a negligible factor in the northern political scene. They possessed a fleet of considerable strength,[1] which implies navigational skill, familiarity with difficult waters, and a knowledge of shipbuilding. They could dominate the Orkneys, they could defeat the Northumbrian army when it was near the peak of its military reputation, and they could hold the boundaries of their kingdom against other northern peoples. Under Angus son of Fergus their forces were able to devastate Dalriada and capture the Scottish stronghold of Dunadd.[2] And in alliance with the Northumbrians they were able to dictate terms to the Britons at Dumbarton.[3] They developed a distinctive style of monumental art which is at once impressive and unique. As Christians they possessed a national church with monasteries and an organised clergy. No Pictish literature has survived, but among the Picts there were learned men who could read Latin and dispute such technical questions as the correct computation of Easter. There is no evidence that they ever produced a Pictish *Beowulf*, a *Historia Ecclesiastica*, or even a set of annals which might properly be called a "chronicle"; but there were scholars and artists among them, and there is no reason to doubt that written records, perhaps mainly if not entirely in Latin, were compiled and kept in the Pictish monasteries. It would be a mistake to regard the Picts as remote and isolated barbarians; they had cultural contacts with Iona and Northumbria, and their kings were men of power and substance. They were not a mean and politically insignificant agglomeration of separate barbarian peoples. Their political unity, though permanently strained by a curious system of succession, was real enough, and their kingdom was both recognised and feared by their neighbours.

That the right of succession among the Picts was different from the right of succession among other nations in Britain may be accepted as a fact. Bede tells us that the Picts, having no wives when they arrived, obtained women from the Scots of Ireland on the express condition that "when the matter was in doubt they would choose their king from

[1] Cf. ATig (RC XVII.235).
[2] AU *s.a.* 735 (*recte* 736); ATig (RC XVII.239).
[3] SD II.40. The date given by Symeon is 1 August 756.

the female rather than from the male royal line".[1] Whether or not Bede fully understood the Pictish system is debatable. It is certain that his story of its origin, which is taken from Irish sources,[2] has no value except as a testimony to the existence of a custom which Irish writers sought to explain by a literary invention of a kind common enough in legend. But Bede's further statement that the custom was observed in his own day is good evidence that the Pictish system of succession was operative in the first half of the eighth century.

The *Pictish Chronicle* cannot by its nature prove that the Pictish right of succession to the throne was matrilinear (i.e. reckoned through the mother), but it does prove that it was not patrilinear. Throughout the whole of the supposedly historical section of the list the fathers of the kings are named, and there is not a single instance of a son immediately succeeding his father as king. Brother succeeded brother occasionally, but this would occur under a matrilinear system, for the principle would be that a man became king through his mother and was succeeded not by his son but by his mother's son (his brother) or by his mother's daughter's son (his nephew). This, so far as one can see, was how the Pictish system worked. It remained operative until the last years of the Pictish kingdom, when Drust and Uuen appear in the list of kings; it may be that their fathers, Constantine and Angus respectively, were the Constantine and Angus who are earlier listed as kings,[3] but in neither case is the father-son relationship between the two kings proved, and in neither case does the son immediately succeed the father. In the last few years of Pictish independence it may be, as Skene suggested,[4] that the ancient Pictish system was tending to fall into line with the patrilinear system of neighbouring states. But there is no evidence, except Bede's phrase, against the view that the normal Pictish system was straightforwardly matrilinear.[5] Bede was accustomed to patrilinear succession, under which, of course, brother often succeeded brother; he may not have realised that brother could also succeed brother under a matrilinear system, and he seems to have believed (wrongly) that the matrilinear system among the Picts came into operation only when a line of brothers failed, at which point, in his eyes, "the matter was in doubt". Perhaps that is why he inserted this curious qualification, which is not present, it should be noted, in his Irish sources.

[1] Bede I.I. See above, p. 10.
[2] Cf. H. M. Chadwick (1949), 84–8.
[3] Cf. H. M. Chadwick (1949), 20–1, 90. A slightly earlier example, Talorcan son of Angus, is an even more doubtful case of a king's son later becoming a king himself.
[4] W. F. Skene (1876), I.307.
[5] The positive evidence is necessarily slight. See H. M. Chadwick (1949), 90.

Julius Caesar and other classical writers comment disparagingly on the marriage customs and sexual practices reported among the peoples of Britain, often specifically among the peoples of northern Britain.[1] It has been suggested,[2] and it may very well be, that these comments are derived from inaccurate and unsympathetic observation of the matrilinear principle in operation. More convincing, perhaps, is the suggestion [3] that the early peoples of north Britain were polyandrous —with the necessary result that their succession was matrilinear— rather than that they had simply a matrilinear system of succession which was misunderstood by classical writers. In either case these classical references are evidence of the existence and practice of a matrilinear system of succession over three hundred years before the historical Picts are mentioned by Eumenius. Their importance in any attempt to establish links between the historical Picts and their predecessors requires no emphasis. Incidentally these references also provide the best evidence that the matrilinear principle applied throughout the social structure, not only to the royal families.[4]

The real point for our problem is whether or not the Pictish system of succession can be defined as characteristic only of non-Celtic or non-Indo-European peoples. Zimmer [5] was convinced that it was not found among Indo-European peoples, and he therefore concluded that the Picts were a non-Indo-European people. Fraser [6] held the view that succession among the Picts was neither matrilinear nor substantially different from succession among the Irish and the Welsh, but his arguments are not convincing. Other scholars [7] have accepted the Pictish system as matrilinear, but they cannot accept the view that it was alien to Celtic peoples. If the system is definitely not found among Celtic or Indo-European peoples, it goes far towards proving that the Picts, or rather certain elements among the Picts, were non-Celtic or non-Indo-European. If this were so we should expect to find non-Celtic or non-Indo-European traces among the linguistic survivals of Pictland.[8] And we should have a fairly reliable indication of at least one element in the racial composition of the Pictish people. Before a firm conclusion can be drawn we need an expert's verdict on the significance and the ethnological provenance of the system of succession as it operated among the Picts, but the general implication at present

[1] MHB i–cv *passim*.
[2] H. Zimmer (1898), 21–7.
[3] K. H. Jackson in private discussion.
[4] The *Pictish Chronicle* and other sources are concerned only or primarily with kings. Therefore it is difficult to find evidence of the extent to which the matrilinear system of succession and inheritance applied to families other than the royal family in historical times. The question is discussed by H. M. Chadwick (1949), 95–8.
[5] H. Zimmer (1898), 13–42.
[6] J. Fraser (1927), 178–82.
[7] E.g. H. M. Chadwick (1949), 92–5.
[8] Cf. below, Chapter VI, especially pp. 152–4.

seems to be that there was at least a strong non-Celtic element in Pictland.

The political significance of matrilinear succession is less open to dispute. The fact that a father was not succeeded by his son would militate against the development of a strong monarchy and would therefore impair the effectiveness of the central authority. The forces which produce dynastic rivalries would be correspondingly strengthened, and it has been noticed that the Pictish kingdom apparently suffered more than neighbouring states from disturbances of this kind. Also, if the husbands of the succession-bearing females were foreigners, that is non-Pictish princes, it follows that Pictish kings would have little Pictish blood in their veins. Talorcan (*d.* 657) was the son of Eanfrith who became king of Bernicia; Brude (*d.* 693) was the son of Bile king of the Strathclyde Britons, and a kinsman (*fratruelis*)[1] of his great enemy Ecgfrith of Northumbria. The fathers of other Pictish kings seem to have been Scots from Dalriada.[2] The nature of the contract, if any, between the Pictish princesses and the foreign princes is obscure; some of the husbands may have been exiles like Eanfrith; others may have been casual visitors at the Pictish court. The point is that Pictish kings often had foreign fathers.[3] It is clear that the system would not be a source of strength and stability to the Pictish kingdom.

So much for problems and evidence the character of which is largely or primarily historical. It will have been noticed that the philologist's assistance is required at many points, not least in the elucidation and evaluation of historical sources and in the checking of identifications such as those proposed for *Monad Croib* and *Druim Derg Blathuug*. Other problems are primarily linguistic, and perhaps the chief of these is that of the language or languages spoken by the historical Picts and by their predecessors in Pictland. Attempts to solve the problem of the Pictish language have produced a formidable literature and a surprising number of theories.[4] The evidence is reviewed and the whole question reconsidered by Kenneth Jackson,[5] whose conclusions will be vital to our study. Neither the historian nor the archaeologist can help in the solution of a problem which, except for the nature of its sources, is entirely philological. But its importance to both, and to our basic problem, can hardly be exaggerated. The linguistic patterns of Pictland may reflect, though not exactly, underlying racial patterns, and

[1] Nennius (MHB 74). [2] See H. M. Chadwick (1949), 90–1.

[3] It is sometimes stated that the succession-bearing Pictish princesses always married foreigners. This may have been so, but it is an assumption for which the evidence is negative and necessarily weak.

[4] The various theories are discussed and summarised by T. F. O'Rahilly (1946), 353–84.

[5] Below, Chapter VI.

they may throw light upon archaeological distributions and historical divisions. If the languages spoken by the Picts and their predecessors can be determined, a great advance will have been made towards the solution of the fundamental problems of race and origin.

Place-names are essentially philological material and in Scotland they present a vast and largely unworked field. Much has been written on the place-names of Scotland; but, apart from Watson's *Celtic Place-names* and one or two smaller regional studies, there is more chaff than grain. Very few of the so-called works on Scottish place-names show any appreciation of the requirements of modern scholarship. When the place-names of Scotland are subjected to an intensive and organised investigation, such as that which is being carried out by the English Place-name Survey, then they will yield a great deal of information relevant to our problems. Identifications will be more soundly based, and linguistic boundaries will become clearer. Light will be thrown on the distribution of various peoples, on the nature and extent of Anglian settlement, on intrusive Scottish influence in Pictland before 843, on later Gaelicisation of Pictish names, on population movements, and on many other problems of immediate importance to our study. Additional light will be thrown on the languages spoken in Pictland and (since place-names frequently preserve fragments of names older than themselves) on languages already forgotten when the Picts appear in history. The future promises much, but results must await an organised survey of the place-names of Scotland.

What of the archaeological contribution? From archaeological remains we may expect information about the material culture of the Picts: their houses and their villages, their domestic animals, their crops, their food supply, their fortresses, their weapons and implements, their attainments in trade and industry, their artistic achievements, and their general cultural level. We may expect information also, less direct but not less valuable, on certain non-material aspects of their lives; a study of their fortifications, for example, will throw some light on political conditions and on the structure of their society, and a study of their graves and grave-monuments will illustrate their attitude to the supernatural. These and many other lines of advance are open to the archaeologist who examines Pictish structures, such as houses and fortresses, and tangible Pictish objects, such as brooches, pottery fragments, and weapons. It all sounds so very simple.

It might be fairly simple if only the archaeologist were in a position to examine such Pictish remains. It is unfortunate that he cannot at present point to a single fortress or to a single dwelling and say with certainty that it is Pictish, i.e. that it was built or used by the historical Picts in the period A.D. 300–850. Without doubt much Pictish material is still hidden from us, but without doubt, also, much has been discovered and not recognised for what it is. The first problem lies in the recognition or identification of material as Pictish. There are many possibilities, even one or two probabilities, but there are very few certainties. The historical Picts, for example, undoubtedly possessed fortresses. Where are they now or, rather, which are they ? Where are the Pictish equivalents of Scottish Dunadd, British Dumbarton and Northumbrian Bamburgh ? Dundurn is a possible candidate; the *Annals of Ulster* note without comment a siege of Dundurn (*obsessio Duin duirn*) in 683 (*s.a.* 682), and today there is what appears to be a Dark Age fortress on the hill. Is it a Pictish stronghold, the military centre of Fortrinn, as Skene [1] suggested ? The fortress on Dumyat is also Dark Age in character ; is it possible to bring this structure, and that on Myot Hill, into a firm association with the Picts or their predecessors ? The fortification on Moncreiffe Hill also belongs to the Dark Ages ; is it Pictish, and was it occupied in the eighth century ? There are similar fortresses in Fife (e.g. Norman's Law [2]) and further north ; are they the Pictish equivalents of Dalmahoy, Ruberslaw and other so-called "Dark Age capitals" in southern Scotland ? Was Dunadd a Pictish fortress before the Scots settled in Argyll ? How do the ring-forts fit into the picture ? Are they Pictish, or does their distribution suggest a Scottish intrusion into Pictland ? Sites such as Dunadd, Dundurn and Moncreiffe deserve special attention because, having a historical context as well as an archaeological background, they offer the best opportunities of effecting equations such as we are seeking. Dunnichen, "the fortress of Nechtan", loomed above Nechtanesmere and probably influenced the result of the battle of 685. It would have been an excellent site for excavation if it had not been quarried away about a hundred and fifty years ago.[3]

The problems are formidable, but advances have been made in recent years. New examples of Dark Age fortifications have been brought to light by the brilliant field-work of officers of the Royal Commission on Ancient and Historical Monuments. And Robert Stevenson, dealing chiefly with southern Scotland, has provided the basis of a possible classification.[4] The whole problem of fortifications and their possible relation to the Picts is reviewed by R. W. Feachem.[5]

[1] Chronicles cxix, cxxxvi ; W. F. Skene (1876), I.264, 342.

[2] The nature of the structure on Norman's Law was apparently not recognised by the officers of the Royal Commission in 1926, but their report (RCAMS XI.193) provides a remarkably convincing description of what would now be recognised at once as a typical Dark Age fortress.

[3] F. T. Wainwright (1948*a*), 94–5.

[4] R. B. K. Stevenson (1949*b*), 186–98.

[5] See below, Chapter III.

But it is extremely difficult to establish equations of the kind that we are seeking. It is one thing to classify a fortress as "nuclear" or "citadel-type", or even to say that it belongs chronologically to the Dark Ages; it is quite another thing to demonstrate that it is Pictish or that its builders spoke a Gallo-Brittonic language.

Even greater difficulties surround the identification of Pictish houses and graves.[1] Houses are not so permanent and were never so conspicuous as fortresses; they are much more easily destroyed, and traces of them are much more difficult to find. Graves are normally permanent structures, but their discovery depends largely upon chance and is usually accompanied by destruction. It may be taken for granted that many Pictish graves have been discovered during the last ten centuries, and it is a fair assumption that some of them are recorded in the *Proceedings of the Society of Antiquaries of Scotland.* But the difficulty is to decide which are Pictish, a difficulty greatly increased by the introduction of Christianity. Many later Pictish burials will lie in what are now country kirkyards, but even if we could see them it is unlikely that we should be able to identify them as Pictish. It may be possible to locate later Pictish graves near deserted chapel-sites, and it may be possible to associate earlier Pictish and proto-Pictish graves with known Pictish settlement-sites—when the latter themselves have been identified. The immediate difficulty is that we cannot recognise archaeological material as Pictish, a word which belongs to history rather than to archaeology. It is probable that historians and archaeologists are referring to the same peoples under different names, and again we are driven back to the need for equations, genuine equations which rest on more than assumption.

There is one group of archaeological monuments to which the label "Pictish" may be applied with confidence. This is the impressive series of symbol stones, the precise significance of which has long been a problem in Scottish archaeology. Romilly Allen and Joseph Anderson[2] divided these monuments into two classes, the first (Class I) being rough unhewn boulders bearing incised linear designs, chiefly geometric and zoomorphic, executed in a highly conventionalised manner, and the second (Class II) being shaped and surface-dressed slabs, carved in relief and bearing crosses and pictorial scenes as well as symbols. The numerous stones found since *Early Christian Monuments* was published in 1903 have in no way weakened this basic classification, though of course it is capable of indefinite and, no doubt, significant subdivision. The point is that these monuments, symbol stones proper,

[1] On which see below, Chapter IV.
[2] ECM *passim.* See also J. Anderson (1881), II.84.

are found almost exclusively in known Pictish territory, and they may be attributed chronologically to the historical Pictish period. The label "Pictish" is attached to symbol stones as safely and as securely as it is ever likely to be attached to any specific body of archaeological evidence.

What do the symbol stones tell us? Their distribution defines with some precision the boundaries of Pictland.[1] The amazing uniformity and the highly stylised execution of their designs imply the existence of a trained band of stone-carvers and at the same time prove a cultural unity which probably reflects an underlying political unity. This in turn raises a point which deserves consideration in any discussion on the chronology of symbol stones, a problem which need not detain us here.[2] Despite the unshakable impression of uniformity conveyed by the series as a whole, however, the various subdivisions apparently represent cultural differences among the Pictish peoples, and these cultural differences may sometimes reflect older political divisions. The traditional Class I and Class II, for example, are not merely stylistic divisions; it is noteworthy that examples of Class I preponderate north of the Mounth and examples of Class II preponderate south of the Mounth. Does this distribution, notwithstanding that it may be partly chronological, preserve an echo of the old "northern" and "southern" divisions of the Pictish peoples? And do the marked concentrations of stones in Aberdeenshire and Angus reflect the shifting centres of political power or merely the tendency of large population groups to seek out the most fertile areas? The meaning of the symbols and the precise purpose of the stones on which they are carved constitute a separate problem. It cannot be discussed here,[3] but its ultimate solution can hardly fail to throw a powerful beam of light on both social groupings and spiritual conceptions among the Picts.

The various figures and scenes depicted on many of these monuments preserve evidence of another kind: they reveal, often in minute detail, the dress, ornaments, arms and equipment of huntsmen, warriors, ecclesiastics and others. An examination of symbol stones from this angle alone would provide valuable information obtainable from no other source. It is surprising that no-one has yet attempted to assemble this full and varied body of easily accessible evidence. Finally, of course, the symbol stones, a distinctive form of art, are worthy of study for their own sake. It may be that analyses of art-relationships and cultural influences will throw a little light on the Picts, their origins, and their neighbours, but the lines of investigation indicated above

[1] See Map 3. [2] See below, Chapter V. [3] See below, Chapter V.

would seem to offer more direct and more promising approaches to the problems in which we are particularly interested.

The amount of relevant information that can be squeezed from symbol stones serves to emphasise the urgency of the need to affix labels such as "Pictish" and "proto-Pictish" to other groups of archaeological material. If an archaeological culture covers the whole of Pictland, coincides roughly with its boundaries and belongs in time to the Pictish period, then its existence presupposes a cultural unity which is probably related to the political unity of the historical Pictish kingdom. Equally important are archaeological cultures which belong to the Pictish period but either cover only part of the Pictish area or extend into the territory of a neighbouring state. In one case the archaeological distribution may indicate a distinct cultural province within Pictland, behind which may lie a political or racial element incompletely absorbed; in the other it may indicate an intrusive culture which may be related to a movement of peoples. Possibilities are numerous and all should be noted; they at once become significant if they can be equated with or related to historical or linguistic divisions or developments. Even archaeological cultures which fall right outside the Pictish period are highly important if there is any reason to believe that they are associated with peoples who later coalesced to form the Pictish kingdom. The distribution of souterrains is a case in point: they seem to fall outside the Pictish period, but the evidence suggests that the descendants of souterrain-builders were Picts.[1] If similar evidence can be produced for brochs and vitrified forts, for example, the distribution of these structures will assume an increased significance in any attempt to isolate the proto-Pictish elements of the Pictish kingdom.

None of the problems raised above belongs exclusively to any one of the separate fields of history, archaeology and philology, but many of them by the nature and occurrence of the evidence belong to one field rather than to the others. Such are the precise nature of the Pictish system of succession (history), the problem of the language or languages spoken among the Picts (philology), and the identification and distribution of material cultures (archaeology). Such, indeed, are most problems concerned with the recognition and identification of evidence. But as soon as it becomes necessary to advance towards a co-ordination, however elementary, then the three major lines of investigation and the various subsidiary approaches tend to merge and run together. Problems involving co-ordination have already been mentioned incidentally or from a particular angle. It may be useful to consider some of them individually here.

[1] See below, Chapter IV.

On the extent and boundaries of the Pictish kingdom Bede is explicit. In 685 Abercorn, near Queensferry on the south bank of the Forth, was "in the territory of the Angles but near the channel which divides the lands of the Angles and the Picts".[1] The Angles had recently conquered and annexed Pictish territory; this was recovered in 685, but there is no suggestion that the Picts then occupied lands recognised as Northumbrian.[2] The Forth was the Anglo-Pictish boundary in Bede's day, and in his opinion it was the traditional southern boundary of the Picts. He tells us that the Scots settled in Pictish territory north of the Clyde and north of the Britons of Strathclyde.[3] And what he means is placed beyond all possible doubt by his further statement that the Picts and the Scots were both separated from the Britons by "two arms of the sea" which can only be the Forth and the Clyde.[4] It is quite clear that Bede accepted the Forth-Clyde line as the ancient southern boundary of the Picts, and there is no reason to doubt his statement that the territories of Dalriada had been Pictish before the arrival of the Scots.

Nor is there any reason to doubt that the Orkneys and the north of Scotland were regarded as falling within the Pictish kingdom. It is true that Aedan mac Gabrain led an expedition to the Orkneys in 580,[5] but the formal overlordship of the islands in this period seems to have belonged to his contemporary, Brude mac Maelchon king of the Picts. This is implied by the presence at Brude's court of an Orkney king or kinglet (*regulus*) to whom Brude was able to give orders concerning the safety of Christian missionaries wandering in northern waters.[6] It would be impossible for any Pictish king on the mainland to maintain uninterrupted control over the Orkneys, but a strong king might enforce

[1] "*. . . in monasterio Aebbercurnig, posito quidem in regione Anglorum, sed in uicinia freti, quod Anglorum terras Pictorumque disterminat*" (Bede IV.24).

[2] See above, pp. 7–9.

[3] "*Est autem sinus maris permaximus, qui antiquitus gentem Brettonum a Pictis secernebat, qui ab occidente in terras longo spatio erumpit, ubi est ciuitas Brettonum munitissima usque hodie, quae uocatur Alcluith; ad cuius uidelicet sinus partem septentrionalem Scotti, quos diximus, aduenientes sibi locum patriae fecerunt*" (Bede I.1). It is clear from the position of Dumbarton, however, that the Britons controlled some territory north of the Clyde. See above, p. 4.

[4] "*. . . duobus sinibus maris interiacentibus, quorum unus ab orientali mari, alter ab occidentali, Brittaniae terras longe lateque inrumpit, quamuis ad se inuicem pertingere non possint. Orientalis habet in medio sui urbem Giudi, occidentalis supra se, hoc est ad dexteram sui, habet urbem Alcluith, quod lingua eorum significat petram Cluith; est enim iuxta fluuium nominis illius*" (Bede I.12).

[5] *Fecht Orc la h-Aedhan mac Gabrain* (AU *s.a.* 579). In the following annal (580, *recte* 581) is the terse entry: *Fecht Orc*. This second "campaign in the Orkneys" is usually taken to be a repetition of the entry in the preceding annal, with the name of the leader omitted. We cannot be sure that this is what it is. It may refer to Aedan's campaign or to another campaign by Aedan or to a Pictish retaliatory campaign. We do not know.

[6] Adamnan II.42.

his will there from time to time, and it is recorded that the islands were devastated by Brude mac Bile in 682.[1] So far as we can judge these events are historical. There are also traditions of doubtful origin and more than doubtful historicity. In the compilation to which the name of Nennius is attached it is stated that the Picts arrived first in the Orkneys (*Orcades*), from which they wasted many regions and occupied the northern third of Britain.[2] A later source, the *Historia Norwegiae*, preserves a curious comment on the Orkneys: "These islands were first inhabited by the Picts (*Peti*) and the Papae. Of these, one race, the Picts, little exceeded pigmies in stature; they did marvels, in the morning and in the evening, in building [walled] towns, but at mid-day they entirely lost all their strength, and lurked through fear in little underground houses."[3] The story is interesting in that it brings together Picts, souterrains, and perhaps brochs, at once explaining the common belief that the Picts were a pigmy people and providing an early example of the mistaken equations implicit in the names "Picts' Houses" (souterrains) and "Pictish Towers" (brochs). But whatever the origins of these stories and however unhistorical they are, they strengthen the impression that the Orkneys were widely regarded as belonging to the Picts.

If one liked to build a theory on Claudian's poetic fancy that "*Incaluit Pictorum sanguine Thyle*",[4] one could pretend that it proves the existence of Picts in Shetland about A.D. 400. It may well be that there were Picts in Shetland at that date, but it would be straining the evidence to treat this and similar references as sober statements of historical fact. We may leave it as a general historical probability that the northern isles, Shetland as well as the Orkneys, were inhabited by peoples known as Picts, and that they, or at least the Orkneys, normally owed allegiance to the kings of the Picts. This was probably the situation in the far north until the arrival of the Scandinavians overwhelmed earlier languages, cultures and political connexions.

According to historical evidence Pictland stretched northwards from the Forth-Clyde line, embracing all of what is now Scotland except Argyll and the islands which formed part of the kingdom of Dalriada. How far is the historian's conception of Pictland supported or supple-

[1] AU *s.a.* 681; ATig (RC XVII.207).

[2] Nennius (MHB 56). Gildas (MHB 10) had said that the Picts were an overseas people (*gens transmarina*) and that they came from the north (*ab Aquilone*). Relying on these sources, and noticing the northern distribution of the brochs or "Pictish Towers", W. J. Watson (1926), 61–6, was led to identify the Picts with the broch-builders. This equation is undoubtedly invalid. For the relationship of the broch-builders to the historical Picts see below, pp. 93–4.

[3] Quoted by A. O. Anderson (1922), I.330–1.

[4] Holder II.994; MHB xcviii.

mented by the evidence of archaeology and philology ? Leaving aside classificatory and other details, it is possible to say at once that the distribution of symbol stones provides support and confirmation. These remarkable monuments are most numerous in Aberdeenshire and Angus, but they are found also in the far north, in Shetland and the Orkneys, and in the western isles. One stone has been found in Edinburgh [1]—where it came from is uncertain—and a "double-disc and Z-rod" symbol has been carved on living rock at Anwoth in Kirkcudbrightshire.[2] Apart from such strays,[3] the distribution of symbol stones coincides with the fertile areas of Pictland and convincingly confirms the reality of the Forth-Clyde boundary.

It is perhaps not surprising that symbol stones should fall so closely into line with the historical evidence. They are, after all, the only series of archaeological remains to which the label "Pictish" has yet been firmly attached. As other groups of remains receive this distinctive label we may expect similar distribution patterns. Souterrains as a class are not "Pictish", as we have defined the term, and we should not expect their distribution to coincide with historical Pictland. Souterrain-dwellers are near to the Picts in more than time, however, and in point of fact the distribution of souterrains is closely related to that of symbol stones and to the known extent of Pictland.[4] Brochs and vitrified forts, by contrast, do not in their distribution reflect the unity of Pictland; they may represent political elements which later formed part of the Pictish kingdom, but they are not specifically "Pictish". Until the label "Pictish" can be applied to a wider range of archaeological material, symbol stones remain the only appreciable body of archaeological evidence for the extent of the historical kingdom of the Picts.

The evidence of place-names is greater in volume but more difficult to interpret in terms of history. Celtic place-names are found all over Scotland, and the ancient names *Orc*, *Orcas*, *Orcades*,[5] preserved today in the group-name Orkneys, suggest that a Celtic-speaking people were settled in the far north by the first century B.C.—by the fourth century B.C., indeed, if Diodorus took the promontory-name *Orcas* from Pytheas.[6] The name Pentland Firth (ON. *Pettaland Fjǫrðr*, "Pictland Firth") shows that the Scandinavians recognised these shores as Pictish, but the age of the Viking raiders begins late in the Pictish period. The most promising line of advance seems to lie in the study of specifically Pictish place-name elements. One such is *pett*, apparently meaning

[1] ECM III.421.
[2] ECM III.477–9. See also below, pp. 43–4.
[3] On which see R. W. Feachem (1950), 206–8.
[4] See below, p. 91.
[5] Holder II.866–8.
[6] See W. J. Watson (1926), 28–30; T. F. O'Rahilly (1946), 355.

"a piece [of land]", as in Low Latin *petia terrae.*[1] It is common in such place-names as Pitcaple, Pitcorthie, Pitewan, Pitglassie, Pitkenny, Pitsligo and Pittenweem. Watson counted about 323 examples, and their distribution is highly significant.[2] They are most common in Aberdeenshire, Kincardine, Angus, Fife and east Perthshire—that is in historical Pictland between the Moray Firth and the Forth. A few are found in south-east Sutherland, but none in north Sutherland, Caithness and the northern isles. Further research will no doubt increase the number of *pett* place-names, but it is unlikely that Watson's distribution pattern will be disturbed. How are we to explain the fact that *pett*, so common between the Moray Firth and the Forth, is not found in the far north? It is interesting and probably significant that the northern area where *pett* is not found coincides in a most remarkable way with the "broch area". Assuming that *pett* is a Pictish word and that its use in the far north is not precluded by its meaning in relation to topographical, agricultural or other conditions of that kind, we are left with two possible conclusions. Either the far north lay outside the Pictish area, a conclusion negatived by other evidence, or the northern part of Pictland formed a separate linguistic province with a vocabulary, perhaps a language, different from that current further south. This is a good example of how a study of the distribution of a place-name element may throw light upon linguistic divisions which may be themselves related to archaeological, political and even racial boundaries. This subject is discussed more fully below where other place-name elements and their distribution are considered.[3]

Historical evidence is explicit that the southern boundary of the Pictish kingdom was the Forth-Clyde line. The evidence of archaeology and philology, though by no means fully available at present, definitely supports this conclusion. But several subsidary questions remain, and three are of considerable importance in their bearing on the extent of Pictland. What precisely do we mean by the "Forth-Clyde line"? Was it always the boundary of the Pictish kingdom? Finally, how and where do the "Picts of Galloway" come into the northern scene?

The generally accepted answer to the second question seems to be that Pictland once extended far to the south of the Forth-Clyde line. H. M. Chadwick says: "South of the Forth there is clear evidence for Pictish occupation in very early times".[4] His evidence, which consists chiefly of "brochs, a vitrified fort and a number of 'earth-houses' (souterrains)", is not admissible. The rarity of brochs and souterrains

[1] Cf. W. J. Watson (1926), 407–14; T. F. O'Rahilly (1946), 356; H. M. Chadwick (1949), 53. See also below, p. 148.
[2] See Map 6. [3] Chapter VI.
[4] H. M. Chadwick (1949), 47.

south of the Forth is much more significant than their sporadic occurrence, but the main objection is that neither can properly be described as Pictish. And vitrified forts have even less claim to be called Pictish. It may be that some of the descendants of the men who built the vitrified forts were among those peoples who in the fourth century were known to the Romans as *Picti*—that is a possible association which should be investigated—and, if they were, then the vitrified-fort-builders, or some of them, could be called proto-Picts. But, even if we could be sure that some of the vitrified-fort-builders were proto-Picts in this sense of the term, it would not follow that the same description could be applied to those who lived south of the Forth or otherwise outside the known Pictish area. It is true, as H. M. Chadwick perhaps meant to imply, that not all the peoples whose descendants were known as *Picti* lived only in the area where the latter are found in historical times, but this could be said of almost any historical people, including the Angles, the Britons and the Scots. Much more serious is A. O. Anderson's reference to "Pictland south of the Forth" and his belief that the Picts, the historical Picts as we have defined them, lived "south of the Forth".[1] For such a view there is no good evidence at all, and we must reject it.

It is least confusing to approach this difficult question from the comparatively sure ground of the eighth century. The Pictish kingdom as Bede knew it did not extend south of the Forth-Clyde line. Pictish traditions, represented by the names of the seven provinces of Pictland and by the seven sons of Cruithne, also recognise the Forth-Clyde line as the southern limit of the Pictish kingdom.[2] We may reject Cruithne's sons as mythical figures, but their names and the names of the seven provinces provide a reliable guide to the territorial extent of Pictland at the time when the "tradition" was invented, which seems to have been late in the period of Pictish independence. It is fairly clear that the kingdom of the Picts was bounded by the Forth-Clyde line in the seventh, eighth and ninth centuries. In the fifth and sixth centuries, the two hundred years which followed the departure of the Roman legions, there are powerful traditions of revived British kingdoms, like Gododdin and Dumbarton, stretching northwards to the Forth-Clyde line.[3] So far as we can see, it was the Britons, "The Men of the North" (*Gwyr y Gogledd*), who controlled the area south of the Forth, and it has been suggested that they "established and policed the earlier frontier" (the Antonine Wall) against the Picts.[4] Future research,

[1] A. O. Anderson (1908), vii–viii. [2] See below, pp. 46–7.
[3] See above, pp. 3–4; and H. M. Chadwick (1949), 137–58.
[4] Mrs Chadwick in H. M. Chadwick (1949), xxiii.

especially archaeological and linguistic, may dictate a modification of this view, but at present we should accept the implications of these British traditions and we should assume that the lands south of the Forth remained in British control until they passed to the Northumbrian Angles. Which leaves the fourth century as the only period in which we may reasonably expect to find the historical Picts in control of areas south of the Forth.

There can be no question that the Picts raided deep into Roman Britain on more than one occasion in the fourth century. Sometimes, as Theodosius realised from experience, it was difficult to eject them, and historical evidence alone cannot determine whether or not permanent settlement resulted from these Pictish excursions. But there is no clear evidence that the *Picti*, or the *Maeatae* before them, were able to gain permanent control of the lands south of the Forth while the Roman power remained unbroken in Britain. The final collapse of Roman authority stimulated the revival of the British kingdoms which, it is suggested, dominated this area in the post-Roman period. It would be unwise to dogmatise in matters so vague, especially as archaeology and place-names have not yet made their full contribution to the problem, but from the admittedly fragmentary evidence at our disposal our tentative conclusion should be that, despite raids and excursions, the permanent homes of the *Picti* were always north of the Antonine Wall. It should be remembered, of course, that the name *Picti* in this volume is reserved for the peoples so described by classical and later writers, the historical Picts who, though they may have been several separate peoples in the fourth century, later achieved a recognisable political unity in the Pictish kingdom. The once wider application of a similar name, which may be inferred from such names as **Priteni*, **Pritani*, *Cruithni*, *Prydyn* and *Prydain*,[1] is relevant to an inquiry into the origins of the Picts, but it is no more relevant than the distribution of vitrified forts to a study of the extent and boundaries of historical Pictland.

What precisely do we mean when we say that the "Forth-Clyde line" was the southern boundary of Pictland ? This is the first of the three subsidiary questions raised above. Bede realised that the "two arms of the sea", the estuaries of the Clyde and the Forth, do not meet,[2] but whether the Anglo-Pictish boundary followed the line of the middle and upper Forth or struck straight across country towards the Clyde is not clear from historical evidence. From place-names and archaeology, however, it appears that the boundary struck inland from the

[1] See T. F. O'Rahilly (1946), 444–52 ; and K. H. Jackson, below, pp. 158–60.
[2] See above, p. 34.

lower Forth, following the strategic line of the Antonine Wall, which divides Britain at its narrowest part. The distribution of *petts*,[1] of which examples are found in Stirlingshire, suggests that the Antonine Wall rather than the middle Forth was the Pictish boundary. And Myot Hill, which we should expect to lie in the territory of the *Maeatae* or *Miathi*, is south of the Forth but immediately north of the Antonine Wall.[2] The Antonine Wall was early abandoned by the Romans as a defended line, but there is good reason to believe that it long retained its importance as a boundary.

We are left with the last of the three questions raised above, that which concerns the "Picts of Galloway". It is a question one would prefer to avoid, if escape were possible, but it must be faced. Another opinion is more justifiable than silence. If the "Picts of Galloway" are not a myth, they certainly lived south of the Antonine Wall, and a long line of scholars do not regard them as a myth. The following writers, differing at many points about the Picts, are among those who have expressed or implied their belief in the "Picts of Galloway": A. O. Anderson (1908, 1922, 1948), H. M. Chadwick (1949), F. C. Diack (1944), W. D. Simpson (1927, 1935), W. F. Skene (1876) and H. Zimmer (1898). The denunciations of Macbain and Watson [3] have made little impression upon what remains the commonly accepted view. It will be well to walk warily.

What is the historical evidence for the existence of Picts in Galloway? There is no contemporary evidence at all. No chronicler makes even an oblique reference to Picts in Galloway until three hundred years after the end of the Pictish kingdom, until a time when, according to Henry of Huntingdon, the Picts and their language were so completely destroyed that a mention of them in earlier writings seemed like a fable.[4] It would never have occurred to modern scholars to seek for Picts in Galloway but for references made to them by two or three writers of the twelfth century. Richard of Hexham, writing about the middle of that century, several times mentions "*Picti*" in connexion with events which occurred in 1138,[5] and once he states clearly that they "are commonly called Galwegians (*Galleweienses*)".[6] A little later Reginald of Durham, another northern English writer, tells us that Kirkcudbright (*Cuthbrictis khirche*) takes its name from St Cuthbert and lies in the land

[1] See Map 6. [2] See above, p. 24.

[3] Cf. W. J. Watson (1926), 174–9.

[4] Henry of Huntingdon (HH 1.8), quoting from Bede's account (Bede 1.1) of the five languages current in Britain (see above, p. 3*n*.), adds his own comment thus: "*quamvis Picti jam videantur deleti, et lingua eorum ita omnino destructa, ut jam fabula videatur, quod in veterum scriptis eorum mentio invenitur*".

[5] RH(Historia) *s.a.* 1138 (Raine, 77–104; Howlett, 151–76).

[6] RH(Historia) *s.a.* 1138 (Raine, 79; Howlett, 152).

of the Picts (*in terra Pictorum sita est*).[1] In describing a curiously unclerical bull-baiting episode at Kirkcudbright he also mentions "priests (*illi clerici*) . . . who in the language of the Picts are called *Scollofthes* (*qui Pictorum lingua Scollofthes cognominantur*)".[2] Apparently Reginald believed that Pictish was still spoken in Kirkcudbright about 1164. Towards the end of the century Jocelin of Furness records a visit by St Kentigern to "the country of the Picts" (*Pictorum patria*) which, he tells us, "is now called Galloway" (*quo modo Galwiethia dicitur*).[3]

How far can we trust these twelfth-century witnesses? It would be easy enough to dismiss them altogether as ignorant blunderers, especially as their contemporaries either avoid the word "*Picti*" or use it in a more natural context. Reginald of Durham is a notoriously unreliable author who, not deigning to make use of earlier sources for matters outside his own knowledge, invents or retails stories which surely raised many an eyebrow, even in his own credulous age. He must be mistaken in his belief that the Pictish language was alive in south-west Scotland at the middle of the twelfth century[4]; *Scollofthes* is clearly a scribal corruption[5]; and what he took to be the *Pictorum lingua* was probably Gaelic. The name Galloway commemorates the *Gall-Gaidil* who appear in Irish chronicles between 850 and 860 as renegade Irish associates of the pagan Norsemen.[6] They later settled in and gave their name to Galloway, but how far they are responsible for the introduction or the strengthening of Gaelic in that area is a matter for the student of language. For us the point is that Reginald of Durham is not a reliable guide. It would be equally easy to discredit Richard of Hexham. In another work, an account of the church and bishops of Hexham,[7] he makes a significant blunder: expanding Bede's comment on Wilfrid's ecclesiastical jurisdiction over the Picts,[8] he adds the mistaken explanation, "because Candida Casa had not yet obtained a bishop of its own". Bede was undoubtedly referring to the Picts of Pictland proper who later received Trumwine for their bishop; Richard apparently thought Trumwine's see was at Whithorn. Since he held such a view, however mistaken, it is not surprising that he equated Galwegians and Picts when he wrote up his account of the troubles of 1138. This, as it stands, is a sufficient explanation of Richard's mistake. W. J. Watson, quoting Galloway traditions about "Creenies" (*Cruithni*) and "Gossocks" (cf. Welsh *gwasog*), explains

[1] RD LXXXIV. [2] RD LXXXV. [3] Jocelin XXXIV.

[4] Compare the opinion of Henry of Huntingdon, quoted above.

[5] Professor Bruce Dickins suggests an association with Old Irish *scolóc*, "student" (editorial footnote to E. MacNeill's article, YCS II.45); Kenneth Jackson proposes to me that *Scollofthes* is a scribal corruption of *scolastes*.

[6] F. T. Wainwright (1948*b*), 158; D. W. H. Marshall (1929), 9–20.

[7] RH(Annotatio) I.vi. [8] Bede IV.3. See above, p. 7.

the twelfth-century English use of "*Picti*" as an attempt to abuse a group of King David's more barbarous subjects. It is true that the Galwegians were especially hated and despised, and it is true that the name "*Picti*", like the modern " Creeny" or "Pecht", would convey the contemptuous disgust which the English chroniclers felt for this section of the enemy. But it is also true that several English chroniclers shared with Richard of Hexham the mistaken belief that Trumwine's see was at Whithorn,[1] a belief which alone would go far towards accounting for these odd references to the "Picts of Galloway". However we explain it, the historical evidence is weak. It cannot stand against Bede's clear statement that the Forth "divides the lands of the Angles and the Picts".[2]

From the historical evidence it looks as if the "Picts of Galloway" are a twelfth-century myth. We might have left the matter there but for the fact that scholars have been inspired to seek, and sometimes to find, evidence which appears to give body to the myth. It has often been claimed that the "Picts who are called *Niduari*" are the "Picts of Nithsdale"; archaeologists have noticed three brochs or broch-like structures in Wigtownshire; and there are the symbols carved on rock at Anwoth (in Kirkcudbrightshire) and engraved on the terminal link of a silver chain found at Whitecleuch (near the Lanarkshire-Dumfriesshire boundary). At first glance these separate pieces of evidence seem to raise the "Picts of Galloway" above the level of a myth. Have they any value as supporting evidence?

In his *Vita Sancti Cuthberti* Bede tells the story of St Cuthbert's midwinter visit "to the land of the Picts who are called *Niduari*" (*ad terram Pictorum qui Niduari uocantur*).[3] An earlier and anonymous Life of St Cuthbert, which Bede followed, gives the saint's destination as "*Niuduera regio*".[4] An eighth-century poem, *Miracula Nynie Episcopi*, places St Ninian's mission among "*Pictorum nationes quae naturae dicuntur*", in which "*naturae*" is an obvious scribal error convincingly corrected to "*Niduarae*" by Dr Wilhelm Levison.[5] We may conclude that the "southern Picts", among whom Bede believed St Ninian to have laboured,[6] correspond to or include the *Niduari*. The details of St Cuthbert's journey to the latter are not sufficient to locate them firmly in any area, but the general indications are that they lived north of the Forth.[7] We should seek them in Pictland proper, probably in the territory annexed and held by Northumbria until the

[1] C. Plummer (1896), II.224.
[2] See above, p. 34.
[3] B. Colgrave (1940), 192.
[4] Ibid. 82.
[5] W. Levison (1940), 288–9.
[6] Bede III.4. See above, p. 21.
[7] See, for example, W. J. Watson (1926), 175–7; B. Colgrave (1940), 320–1; W. Levison (1940), 289.

disaster of 685. They may have lived in Fife, possibly even further north, and our best chance of settling this problem lies in a comprehensive study of place-names. At present there are no good grounds for calling them the "Picts of Nithsdale" or for locating them in south-west Scotland. It is doubtful if such a suggestion would have been made but for the assumption that there were Picts in Galloway.[1] It may be that future research, contradicting present expectations, will place the *Niduari* in the south-west, but it would be illogical at this stage to allow a suggestion which arises from an assumption to count as evidence in support of that assumption. On the evidence at our disposal we must conclude that the *Niduari* bring no support to the twelfth-century myth.

The three broch-like structures of Wigtownshire, by a similar argument, must be rejected as evidence supporting the "Picts-of-Galloway" theory. Whether or not they are all brochs is still disputed among archaeologists, but that need not concern us here. What has been said about vitrified forts [2] applies with special force to any brochs that may be found in Galloway. If broch-builders within the Pictish area are proved to be proto-Picts, in the sense defined above, it will not follow that broch-builders everywhere are proto-Picts. Indeed it would be hazardous to apply that term to broch-builders outside the known Pictish area. And the folly of using an assumption (that there were Picts in Galloway) as indirect evidence of its own validity requires no further emphasis.

Symbols fall into quite another category. They may be accepted as Pictish, and the only tangible trace of Picts in south-west Scotland is provided by the two symbols engraved on the silver chain from Whitecleuch [3] and by the "double-disc and Z-rod" symbol carved on a rock surface at Anwoth.[4] Are we justified in dismissing these symbols as strays? Or should we assume, with F. C. Diack,[5] that they indicate Pictish settlement in Galloway? The Whitecleuch chain, now in the National Museum, is a valuable and portable object which might have come from anywhere in Scotland. It has no significance in this context. It is not possible to impugn in this fashion the evidence of the symbols cut into natural rock at Anwoth, but whether or not they are Pictish,

[1] A. O. Anderson (1948), 44–5, has recently raised the old question in a new form by cautiously suggesting that the "southern Picts" converted by Ninian may have lived in Galloway, in which case they could be equated with the "*Niduari*" or "Picts of Nithsdale", who would thus become the "Picts of Galloway". In a field where so much is vague one can only say that there are no good reasons either for removing the "southern Picts" from their generally accepted homes north of the Forth or for transferring the "*Niduari*" from Pictland proper to Galloway. Bede's testimony and the balance of the evidence are against both parts of the suggestion.

[2] See above, p. 38.

[3] ECM III.472–3.

[4] ECM III.477–9.

[5] F. C. Diack (1944), 22.

that is cut by Picts in the Pictish period, is a question which might be debated. Much more significant at this stage, however, is the fact that Whitecleuch and Anwoth have provided symbols but not symbol stones. We know that Pictish symbols are occasionally engraved on metal and we know that symbols are found in caves, but the outstanding feature of symbol stones as such is that they are individual stone monuments, not mere decorative designs applied to metal or immovable rock surfaces. The controlling purpose behind them apparently required monuments that could be erected at selected places in the open air. Viewed from these angles of character and function, the Anwoth and Whitecleuch symbols are obviously sports or strays. South-west Scotland has not yet produced a single example of the symbol-stone monument that is so characteristic of Pictland. Two sets of symbols, divorced from their normal setting, are not what we should expect to find if Picts had lived in this area during or immediately after the Pictish period.

It has been shown that the twelfth-century references to the "Picts of Galloway" cannot stand unless they are supported. They are not supported, either historically or archaeologically, and so they fall. Those who wish to regard the question as open may take comfort from the fact that archaeological and philological studies will undoubtedly increase the volume of evidence available for consideration. The study of place-names alone will go far towards settling the question ; if there was Pictish settlement on any scale in south-west Scotland, place-names, however heavily Gaelicised or Anglicised, will reveal it. W. J. Watson found no *pett* place-names in the counties of Wigtown, Kirkcudbright and Dumfries. A more intensive survey may produce examples both of *pett* and, when they have been isolated, of other distinctively Pictish test-words. If the unexpected happens and the place-names of south-west Scotland reveal considerable traces of Pictish influence, then we shall have to revise our present opinion. But if an opinion is required today it can only be that on the evidence available the "Picts of Galloway" are a myth. So far as can be seen the historical Picts of Pictland played no part in the settlement of Galloway.

The internal divisions of Pictland raise a series of problems allied to but distinct from those discussed above. It is probable that the Pictish kingdom represents the political amalgamation of once separate peoples, and it is possible that the territorial distribution of these peoples, surviving their political amalgamation, underlies the provinces or internal divisions of historical Pictland. Bede, writing of St Columba's mission, believed that the Picts at that time were divided into two groups, the "northern Picts" (*septentrionales Picti*) and the "southern Picts" (*australes Picti*). He also understood that the "southern Picts" had been converted to Christianity by St Ninian. We may infer, therefore, that the division was recognised from about A.D. 400 to about A.D. 600; it may be much older than 400, and it was certainly remembered long after 600. The title *rex Pictorum citra Monoth*, which seems to be applied to Dubthalorc who died in 782,[1] may suggest that it was more than an academic memory in Bede's day. The boundary between the two groups is not defined with precision, but details provided by Adamnan and Bede strongly suggest that it was the Mounth.[2] We should accept the view that the "northern Picts" lived north of the Mounth and that the "southern Picts" lived between the Mounth and the Antonine Wall.

This division is based upon historical evidence. How far is it supported by archaeology and philology? Symbol stones demonstrate that the Mounth was a cultural boundary but not an insurmountable cultural barrier. They show that the cultural unity which they represent embraced both north and south Pictland, but the marked predominance of Class I monuments in the north and the marked predominance of Class II monuments in the south emphasise artistic and cultural divisions which cannot be ignored. The precise significance of this distributional variation need not be pursued here; it is enough to note that symbol stones strongly support the view that the Pictish peoples were recognisable as two cultural groups, separated by the Mounth, long after they had gone far towards achieving artistic and cultural unity. At the time when *pett* place-names were being formed, on the other hand, the Mounth seems not to have existed as a linguistic boundary. Their distribution implies a certain linguistic unity stretching from the Antonine Wall to the Moray Firth but, unlike that of symbol stones, not reaching the far north.[3] The two lines of investigation do not clash; it is simply that we cannot at present see how they are related. If the formation of *pett* place-names was contemporaneous with the erection of symbol stones we should have an interesting example of linguistic and cultural divisions overlapping and yet cutting across each other. Which might, but need not, imply the existence of two distinct peoples, perhaps within a single political framework. At

[1] See above, p. 22.

[2] Adamnan II.33, 35; Bede III.4. For A. O. Anderson's suggestion that the "southern Picts" lived in south-west Scotland, see above, p. 43*n*. It has also been suggested that Bede, misled by Ptolemy, uses "northern" and "southern" as we should use "western" and "eastern". This would confine the "northern Picts" (and St Columba's mission) to the western fringe of Scotland, and allow the "southern Picts" (and St Ninian) to roam at will from the Forth to Caithness. The suggestion may be ignored; it is only one of many worthless opinions expressed by a writer, now deceased, who has been justly described as a "Pictomaniac".

[3] See above, p. 37, and Maps 3 and 6.

present, however, we cannot date either the erection of symbol stones or the formation of *pett* place-names closely enough to see even the chronological relation between them. The historian knows too little about their local characteristics and about similar distributional details to pursue the problem further. The final picture will include other archaeological material, both Pictish and proto-Pictish, and other linguistic criteria which are still unrecognised.

There are also the seven provinces of Pictland. These are listed in a survey which forms part of an account of Scotland known as *De Situ Albanie* [1] and attached, as a kind of preface, to the *Pictish Chronicle* in MS A. The manuscript seems to have been written in the fourteenth century, and there is evidence that *De Situ Albanie* assumed its present form in the second half of the twelfth. The survey itself covers only Pictland, omitting Argyll and the lands south of the Forth, and therefore refers to the historical kingdom of the Picts before 843.[2] The seven provinces are listed as follows and, except in one instance, the names survive today [3]: *Enegus cum Moerne* (Angus and the Mearns), *Adtheodle et Gouerin* (Atholl and Gowrie), *Sradeern cum Meneted* (Strathearn and Menteith), *Fif cum Fothreue* (Fife and Kinross), *Marr cum Buchen* (Mar and Buchan), *Muref et Ros* (Moray and Ross), *Cathanesia* (Caithness). Another and apparently older form of the same list is preserved in the names of Cruithne's seven sons, which appear, with variant forms, in Group I manuscripts of the *Pictish Chronicle.*[4] They are: *Fib* (*Fibaid*, *Fibh*, *Fidbaiid*), *Fidach* (*Fidac*, *Fidaich*, *Fidhach*), *Fotla* (*Fodla*, *Floclaid*, *Foltlaid*, *Foltlaig*), *Fortrenn* (*Fortreann*, *Fortrend*), *Cait* (*Caitt*, *Gatt*, *Got*), *Ce* (*Cee*), and *Circinn* (*Circin*, *Circing*, *Cirig*, *Cirigh*, *Ciricc*).[5] These seven sons are eponyms derived from the seven provinces of Pictland. Five of them may be equated at once with five of the provinces listed in *De Situ Albanie.* The other two, Fidach and Ce, have given much trouble, but if it is true that Ce is associated with Aberdeenshire,[6] then the two lists may be equated thus:

1. Circinn	:	Enegus cum Moerne
2. Fotla	:	Adtheodle et Gouerin
3. Fortrenn	:	Sradeern cum Meneted

[1] Printed by W. F. Skene in Chronicles 135–7.

[2] *De Situ Albanie* also contains what amounts to a second survey, associated with the name of Andrew, Bishop of Caithness. This introduces Argyll (in place of Caithness) which, if not a mistake, implies that it refers to a period later than 843.

[3] For the names, and the boundaries, see W. J. Watson (1926), 107–17.

[4] See above, pp. 16–17.

[5] Some of these names are in the nominative case; others (e.g. *Fortrenn*) are in the genitive. The forms are given as they occur.

[6] Margaret E. Dobbs (1949), 137–8.

4. Fib	:	Fif cum Fothreue
5. Ce	:	Marr cum Buchen
6. Fidach	:	Muref et Ros
7. Cait	:	Cathanesia

The first four provinces lie south of the Mounth and their boundaries may be drawn with some precision. Ce, Fidach and Cait, the three provinces north of the Mounth, do not coincide with modern territorial divisions—Cait or Cathanesia, for example, seems to have included at least part of Sutherland—but the general impression, as worked out by W. J. Watson, is clear enough to give us a very good idea of the extent and boundaries of the seven provinces of Pictland.

The above list obviously refers to Pictland before 843, but it would not be easy to prove that a written version of it existed much before that date. The usual argument is that the legend of Cruithne's sons succeeding their father as kings would not have been acceptable in Pictland until, in the last phases of independence, the principle of matrilinear succession was being abandoned. But the age of the divisions themselves is another matter. They are obviously older than the legend. The province of Fotla (*Adtheodle et Gouerin*) is mentioned in 739, a hundred years before the extinction of the Pictish kingdom, as *Athfotla* or *Athfoithle* (Atholl)[1]; Fortrinn or Fortriu (gen. *Fortrenn*) is mentioned from 664 onwards[2]; and Circind (Circinn) appears before 600 as the area in which Aedan mac Gabrain fought the battle of Circind.[3] It is clear that the divisions are ancient. Some of them may be older than the Pictish kingdom itself. It will be interesting to see if archaeological and linguistic distributions, when they are worked out, bear any relation to these known historical boundaries. It will be especially significant if proto-Pictish distributions coincide with them, for then we should be able to establish equations of the first importance. And we ought to keep these divisions in mind when we try to locate historical proto-Pictish peoples such as those named by Ptolemy.

The name *Athfotla* (Atholl), recorded in 739, means "new Ireland" or "second Ireland". It implies the existence of a considerable body of Irish (Scottish) settlers in Pictland long before the Pictish kingdom came to an end in 843. Throughout the whole of the historical period Pictland was subjected to powerful Irish influences. Scots were probably settling in north Britain before the kingdom of Dalriada was founded, even before the authority of Rome was seriously shaken.

[1] AU *s.a.* 738; ATig (RC XVII.243). [2] AU *s.a.* 663, 692, 767.
[3] ATig (RC XVII.160). See above, p. 5, and below, pp. 51–2.

The pressure seems not to have slackened. Circind was reputed to be the home of the Eoganacht of Magh Gerginn, a branch of the Munster family from which Angus, probably Angus son of Fergus (*d.* 761), is said to have been descended. It may not be without significance in this context that in *De Situ Albanie* Circinn (*Enegus cum Moerne*) is placed first and described as the most important (*pars principalis*) of the seven provinces. If W. J. Watson's suggestion—that the name Gowrie is associated with Gabran, father of Aedan [1]—is accepted, this might indicate Irish influence in the area during the sixth century, and similar doubtful interpretations have been held to indicate Irish influence in Fife. How far the expeditions and conquests of a king like Aedan mac Gabrain strengthened Scottish influence is a matter of opinion, but it is probable that Scottish cultural penetration of Pictland was facilitated by the Pictish system of matrilinear succession. And after 565 the influence of the Columban church on culture, even on language, must have been tremendous. Altogether there is a considerable amount of evidence for the intrusion of Scots and Scottish influence into Pictland before 843, but its quality is not always of the highest; much of it is late or legendary or transmitted through dubious Irish sources. Most of it has been assembled by W. J. Watson,[2] but the sifting process has hardly yet begun.

The linguistic evidence for Scottish intrusion is represented chiefly by place-names, hill-names, river-names and district-names. Traces of Scottish settlement in Pictland before 843 are considerable in all the four southern provinces and by no means negligible north of the Mounth. Gaelic names are common everywhere, of course, and the chief difficulty is that of determining which arose during the Pictish period. Into the final picture, also, must come ring-forts, Ogam stones and much else. The problem of Scottish intrusion into Pictland is a good example of a field in which archaeological-historical-philological co-operation holds out high hopes of success. The problem is also important in itself. Already it is clear that the Gaelicisation of Pictland had gone far by 843, a fact which helps to explain the rapid disappearance of the Pictish language. It is probable that the language (or languages) and other distinctive cultural characteristics of the Picts were doomed to extinction before the accession of Kenneth mac Alpin introduced the final wave of Scottish influence which overwhelmed Pictland.

The problem of Pictish origins overshadows this volume. We are

[1] W. J. Watson (1926), 112–13.

[2] W. J. Watson (1926), 109–13, 213–34. See also T. F. O'Rahilly (1946), 370–3; A. O. Anderson (1948), 33–6; H. M. Chadwick (1949), 120–6.

carried to the fringe of it again by the last questions raised here, those which concern the proto-Pictish peoples of history. The importance of isolating proto-Pictish archaeological cultures and of recognising proto-Pictish linguistic survivals has been sufficiently stressed. Equally important in any attempt to see beyond the Pictish period are the proto-Pictish historical peoples. We know several by name, and we can safely label them "proto-Pictish". To define their relationship to the Picts of history would seem to be a simple matter, but nothing about the Picts is simple. And, since we are dealing with names, the problem is philological rather than historical.

Tacitus, writing of Agricola's campaigns at the end of the first century, knew and used the word *Caledonia*, but to him the inhabitants of northern Britain were *Britanni*. Other writers, Lucan, Martial, Valerius Flaccus, Pliny, Solinus, Statius and their successors,[1] refer to Caledonian Britons (*Caledonii Britanni*), the Caledonian Ocean (*Caledonius Oceanus*), the Caledonian Forest or Forests (*Silva Caledonia*, *Calidoniae Silvae*), the Caledonian Promontory (*Calidoniae Promontorium*) and the Caledonian Plains (*Calydonii Campi*). It is clear that the *Britanni* of Tacitus are the *Caledonii* (*Caledones*) of other writers. Both are group-names which cover a number of separate peoples. Tacitus mentions only one by name, the *Boresti*, but there were others, and it is politically significant that they were able to combine in a confederacy against Agricola. Ptolemy provides the names of some thirty-three separate peoples who lived in Britain early in the second century. Sixteen of them belong wholly or mainly to what is now Scotland, and W. J. Watson[2] has listed them in the following forms: *Caereni*, *Cornavii*, *Lugi*, *Smertae*, *Decantae*, *Carnonacae*, *Caledonii*, *Vacomagi*, *Taexali*, *Venicones*, *Creones*, *Epidii*, *Damnonii*, *Novantae*, *Selgovae*, and *Votadini*. The first eleven or twelve of these peoples, together with the most northerly divisions of the *Damnonii*, lived north of the Forth-Clyde line. We may fairly describe them as proto-Picts in the sense that their descendants were historical Picts, though some of them occupied that part of north Britain which later became the Scottish kingdom of Dalriada. By the end of the third century the group-name *Caledonii*, by which they were collectively known, had given place to *Picti*.

The confederacy of the northern peoples against Agricola illustrates the tendency towards political amalgamation which, increasing with time and under external pressure, finally produced the historical

[1] For references to evidence here quoted see Holder 1.555–6, 691–4, and MHB i–cxlv.

[2] W. J. Watson (1926), 15–28.

kingdom of the Picts. At the beginning of the third century, over a hundred years after Agricola's campaigns but a hundred years before the name *Picti* appears, we are told that the *Caledonii* (Καληδόνιοι of Xiphilinus) and the *Maeatae* (Μαιάται) are the greatest peoples among the (northern) Britons and, perhaps more important, that the names of the other peoples have been merged into these two. We are also told that the *Maeatae* "live close to the wall that divides the island into two parts"; that the *Caledonii* are "beyond them"; and, finally, that these two peoples are co-operating against the Romans.[1] A hundred years later (*c.*310) there is a reference to "*Caledones* and other Picts"[2]; and by 368, Ammianus Marcellinus tells us, the *Picti* are divided into two peoples, the *Dicalydones* and the *Verturiones*.[3] In these references we may see the Pictish and proto-Pictish peoples advancing towards a political unity which was clearly foreshadowed before the Romans left Britain. There were still two divisions (*Dicalydones* and *Verturiones*) in the fourth century, however, and there were still two divisions ("northern Picts" and "southern Picts") in the sixth.[4]

Tacitus believed that the inhabitants of north Britain were different, at least in appearance, from the inhabitants of the south, but he described them all as *Britanni*, a name later reserved for the native peoples of the Roman province. Whether or not he meant to imply that they were all of one race is doubtful and perhaps unimportant. But the names *Cornavii* and *Damnonii* carry the suggestion that the peoples to which they were applied were related to the *Cornovii* and the *Dumnonii* of southern Britain. Such a relationship is inherently probable in the case of the *Damnonii*, who were later associated, it would seem, with the British kingdom of Dumbarton. But the *Cornavii* lived in the far north, in the area that later became part of Pictland. The *Decantae*, another proto-Pictish people, also seem to have had affinities in the south. The possible implications are obvious.

The evidence of names alone often misleads those who try to force precise political and racial conclusions from them. Changes in names, in political balances, and in the racial fabric, frequently occur independently of each other. The limitation of the name *Britanni*, for example, has no racial significance. Nor, so far as we can see, has the introduction of the names *Caledonii* and *Picti*. *Caledonii* as a name has at least two quite different applications: it was a group-name applied collectively to all the peoples later known as *Picti*, and from

[1] Dio Cassius, as abridged by Xiphilinus. See Holder I.693; II.388–9; MHB lx–lxi.

[2] See above, p. 2. [3] See above, p. 3. [4] See above, pp. 20–21.

Ptolemy we know that it was also the name of a single people whose territories stretched from south-east Perthshire to the Beauly Firth. *Verturiones* as a name has been convincingly equated with *Fortrinn*; but the *Verturiones*, one of the two divisions of the Picts in the fourth century, certainly controlled more than the Pictish province of Fortrinn. And *Fortrinn* itself had two meanings: strictly it was the name of a single province, but it could be a synonym for Pictland, as when Brude mac Bile was described as "king of Fortrinn". These examples provide a warning that, even when names have been equated, the equation of underlying political and racial implications cannot be assumed.

It is of the first importance, however, to equate names, especially names of the pre-Pictish period with names of the Pictish period. Ptolemy's **Votadini* ('Ωταδινοί) are found in the Pictish period as *Guotodin* and *Gododdin*, but they are outside the Pictish area, and the peoples to which they refer were neither Picts nor proto-Picts. More to the point is Ptolemy's *Caledonii* (Καληδόνιοι), for it is the name of a presumably proto-Pictish people and it survives as a name, with changed political implications, into the Pictish period. Names of other proto-Pictish historical peoples may be preserved in place-names, hill-names and river-names, but none of those listed by Ptolemy, except *Caledonii*, survives as the name of a people in the Pictish period—unless we accept O'Rahilly's suggestion that *Venicones* (in a variety of manuscript spellings) is merely a bad scribal corruption of *Verturiones*.[1] If O'Rahilly is right, we have the significant association of the names *Venicones*, *Verturiones* and *Fortrinn*. The *Venicones*, it may be noted, seem to have occupied the coastlands of east Scotland from the Forth to the Mounth or, as O'Rahilly suggests, from the Forth to the Dee.

The *Maeatae* (Μαιάται) of Dio Cassius and Xiphilinus may be safely equated with the *Miathi* of Adamnan.[2] There is no reason to doubt the statement of Dio Cassius that the *Maeatae* lived near the Wall,[3] and it seems clear enough that he meant the Antonine Wall.[4] Dumyat and Myot Hill, near Stirling and north of the Antonine Wall, probably mark (archaeologically as well as linguistically) the southern limits of their territory.[5] If the "battle of Circind" is the same as

[1] T. F. O'Rahilly (1946), 382.
[2] Adamnan 1.8. See W. J. Watson (1926), 58–9.
[3] See above, p. 50.
[4] A. O. Anderson (1922), 1.96–7, and W. J. Watson (1926), 8–9, 57–8, both think that Dio Cassius was referring to Hadrian's Wall, but a reading of Dio Cassius, as abridged by Xiphilinus, confirms the view that he was referring to the Antonine Wall. Cf. R. G. Collingwood (1937), 157.
[5] See above, pp. 24, 40.

Adamnan's *Bellum Miathorum*,[1] it would seem that in the sixth century the *Miathi* occupied Angus and the Mearns. It is sometimes thought necessary to assume that the *Maeatae* moved northwards between 200 and 600,[2] but this is an attempt to explain what perhaps requires no explanation. If we must assume something, we could assume that the name *Maeatae* covers all the peoples who lived between the Mounth and the Antonine Wall at the beginning of the second century. After all, we know from Dio Cassius that the *Maeatae* were not a single small and insignificant people but a group of peoples, one of the two great divisions of the north.[3]

Few firm political conclusions can be drawn from the evidence and the equations at present available, but one certainty shines clearly through the doubt and the confusion. The Picts, and the proto-Picts before them, fell into two distinct political divisions from about A.D. 200 onwards. In 200 the two divisions were *Caledonii* and *Maeatae*; about 310 there were *Caledones* and *alii Picti*; about 368 there were *Dicalydones* and *Verturiones*; and, if we trust Bede's information, from about 400 to about 600 there were "northern Picts" and "southern Picts".

It is usually assumed, on insufficient evidence, that the boundaries of these political divisions changed with their changing names. It could be assumed, on the same insufficient evidence, that beneath the changing names the divisions themselves remained fixed and permanent. If the *Maeatae* occupied the lands between the Mounth and the Antonine Wall, as suggested above, then perhaps the "*Caledonii*" of Dio Cassius lived to the north of the Mounth. We know, of course, that Ptolemy's "*Caledonii*" occupied much of Perthshire, where their presence is independently attested by the names Dunkeld, Rohallion and Schiehallion, but their territory also extended north of the Mounth to the Beauly Firth. And Dio Cassius explicitly states that his "*Caledonii*" and "*Maeatae*" had replaced the names of the separate northern peoples. It is at least possible, though it has never been suggested, that the "*Caledonii*" of Dio Cassius, as distinct from both the specific "*Caledonii*" of Ptolemy and the all-embracing "*Caledonii*" of other writers, were those peoples who lived north of the Mounth, including only the northern part of Ptolemy's "*Caledonii*". If this were so, the *Maeatae* would include all the southern proto-Pictish peoples, including those who lived in Perthshire. As a possibility this may gain a little support from the fourth-century divisions of *Dicalydones* and

[1] It cannot be proved that the two battles are the same, but the identification should not be rejected out of hand as by A. O. Anderson (1922), 1.96–7. Geographical considerations alone do not justify its rejection, as is recognised by T. F. O'Rahilly (1946), 505.

[2] Cf. W. J. Watson (1926), 58.

[3] See above, p. 50.

Verturiones. The *Dicalydones* are clearly related in name at least to the *Caledonii* or *Caledones*, and the curious prefix is usually held to imply that their lands lay on both sides of Druim Alban. It is worth noting again that the "*Caledonii*" of Ptolemy occupied lands on both sides of the Mounth. The *Dicalydones*, taking their name from the northern half of Ptolemy's "*Caledonii*", may be the same people as the "*Caledonii*" of Dio Cassius. This, in turn, would leave the whole of Pictland south of the Mounth to the *Verturiones*, who could be equated politically with the earlier *Maeatae*. Indeed, the *Verturiones* ought to cover just such a wide area if their name has anything more than a mere linguistic connexion with the name of the *Venicones*, who occupied the coastlands from the Mounth to the Forth, and with the name of Fortrinn, which even as a single province stretched westwards across Perthshire to Druim Alban.

The suggestion thrown out in the last paragraph is that from about A.D. 200 the proto-Picts, and later the Picts, were recognised as falling into two divisions which, despite changing names, remained static as political conceptions; that the "*Caledonii*" and the "*Maeatae*" of Dio Cassius may be equated with the "*Dicalydones*" and the "*Verturiones*" of Ammianus Marcellinus; and that the boundary between the two divisions was the Mounth. Then, from 400 to 600, we have the "northern Picts" and the "southern Picts", separated by the same boundary and, if the suggestion comes anywhere near the truth, perpetuating ancient divisions which go back at least to the end of the second century. But the suggestion is little more than a guess, and it would be surprising if it retained its present form without modification.

Peering beyond the Pictish period, we have been attracted to assumed and questionable equations which might be misleading if they were not so clearly labelled, and we have been drawn towards problems which lie outside the scope of our inquiry. But an excursion into conjecture is perhaps the best way to emphasise the fundamental importance of establishing reliable equations between historical, archaeological, linguistic and other conceptions. That is our great need. Until it is satisfied we shall not be able to advance with confidence towards the tantalising problem of the origins of the Picts.

Chapter II

THE ARCHAEOLOGICAL BACKGROUND

Stuart Piggott

THE historical Picts are known to us from documentary sources, epigraphy, and an art-style mainly manifested in low-relief stone sculpture and a certain amount of surviving metal-work. The attribution of other aspects of material culture to these people—forts, settlements, burials and so forth—must remain inferential in the present state of our knowledge, and Pictish archaeology as such can hardly be said to exist. We can point to certain distributions (as for instance that of the carved stones) which by-and-large conform to boundaries approximating to those of the historical Pictish kingdom, or we can show that certain objects within the same area may be dated within the known chronological range of Pictish hegemony and so be presumptively of Pictish origin. But for the rest, we can at present do no more than examine the prehistory of Pictland with a view to assessing the component elements which are likely to have been present in greater or less degree at the time when the Pictish people emerge into the uncertain light of early historical record. If these antecedents can be truthfully estimated, they may in their turn give us a clue to the likely nature of certain aspects of Pictish culture.

We cannot consider north-east Scotland in isolation, either from the rest of Scotland or from the British Isles as a whole. The prehistory and history of these islands is inextricably bound up with that of the European continent, and Britain may best be considered as the meeting-place of three main zones of influences, from the Atlantic, the North Sea and the Channel coasts respectively. To these should be added a fourth cultural zone, that of the Circumpolar regions, within which archaeology shows the Shetlands, the Orkneys and parts of the northern mainland of Scotland to have come in ancient times. In Scotland north of the Forth-Clyde isthmus, the Atlantic and North Sea provinces are separated by the great massif of the Highlands (through which, however, a highway of communication from west to east is afforded by the Great Glen), and elements of Circumpolar culture appear to penetrate southwards down the eastern coasts rather than those of the west.

We may conveniently start our survey of human settlement in Scotland in the middle of the second millennium B.C., a date which may seem unnecessarily early as a prologue to the Pictish Dark Ages, but which, as we shall see, is in fact justified. By about 1500 B.C. agricultural colonies had been established along the Atlantic sea-ways for four or five centuries and, if wholly stone-using in their earliest phases, had soon become involved in the trade and production of copper, bronze and gold for tools and adornment.[1] The settlements of these people are mainly marked today by their monumental family vaults, or chambered cairns, in the Hebrides, Orkney, Shetland, and (as a result of traffic up the Great Glen) in the North Sea area round Inverness and northwards to Caithness. Such tombs appear to belong to the first stages of colonisation by immigrant groups of Iberian and West French antecedents; but the early establishment of centres of metal-working in Ireland, at least by 1700 B.C. or so, was soon to bring the Atlantic province of Scotland, as well as areas outside it, within the ambit of a common Hiberno-Scottish school of metallurgy.

It is likely that the colonists arriving by the Atlantic routes found, and absorbed into their economy, a sparse and scattered population of stone-using hunter-fishers in the Western Isles, heirs to the ancient traditions of the Palaeolithic and Mesolithic cultures of northern Europe, and that cultures of mixed tradition ensued. In Orkney and Shetland these cultures (as seen for instance at Skara Brae) can be recognised as specifically including elements proper to the whole Circumpolar region of Eurasia and the northern coasts of the American continent, and an extension of this province southward into the eastern woodlands of Scotland can be traced, now mingled with agricultural traditions derived either from Atlantic colonists or from north-easterly extensions of southern English Neolithic cultures, which can be traced via Yorkshire to Aberdeenshire. The hunter-fisher traditions can be reciprocally distinguished as far south as the mouth of the Thames. The well-known carved stone balls of north-eastern Scotland belong to this Skara Brae type of culture.

Within the first quarter of the second millennium B.C., and concurrently with much of the Atlantic colonisation just described, eastern Scotland was, in common with eastern England, also receiving immigrants from the North Sea area, coming from homelands likely to have been in the main between the Elbe and the Rhine. These colonists were largely stone-using but had some knowledge of metallurgy and a sufficient interest in metal tools to acquire them by trade when possible, and they are distinguished in the archaeological record by their custom of single-grave inhumation, rather than that of collective burial in the

[1] Fully documented in W. L. Scott (1951).

Atlantic tradition, their graves being either simple pits, or more often these lined with stone slabs to form a cist, in Scotland usually without a covering mound, but sometimes beneath a barrow or cairn, though in England south of the Tyne tumulus-burial was the normal custom. In these graves, the crouched burial could be accompanied by a pot, either of the Beaker or the Food Vessel type, or tools and weapons appropriate to the two sexes: stone battle-axes or bronze daggers with men; necklaces, small flint knives or bronze awls with women. In Europe the cultures ancestral to these in Britain had affiliations with the Warrior Cultures widely spread from northern Europe to the south Russian steppe, and a case has been made for regarding such cultures as representing an early dispersal of peoples speaking Indo-European dialects.[1]

These then were the cultural components about 1500 B.C. in the area later to be that of the Picts: surviving hunter-fisher traditions of Mesolithic origin, mingled with intrusive agricultural economies; a powerful element represented by the single-grave burials; and, especially in the north of the area, an Atlantic-derived component. Subsistence was based on rudimentary hoe-cultivation, and barley seems to have been the staple crop; communities would have been small and impermanent, moving as land was exhausted, and through the whole area would have moved the traders in metal and other commodities, bringing with them news and strange tales.

The pattern so set changed little for many centuries. By the early first millennium B.C. the Atlantic influence had dwindled except in so far as Irish metal-smiths still used the old routes, and the Circumpolar hunter-fisher elements must have been totally absorbed in what were now fully Bronze Age agricultural communities in eastern Scotland. For unknown reasons, cremation had replaced inhumation as a burial rite and although in the middle of the second millennium the opening up of trade connexions with Saxo-Thuringia had brought about notable local innovations in the aristocratic and mercantile culture of Wessex, such events only slightly touched north Britain. For most of Britain it was a period of insular development, often, it seems, of technological stagnation.

But in the couple of centuries round 600–400 B.C. there is evidence of at least trade contacts between eastern Scotland and north-west Germany, then in the iron-using Hallstatt C and D phases of its prehistory. Although the beginnings of a true Early Iron Age in England is marked by immigration from across the North Sea by settlers who came at least as far north as Yorkshire round 450–400 B.C., the Scottish

[1] V. G. Childe (1935, 1946) and S. Piggott (1949, 1954).

evidence appears to show only imports, into a bronze-using economy, of occasional personal possessions of Hallstatt type.[1]

It has however been claimed that there is evidence, in Scotland, northern England and Ireland, of something more than trade at this time, and that in a type of Late Bronze Age pottery, rather unsatisfactorily called "Flat-Rimmed Ware", we may recognise a novel ceramic style which can only be attributed to an intrusive population with likely origins in north Germany.[2] The evidence is not, however, at all clear, and it can be interpreted in more than one way. The pottery in question is normally represented by undecorated bucket-shaped pots of coarse ware, sometimes but not always with flattened rims, and it is this very lack of really distinctive features which renders the problem a difficult one at the outset. Such simple forms could have a local origin in degenerate native Bronze Age types, and the presence of somewhat similar pottery in north Germany may be nothing more than a parallel devolution there. Sprockhoff indeed regards the apparent resemblances between the German and the British material as no more than a lowest common denominator of bad pottery—*kümmerkeramik*.[3]

On the other hand, a small proportion of sherds within this Flat-Rimmed group are of harder, grittier paste than that normal to the British Bronze Age wares or their derivatives, and this may indicate the introduction of new methods of pottery manufacture. The question is not the archaeological quibble it may appear at first sight, but one of some importance. A few metal ornaments or weapons of Hallstatt or Hallstatt-derived types need mean nothing more than trade contacts between north Germany and the old Bronze Age population of north-east Scotland, but innovations in pottery manufacture can hardly result from anything but the arrival of immigrants, in however small numbers, bringing with them distinctive techniques in the domestic crafts normally associated with the women of the community. In fine, upon the ambiguous pottery evidence just discussed rests the question as to whether north-east Scotland (and certain other areas of Britain) continued in a native Bronze Age tradition unaltered until the end of the first millennium B.C., or whether this tradition was modified by the arrival of newcomers of Hallstatt antecedents in the fifth and sixth centuries B.C. And since such hypothetical Hallstatt colonists are likely to have spoken a Celtic dialect, the bearing of the problem upon the questions discussed by K. H. Jackson in Chapter VI becomes immedi-

[1] Listed by V. G. Childe (1935), 163–5, with additions by Cecily M. Piggott (1948).
[2] V. G. Childe (1935), 170–3; R. B. K. Stevenson (1944), 124–5; H. O'N. Hencken (1942).
[3] E. Sprockhoff (1941), and in conversation 1950.

ately apparent. Unfortunately, on the available evidence, the problem must remained unresolved.

We have seen that immigrants bringing in a version of the Continental Hallstatt iron-using cultures arrived in England in the middle of the fifth century B.C.; such immigrations continued, and in the mid-third century B.C. were augmented by further contingents representing the La Tène phase of the European Iron Age. But the effective colonisation of these peoples, and of the subsequent insular versions of the British Iron Age, did not extend north of Yorkshire much before the first century. Finds of aristocratic metal-work, such as sword-scabbards and chariot-gear, suggest that south-west Scotland may have shared at least in trade with Ulster, where warrior overlords, apparently coming from Yorkshire, had established themselves perhaps as early as the middle of the second century B.C., but in general the evidence at present available suggests that the arrival of Iron Age peoples in the region north of the Tyne was an event not likely to date before the first century B.C. Linguistically, we are for the first time dealing with persons who undoubtedly spoke a Celtic tongue.

The appearance of the Iron Age Celts in southern Scotland is marked in the main by the archaeological evidence for the arrival of a warrior aristocracy—fortifications, fine metal-work, weapons and chariot-gear. Stylistically it is immediately apparent that these elements were not brought direct from the Continent, but are characteristically southern English in all respects. The unsettled state of England in the first century B.C., with the Belgic invasion of *c.*75 B.C., the probable influx of refugee chieftains from the Venetic tribal area after 56, and Caesar's raids of the next two years, to say nothing of the knowledge in the Celtic courts of the irresistible establishment of Roman power in Gaul, would all have combined to create a situation when refugees might well set out northwards hoping for respite. The distribution of archaeological material indicative of such action suggests that the great tribal confederacy of the Brigantes, stretching from sea to sea south of the Tyne-Solway line, at first inhibited the passage of refugees through its territories, and access to the northern lands was gained by sea.

By the North Sea route there seems to have come some form of invasion which entered the Lowlands by means of the Tweed and, spreading up the valley of this river and those of its tributaries, established strongholds and built fortifications in the foothills of the Cheviots and adjacent hill-masses. The evidence of changes in fortification technique in that area suggests that more than one movement may have been involved, and to the earlier belong forts with a sheer-faced stone wall as defence, which may on occasion be laced with horizontal and vertical timbers. As one moves north-east from the Tweed basin forts become far fewer, but the timber-laced wall is characteristically represented in the so-called *murus gallicus* and vitrified forts of Scotland north of the Forth-Clyde isthmus.[1] These, well known within the Pictish area, are further discussed below in Chapter III.

Along the Atlantic route colonists reached the Western Isles from regions which probably included north-west England, and possibly west France, at a time likely to be contemporary with or later than the North Sea movements just described. Here the evidence of pottery, and still more the specialised weaving techniques and house-types, imply a more complete migration than that affecting the Tweed basin, with entire families taking the road to the Isles. From the Hebrides, colonisation extended to Orkney, Shetland and the northern mainland of Caithness and Sutherland, marked particularly by defensive circular tower-houses of a kind evolved from the round stone-walled farmhouse in Scotland and known as a broch.[2] In this connexion we may note a valuable piece of dating evidence contained in the historical record. A statement in Orosius may imply that at the time of the Roman conquest in A.D. 43 the chieftains of the Orkneys made formal submission to Claudius in a manner common to Celtic tribes on the immediate fringes of the Roman province who wished to become client kingdoms. Now a knowledge of such procedure would be appropriate only to tribes recently in contact with the Romans, and this implies that the Orcadian chieftains, who can hardly be other than the builders of the brochs, had recently arrived in the north from some more southerly region.[3]

In 1935 Childe demonstrated the close affinities between a series of bone tools characteristic of the Atlantic Iron Age of Scotland and others equally representative of the south-west English Iron Age B cultures.[4] Scott, in 1948, in an analysis of the Iron Age pottery from the Hebrides, found certain analogies in techniques and arrangement of ornament between it and the south-west English Iron Age B styles.[5] But the bone objects in question—weaving combs, shuttle bobbins, oblong dice and so-called toggles, and other less distinctive forms—are equally characteristic of the Iron Age B culture of Yorkshire and farther north, and with a similarly well-defined group of harness equipment and other metal types such as swords they can be regarded as Brigantian in origin, with a later (first to second century) spread into the Scottish Lowlands. There is no need, therefore, to bring these elements in the Atlantic

[1] Cecily M. Piggott (1950), 129–35. R. E. M. Wheeler (1952) has urged the limitation of the term *murus gallicus* to the elaborated type described by Caesar in Gaul.

[2] W. L. Scott (1947, 1948).

[3] Quoted by V. G. Childe (1946), 129.

[4] V. G. Childe (1935), 238–42.

[5] W. L. Scott (1948), 57.

Iron Age from as far south as Somerset, since they also occur as a constant feature in Brigantia, two hundred miles farther north.[1]

Scott, in his paper quoted above, was careful to point out that no really exact parallels existed between the Scottish and the south-west English pottery, and he hinted that we might have to look for partial origins at least in western France. It is in fact very difficult to perceive more than a few generalised similarities in decorative techniques common to the two groups of pottery, which are both highly individual and elaborate. This is not the place to go into the matter in detail, but it is sufficient to say that the pottery of the Scottish Atlantic Iron Age suggests a derivation either from local Bronze Age or even Late Neolithic styles or from retarded Hallstatt or even Late Bronze Age traditions. An origin has been suggested in western France (though direct evidence is lacking), and its antecedents cannot at present be seen convincingly in any British group. It is therefore possible that the Orcadian chieftains' knowledge of the Roman world had been gained by themselves or their immediate ancestors in some region other than in southern Britain, and that the peculiar weaving equipment and other specifically British Iron Age traits are likely to have been acquired from the western sea-coast of Brigantia, perhaps as the result of a secondary migration following the Roman occupation of that region.

So far as the archaeology of the northern Pictish area is concerned, therefore, we may say that by the early centuries of the Christian era there was, in addition to peoples of ancient Bronze Age stock, a considerable population of iron-using, presumably Celtic-speaking immigrants who had only recently colonised Orkney, Caithness and the coastal fringe of Sutherland, and whose characteristic architectural monument was the circular defensive tower-house or broch. Here we may be dealing with a mixture of intrusive and local traditions together evolving the broch architecture, but there is an important component representing the British Iron Age B cultures of La Tène derivation and in this instance probably originating in Brigantia.

With the exception of a few scattered examples as far south as the Lowlands, the broch-builders' province in eastern Scotland lies north of the Black Isle. Immediately to the south of this, in the Beauly-Firth:Loch-Ness:Strath-Nairn area, appear timber-laced defences represented by the "vitrified" forts which, as Childe demonstrated, are the result of accidental or deliberate firing of timber-framed walls built of readily fusible stone.[2] Eight or ten similar forts, or those in which the

[1] Compare distribution maps of weaving combs in Audrey S. Henshall (1950), 147, and of swords in S. Piggott (1950), 23. Much of the northern English and Lowland Scottish material is unpublished, and its significance hitherto unrecognised.

[2] V. G. Childe (1938).

timber-channels have been recovered by excavation, lie in Aberdeenshire and between the Tay and the South Esk; one or two are known in the Lowlands, and a couple of dozen are scattered along the west coasts of Scotland from Fort William to the Solway.

These forts constitute a cardinal problem in Scottish prehistory. The distribution indicated above may in fact be delusive, since while vitrified examples can be recognised on the ground without excavation, timber-laced walls which have not been burnt can only be identified by careful excavation,[1] and many more are likely to exist than those at present on record. In 1935 Childe pointed out the affinities of the timber-laced construction with the *muri gallici* described by Caesar, suggested that the Scottish forts represented a direct immigration from Gaul to the Moray Firth and, stressing the absence of Roman finds from excavated examples and the occurrence of brooches of early La Tène types in them, suggested that they might mark "the earliest landings of La Tène Kelts in Scotland",[2] perhaps in the third century B.C. But in 1946, when evidence of the late survival of the brooch-types in question in the south of England had become available, he inclined to an origin in southern England, and to a date near 100 B.C. for their inception in Scotland.[3] In 1949 the writer, taking into consideration similar timber-laced forts recently excavated in the Welsh Marches and known in vitrified form as far north-west as the Vale of Clwyd in North Wales, suggested that the arrival of these fort-builders in Scotland might have been by a west-coast Atlantic route from a point around the mouth of the Cheshire Dee, and that the east-coast examples were the result of subsequent movement up the Great Glen.[4]

A subsequent reappraisal of the characteristic metal types which had been classed by Childe, with the forts, as components of his Abernethy culture, has led Mrs Piggott to emphasise the southern English character of the culture, and to reaffirm a date not before 100 B.C. for its implantation in Scotland by whatever route—a question which must remain uncertain in view of the unsatisfactory evidence afforded by distribution maps.[5] She also stresses the personal character of the imported objects (La Tène 1*c* brooches, ring-headed cloak pins, spiral finger- or toe-rings) as appropriate to a warrior invasion, bringing with it too its peculiar type of fortification technique. As we know from excavation, there is no sign of a change in pottery traditions which would have been expected from more wholesale immigration.

The use of timber-lacing as a reinforcement to a rubble or earthen

[1] As at Castle Law, Glencorse (Midlothian), detected by excavation in 1948. See S. Piggott (1952).

[2] V. G. Childe (1935), 193–7.

[3] V. G. Childe (1946), 129–30.

[4] S. Piggott (1949).

[5] Cecily M. Piggott (1950), 129–35.

rampart, particularly when constructed so as to produce a vertical wood-shored outer face, appears to be a technique of Hallstatt origins on the Continent, and versions of it appear in southern English forts of the Iron Age A culture in the third or even fourth centuries B.C. Wheeler has rightly warned us recently against confusing all types of timber-laced ramparts together under the term *murus gallicus* or "Gallic Walls", a phrase appropriate only to the elaborate type built by the Gauls in the first century B.C. for the specific purpose of opposing the Roman battering-rams and incendiary parties—*ab incendio lapis et ab ariete materia defendit.*[1] He rightly points out that the only Scottish fort approximating to such a sophisticated construction is that at Burghead on the Moray Firth, referred to again below, which alone of British forts had the internal beams nailed or bolted together with iron in the Gaulish manner. The Scottish timber-laced forts in general he would regard as ramshackle versions of a half-forgotten Gallic Wall technique, built in the first century A.D.; and, following a hint of Childe's, he suggests that the vitrified forts may have been burnt as part of a deliberate Roman policy of slighting the native strongholds.[2]

The long-standing Hallstatt tradition of the use of timber-lacing in a wall or rampart makes it questionable, however, whether the Scottish forts can be regarded as degenerate versions of Gallic structures; furthermore, their associated material culture, where it has been recovered, shows links not with Gaul but specifically with southern England, where the true *murus gallicus* is unknown. Timbering in walls and ramparts is, however, known in hill-forts in northern England and on the Welsh marches,[3] none likely to be earlier than the beginning of the first century B.C., and these, and the Scottish examples of the same technique, would be best explicable as representative of the old Hallstatt tradition lying behind the British Iron Age A group of cultures, surviving unaffected by the changes in hill-fort architecture introduced by the Iron Age B people of La Tène affiliations. On the other hand it must be remembered that timber-laced walls have a long history in continental Europe, and examples of the Dark Ages and early medieval period are known in Poland, Czechoslovakia, north Germany and Denmark. There is no inherent reason why some or many of the Scottish forts under discussion should not in fact belong to the period of the historical Picts.

The second Iron Age component within the Pictish area could then be interpreted as one of British Iron Age A, and ultimately Hallstatt,

[1] R. E. M. Wheeler (1952), quoting Caesar (BG VII.23).
[2] V. G. Childe (1946), 216; R. E. M. Wheeler (1952), 78.
[3] W. J. Varley (1948) and references.

derivation, though including in its material culture such items as brooches of La Tène types. As with the brochs, the timber-laced and vitrified forts can hardly have been built in Scotland before the first century B.C., and their construction could, as we have seen, have continued for a long period of time.

The situation in north-east Scotland at the time of the Agricolan advance at the end of the first century A.D. was then that of a Bronze Age substrate population with, in the north (Orkney, Caithness and Sutherland), a considerable component of uncertain but probably composite origins though including elements present in the English Iron Age B culture-area. Elsewhere, south of the Great Glen, a certain number of chieftains, at least, were causing the construction of forts in techniques ultimately derived from those of Iron Age in Wessex or Sussex and, at less remove in space and time, from those of Yorkshire and the Welsh borders. Neither group of Iron Age settlers, both of which may be presumed to have been Celtic in language and traditions, is likely to have been in the north-east Scottish area for much more than a hundred and fifty years or so by A.D. 80.

It is not the purpose of this essay to do more than outline the antecedents of what was to become the Pictish population, and structures within the area of their settlement known to date from the early centuries of the Christian era, such as the "earth-houses", are discussed elsewhere; we must remember, too, that the building and occupation of brochs clearly continued well into and beyond the period of the Roman occupation of southern Scotland. There remains for comment, however, a group of metal-work in the La Tène tradition, consistent in its stylistic qualities and with its distribution centred on the Pictish area.

This Caledonian metal-work, as it may conveniently be called, is represented in the main by two types of massive bronze bracelets or arm-rings, and a distinctive form of terret or fair-lead on horse-harness.[1] These need not be discussed in detail, and it is sufficient to say that associated finds suggest a date not earlier than the second century A.D. for any of the types. The terrets are copies of Roman military equipment of forms known to have been current on the Continent in the second and third centuries, and one group of bracelets, those in the form of a snake, again probably copy Roman prototypes and employ Roman decorative motifs. The other group, exemplified by the pair from the Castle Newe earth-house, derives at some remove from native Iron Age torcs of the first century A.D.,[2] and on occasion they have

[1] H. E. Kilbride-Jones (1935).
[2] For these prototypes see R. R. Clarke (1949).

coloured enamel inlay in the Roman manner. The whole group, with one or two odd pieces in comparable style, represents a Romano-Celtic tradition, probably in the main of post-Antonine date, developing in north-east Scotland in a localised and distinctive form. What should be noted is that the style cannot be regarded as ancestral to the "Celtic" elements embodied in the art of the Pictish sculptured stones and metal-work, but represents a tradition which may have been relatively short-lived and which died out without leaving its mark on later work.

It remains therefore to sum up the somewhat ambiguous archaeological evidence we have surveyed. The earlier populations of the Pictish area, from the early second millennium B.C. onwards, combined traditions from the ancient Eurasian hunter-fisher areas of the Circumpolar north, the builders of chambered tombs from Atlantic Europe, and the Warrior Cultures of the north European plain. What contributions these peoples may have made to historical Pictish culture is obviously a matter of inference, and little more, but their importance as a substrate population should not be underestimated. Linguistic affiliations must be a matter of guess-work, but a predominantly non-Indo-European tradition until the Late Bronze or Early Iron Age is inherently likely, although the likelihood of some Indo-European language being spoken by peoples of the Warrior Cultures must not be forgotten. By analogy, the social unit should be that of the homestead rather than the village, and agriculture that of primitive hoe-cultivation of cereal crops and stock-breeding.

The circular house-type (in timber as at Scotstarvit [1] and in stone in innumerable hut-circles) goes back to this period, even if known examples cannot be dated in our area before the early centuries A.D., and it is just possible that in the tradition of subterranean or semi-subterranean structures we may see traces of the early Circumpolar manner of house-building evolved to combat adverse climatic conditions. By the end of the second millennium B.C. the rite of cremation had become universal, and there is evidence of the survival of the practice into post-Roman times in Scotland.[2]

The arrival of iron-using Celtic peoples in the region can hardly have been before the latter part of the first century B.C., and may have been later, and while it may possibly have included some elements from west France, this new immigration was predominantly a refugee movement from England, and combined traditions from the Hallstatt-

[1] G. Bersu (1948*a*). A case could be made for dating this house as Late Bronze Age on the available evidence.

[2] See D. Ure (1793) for cremation burials in urns of Late Bronze Age type, one containing a bone comb of post-Roman type and all probably secondary to an Early Iron Age burial. See also V. G. Childe (1946), 130–1, for this and other examples.

derived Iron Age A and the La Tène-derived Iron Age B cultures. The circular house-type had been adopted by these peoples, and what we know of their burials shows that both inhumation and cremation were practised. In Scotland their outstanding monuments are those of fortifications, either defensive tower-houses of the broch type or hill-forts including those with timber-laced walls. There is little evidence of the growth of homesteads into villages, though in the Lowlands such larger units, with up to fifteen or so circular houses within a palisade or earthwork enclosure, seem to have come into being before the Roman conquest.[1] During and after this event such villages (normally with stone-built circular huts) become common. Agriculture, however, appears to have remained at the level of hoe-cultivation, and evidence for the use of the traction plough is very slight and may be due to Roman influence.[2] Such pieces of La Tène art as are exemplified by the metal-work which characterise the Pictish area all appear to belong to the second or third centuries A.D. and to belong to a different stylistic tradition than that expressed in the Pictish metal-work and carved slabs of the historical period.

[1] As at Hayhope Knowe in Roxburghshire (pre-Roman) and Braidwood in Midlothian (occupation into second century A.D.). See Cecily M. Piggott (1949) and R. B. K. Stevenson (1949*a*).

[2] Plough-shares of Belgic type occur in the south-east Lowlands. F. G. Payne (1948).

Chapter III

FORTIFICATIONS

R.W. Feachem

THE inferential character of any attempt to ascribe particular types or classes of fortified structures to the Picts is clearly established in Chapters I and II; and there is no need for further consideration here of the prehistoric background to the period under review or of the profound and irrevocable changes which were brought about by the arrival in Scotland of populations whose cultures embodied Halstatt and La Tène elements. Briefly, the older and the newer peoples may be said to have merged to form a heterogeneous proto-Pictish population from which the historical Picts appear eventually to have sprung. The coming of the later arrivals brought an end to the generally prevailing nomadic mode of life in which no necessity for fortifications seems to have existed, and gave rise to a political development under which it became necessary for some members of the community, at least, to possess strong defensive establishments. Stuart Piggott describes [1] how, in pre-Pictish times, the broch fulfilled this requirement in the west and north ot Scotland, in Orkney and in Shetland, and how another class of fortified structure, the small hill-fort, was developed for the same purpose in the Lowland area.

The geographical region which can be called the main Pictish area stretches from the Moray Firth in the north to the Firth of Forth in the south, from the North Sea coasts in the east to the inhospitable Highland massif in the west. Within this area, there are only six known brochs—those at Castle Spynie (Inverness-shire), Drumsturdy Hill near Monifieth and Hurley Hawkin at Liff (Angus), Drumcarrow (east Fife), Coldoch near Doune (Perthshire), and Torwood near Larbert (Stirlingshire)—and there are comparatively few hill-forts of the type so widely distributed throughout the Lowland region. There are numerous other fortified structures in the main Pictish area, however, and if we may assume that the Picts had fortifications, then it is among these that a search for them must be made.

Nevertheless it may not be out of place to make further reference to the brochs. For, although they may be said to belong to the period during which the peoples eventually to be called the historical Picts had not yet emerged from the welding of separate population groups,

[1] See above, Chapter II.

it is very likely that the broch-builders were an important element among those groups.

The majority of the brochs—of which the known total is in excess of 500 [1]—are located in the regions mentioned above, which constitute what can be called the main broch area. In addition to these, there are a few, some of doubtful character, in the south-west of Scotland; the six, referred to above, in the main Pictish area; and four more in the Lowlands.[2] The fact that the known distribution of brochs runs counter to that of symbol stones serves to emphasise the probability that their builders preceded the historical Picts.

Examinations of brochs by excavation have unfortunately been such as to have merited, in most cases, the severe stricture proclaimed by Scott [3]: "No ancient sites have been more excavated than those of the brochs, and . . . none with less result. The extensive early excavations are inadequately reported, if at all, and were not conducted so as to yield systematic evidence of stratification". It is at least known, however, that the dwellers in many of the brochs were at one time or another in the course of their history in contact with the Romans,[4] if only, in many cases, by the processes of trade. Such peoples, whether the builders or the immediate descendants of the builders of the brochs, must therefore have belonged among the sixteen or eighteen tribes mentioned by Ptolemy as having lived in Scotland in the second century of the Christian era,[5] and so, presumably, to either the *Maeatae* or the *Caledonii*, the two divisions into which the whole population of the country was later merged, according to Dio Cassius as abridged by Xiphilinus.[6] These peoples were certainly elements in the heterogeneous groups which eventually formed the historical Picts.

Of the brochs themselves, it will suffice to notice certain general characteristics of their situation and structure. It is evident that in many cases the brochs are situated in such a position as to overlook an area of land which could be farmed; this applies in particular to brochs in the main broch area, where expanses of land suitable for farming are not omnipresent as they are in the lowland regions.[7] In the main area, a broch is often found at the head of a small plain or glen, bordered by rocky slopes or by the sea and its arms, and there can be little doubt that in many cases the broch is a house which was built and occupied by a farmer and his household. There are, of course, cases in which the situation of the broch suggests that its

[1] A. Graham (1947).
[2] See Map 2.
[3] W. L. Scott (1947), 3*n*.
[4] S. Piggott (1951); S. Laing (1867), 69.
[5] W. F. Skene (1876), 1.70–6.
[6] Ibid. 82–3.
[7] W. L. Scott (1947).

occupants might have gained their livelihood by fishing or, perhaps, by some less reputable occupation such as trafficking in slaves or piracy. There are no good reasons at the present time to suppose that brochs thus situated were built either earlier or later than the majority. It may not be unreasonable to suggest that, after the most suitable territories had been claimed, later builders were forced to select less satisfactory situations, where life could only be supported by means other than farming. However this may be, in the great majority of cases the broch is situated so as to warrant its being called the dwelling of a farmer or a fisherman.

The method of construction of the broch implies that it was a strongly defended and, in that sense, a fortified dwelling-house. But, however high a broch may have been—fifteen or fifty feet as the case may be—the complete lack of any aperture in the outer face of the wall, except for the entrance, rendered active defence impossible. It is not considered likely that a parapet walk ran round the top of the broch wall. In general, the term "fortification" describes not only a structure into which an intruder will find it hard to make his way, but also one from the security of which the proprietor will be able actively to discourage an attempt at entry. The broch, which fulfils the former qualification admirably, entirely lacks the latter, and may therefore be described as a defensive dwelling if not as a fortification.

Any fortifications which the historical Picts may be supposed to have used during a period of some 500 years must have included structures which varied enormously in character according to the necessities which they served, the period in which they were built, and the habits of the particular section of the heterogeneous population responsible for them. In an examination of Dark Age records, Graham [1] has listed seventeen different words by which structures considered to come under the classification of forts were distinguished, although no specific description of any particular kind of structure can be attached to any one word.

The most conspicuous and the best-known structures in the main Pictish area are the oval or oblong forts with heavy stone walls. In some cases these walls are known to have contained timber frameworks as an integral and important part of their structure, and examples are widely known wherein combustion of such timber-laced walls can be seen to have caused vitrifaction. But so many stone-built forts have yet to be examined that it is impossible to draw any conclusions from the known distribution of them throughout Scotland; and no adequate body of evidence exists from which even a general indication of the

[1] A. Graham (1951), 65–8.

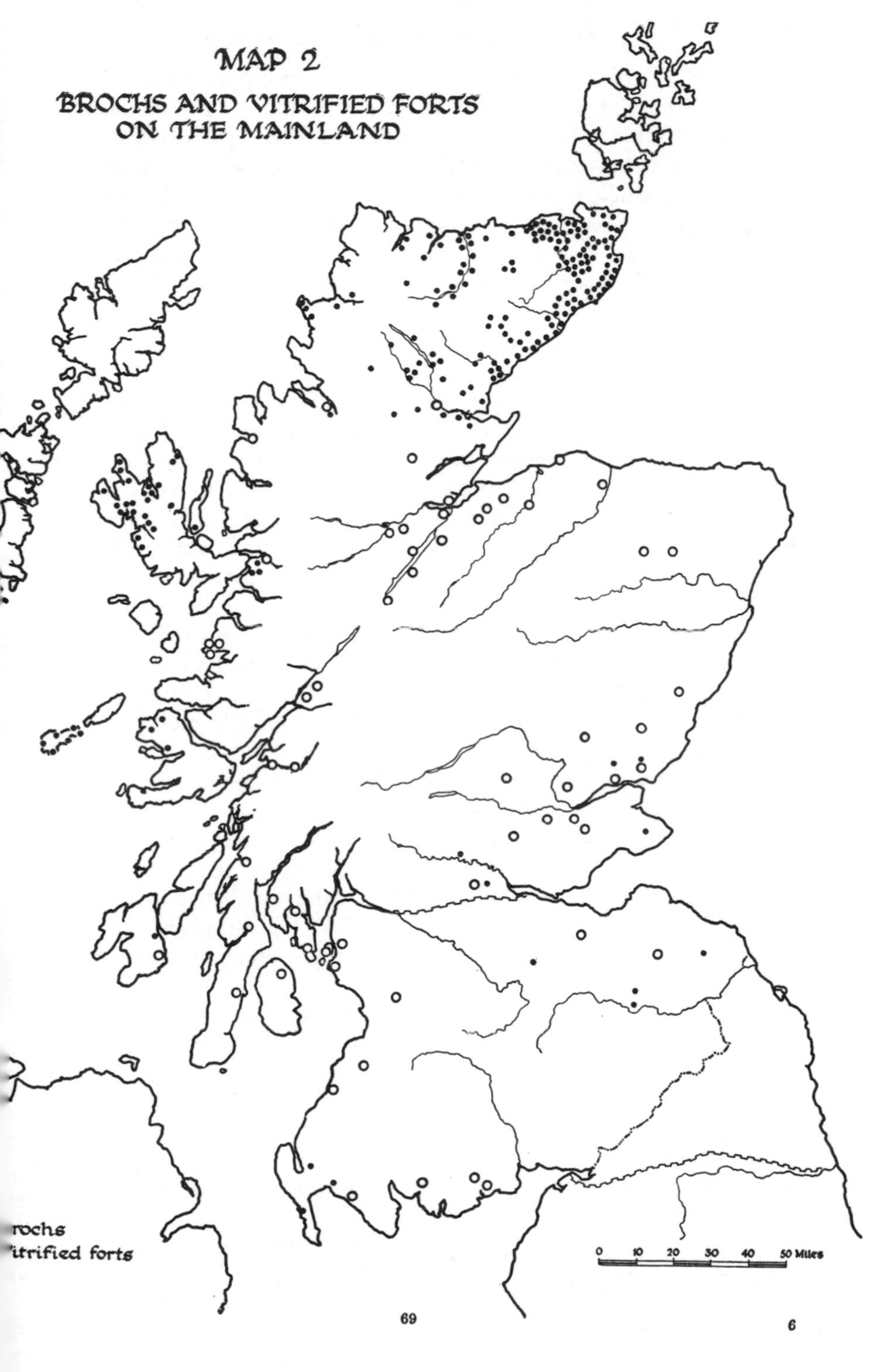
MAP 2
BROCHS AND VITRIFIED FORTS
ON THE MAINLAND
rochs
itrified forts
0 10 20 30 40 50 Miles

period or periods at which any considerable group of these structures were built can be inferred. It is only necessary to re-emphasise the possibility that timber-laced stone walls, whether now vitrified or not, could probably have been built at any time during the last three centuries B.C. and the whole of the first millennium of the Christian era.[1]

Despite the generally incomplete nature of existing information about these forts, it may be of use to observe that the majority of the large oval or oblong examples seem to lie within the main Pictish area. If this should eventually be confirmed to be a fact, then the reason for such a distribution might be attributable to one of the following possibilities, amongst others. Either the builders of a significant proportion of the forts must have arrived directly on the east coast of Scotland, presumably from England or from the north coasts of continental Europe, and so have represented a strong element among the heterogeneous proto-Pictish population; or a substantial number of the forts may actually be the work of the historical Picts. If, in the case of the first possibility, the fort-builders arrived from the west and moved across to develop the eastern lands, the same result would ensue.

However this may be, two forts of this type can be mentioned as bearing upon the problem under review. At Drumsturdy Hill, near Monifieth in Angus, the lowest courses of a ruined broch lie partly within and partly upon the ruined vitrified wall of an oblong fort.[2] In this case the ruin or disuse of the fort unquestionably took place prior to the building of the broch. This particular fort, therefore—and, by reasonable supposition, some others of the same type—can be dismissed from consideration as a work of the historical Picts.

But at Burghead, in Moray, where until recently there were the ruins of a *murus gallicus* fort,[3] the recovery is recorded of linear representations of bulls and of other undeniably Pictish relics. The possibility must therefore be allowed that the Burghead fort—and perhaps some others—was used, if not actually built, by the historical Picts.

The area in which fortifications attributable to the Picts must be sought, among the structures remaining after the deletion of Early Iron Age hill-forts, brochs and forts with timber-laced stone walls (whether vitrified or not), has not yet been covered by an adequate field survey, although the results of certain regional studies are available. Practically no excavation has been attempted, and the few reports which have been published throw little or no light upon the problem. At present,

[1] See above, p. 62.

[2] D. Christison (1900), 82–5.

[3] J. Macdonald (1861); A. Mitchell (1874); J. Anderson (1889); H. W. Young (1890, 1891 and 1893).

therefore, any study of the fortifications in the main Pictish area must be based upon insufficient information, and any attempt to ascribe given structures to the historical Picts must be proclaimed as purely conjectural. Likewise, with so little assistance from work already accomplished, it is impossible to produce a map of the distribution of fortified structures which would serve any purpose except that of demonstrating the narrow limits of present knowledge. But the examination of various classes of structures which follows may serve as a basis for a general study of works of this kind.

It is notable that all the types of fortified structures to be described, as well as forts with timber-laced stone walls, are found both inside and outside the main Pictish area. This may imply that, as in subsequent times, structural fashions extended impartially across political divisions.

The simple circular structures known as ring-forts are an example of this. They occur well within the main Pictish area—for example, at Kingennie, six miles north-east of Dundee, and on Turin Hill, four miles north-east of Forfar—as well as marginally in Glen Lyon and Strath Tummel [1]; but they are also found along the western seaboard [2] and in other regions.

In its simplest form the ring-fort stands alone, without any additional defences. In many cases the structure is placed close to the brink of a steep rocky descent, thus gaining an added security on at least one flank; but examples are found on open hill-sides and on low ground. The wall of the ring-fort is usually well built, the facing stones being large and more or less rectangular in section. They are carefully laid to form smooth faces, and the space between is filled with tightly packed rubble. The width of the walls varies considerably from one fort to another, but a measurement of about 12 feet is not uncommon. Similarly, the internal diameter varies very much, from about 40 feet to about 80 feet. The forts have single entrances and, on the surface, featureless interiors.

Apart from using the natural defensive strength provided by the lip of a rocky descent, the wall of the ring-fort is often so constructed as to include within its fabric natural features such as outcrops or large boulders. An example of this is seen at the structure known as Castal an Dui, in Glen Lyon, of which a plan is shown in Fig. 1. In this case the boulder stands to a height of 11 feet above the surface of the ground, and measures 20 feet in length and 10 feet in width. The use of natural features in the construction of a wall is typical of the structural habit observed in other works believed to be of Dark Age

[1] W. J. Watson (1913, 1915). [2] D. Christison (1889, 1904).

date, and is further described below in connexion with larger structures.

Very little information about ring-forts has become available from chance finds or from excavations. Watson made a study of these structures [1] in the course of which he excavated an example at Borenich in Strath Tummel (Fig. 1). From three to four men were employed for two weeks to dig out the whole of the interior of the fort down to the level of the natural soil. All the debris removed was riddled, but there is no record of any attempt having been made to watch the progress of the excavation for signs of stratification or of internal structures. The relics discovered in this way were described as few in number and poor in quality, and from them Watson was able to deduce only that the

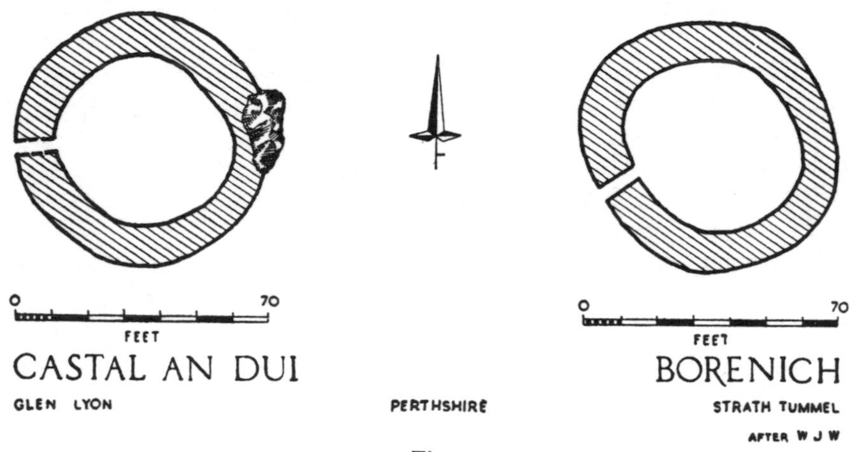

Fig. 1

ring-fort had been occupied by people who had the use of iron, grew corn and probably bred sheep. Such evidence might indicate that the structure was inhabited at any time during the first millennium of the Christian era, but nothing more precise can be deduced from it.

At the present time, the lack of records forbids the construction of a distribution map of ring-forts, but the information available suggests that they do not appear in any great degree of concentration throughout the main Pictish area. From this it might be permissible to suggest that while some ring-forts may very well have been the work of Picts, or even of proto-Pictish elements, others might have been built by peoples moving eastwards from the western seaboard. If the latter supposition could be supported by any evidence, there would arise the possibility that the builders might have been Scots.[2]

[1] W. J. Watson (1913, 1915).

[2] See above, pp. 30, 47–8.

In addition to free-standing ring-forts, there are examples which are situated within the protection of additional defensive works such as walls, ramparts and ditches. A monument of this kind can be seen at Tillicoultry (Clackmannanshire), several miles to the north of the Firth of Forth, the southern boundary of the main Pictish area.[1] This ring-fort (Fig. 2) is situated at a height of 550 feet above sea-level on Castle Craig, a low spur which protrudes from the steep southern face

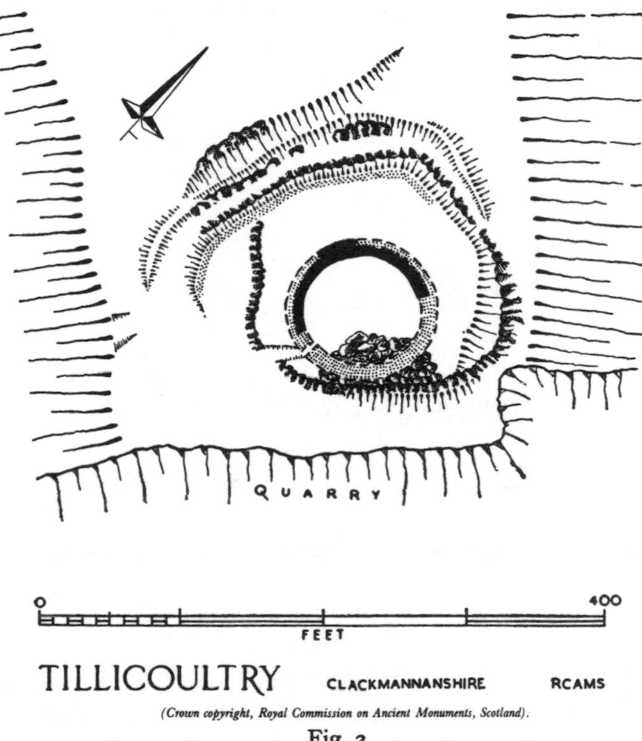

(Crown copyright, Royal Commission on Ancient Monuments, Scotland).

Fig. 2

of the Ochil massif. The surface of the spur, an uneven rocky shelf, is joined to the main hill-side by a gentle slope down from the north-west, but on all other sides it is girt by steep descents, in parts precipitous. The shelf measures about 300 feet in width in each direction. The fort is placed a little to the north-east of the centre of the shelf, and consists of a circular stone wall 12 feet in thickness with an internal diameter of 82 feet. Although ruinous and much robbed, the remains of the wall reflect a high degree of technical ability in the builders, the facing stones being carefully chosen and well laid to form even external surfaces. The south-eastern sector of the wall runs up to and includes

[1] See above, pp. 34–40, 51.

a rocky outcrop. The slope from the north-west, which would give easy access to the fort, is crossed by a wide rock-cut ditch, on the inner lip of which is the ruin of a stone wall. There is no reason to suppose that the ring-fort and the outer defences were not contemporary.

Ring-forts, whether free-standing or defended, are not found only on sites which were previously unused by builders of defensive works. Instances are not infrequently found where a ring-fort has been built on a site already occupied by another defensive structure, often an Early Iron Age contour fort. A splendid example is situated on Turin Hill, near Forfar (Fig. 3). The visible remains of fortifications on this

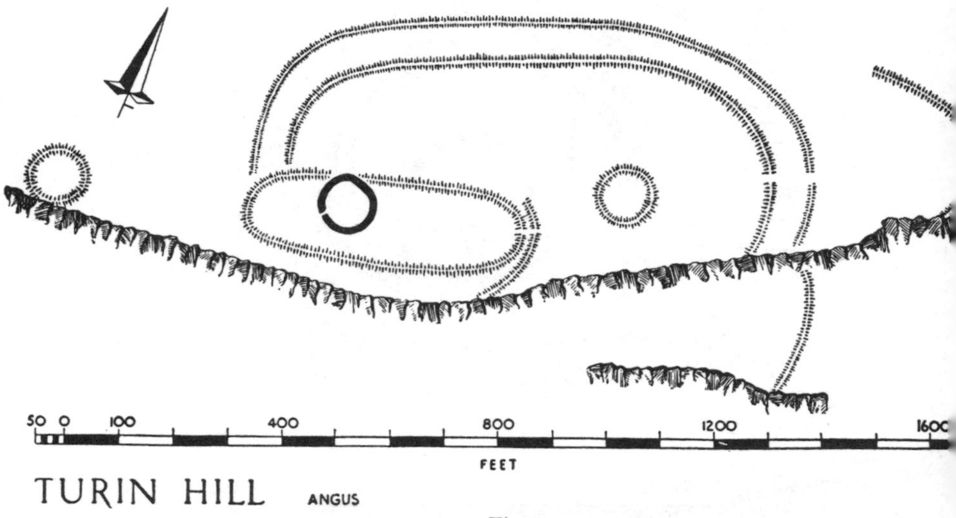

Fig. 3

hill include a series of partly superimposed works, the earliest being a large enclosure, presumably Early Iron Age in date, which measures about 900 feet in length by about 400 feet in breadth within two concentric ramparts. Secondary to this, and overlying the south-west sector of its defences, there is the ruin of an oval fort which measures about 500 feet in length by about 130 feet in breadth within a single rampart. The ruin of the rampart is spread to as much as 30 feet in width at a point in the west arc where it is 6 feet in height; it is so overgrown that it is impossible to tell from surface examination whether it was originally a rubble-filled wall or a stone-faced rampart. The amount of stone visible suggests, however, that it might have been a wall, while the shape and size of this structure of the second phase recalls certain of the forts with timber-laced walls.[1]

[1] D. Christison (1900), 99.

Secondary to this fort, the third structure on Turin Hill is a ring-fort which lies partly within the second-phase fort and partly upon a section of its rampart, on the north-west side. Thus, the chronological relationships between the three works are evident. The ruins of the ring-fort are very similar in character to those of the example at Tillicoultry; the well-built wall is about 12 feet in thickness and surrounds an area about 80 feet in diameter.

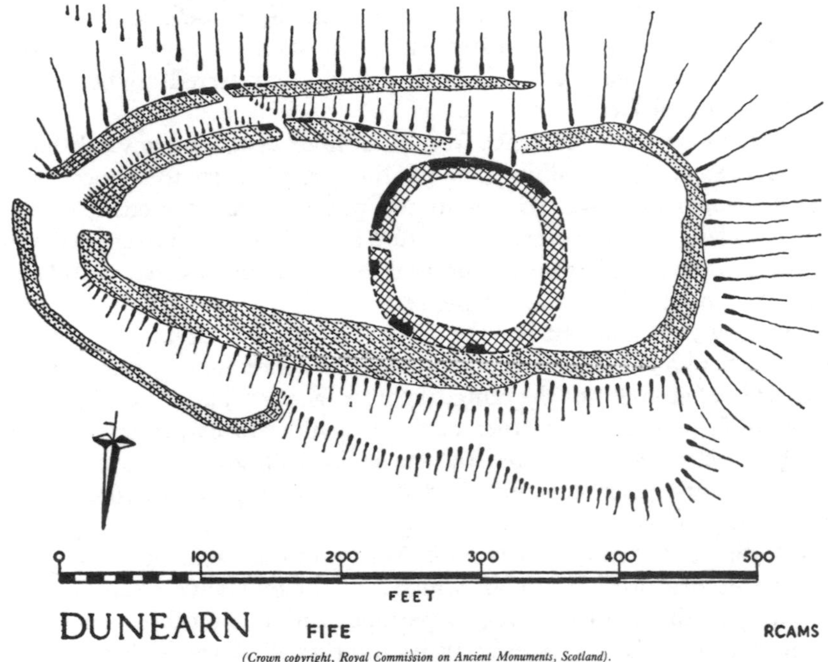

(Crown copyright, Royal Commission on Ancient Monuments, Scotland).

Fig. 4

Another example of this juxtaposition of a ring-fort and an earlier defensive work can be seen on the hill named Dunearn, near Burntisland in Fife (Fig. 4). In this case the combined structure assumes, even more than that upon Turin Hill, the appearance and character of a single work, despite the fact that the secondary structure, which can be called the citadel, lies partly within and partly upon the ruined inner rampart of the fort.

It is reasonable to assume that the placing of ring-forts as citadels within disused defensive structures was not done purely from considerations of topography. For, in addition to the excellence of the situation, the builders freely obtained the additional advantages of a plentiful supply of building material among the ruins and, perhaps more important, of existing lines of walling or ramparts fit to be used either as enclosures or as defences. The hybrid structures that resulted may perhaps be said to reflect the existence of a need for larger premises and greater defensive strength than a simple ring-fort could afford, such as might arise under conditions of an expanding economy and a maturing social structure. It might not be too fanciful to suggest that the three classes of structures described above—the free-standing ring-forts, the ring-forts with comparatively small contemporary defences, and the ring-forts combined as citadels with earlier defensive works—could possibly reflect successive stages in such an expansion. And further, that the society to which they could be referred might be that of the historical Picts.

There is as yet no evidence from datable relics to lend any substance whatsoever to this possibility, nor is there any reason to suppose that the development suggested was in any way peculiar to Pictish society. Nevertheless, the next class of structure to be considered may very well have been developed from a structural sequence such as that postulated above, or at least from the last phase.

Both within and outside the main Pictish area there are fortified works wherein the citadel is surrounded by contemporary outworks of the order of strength of the ramparts or walls of an Early Iron Age fort. The whole of such a structure occupies a hitherto barren site chosen, unlike most of those selected by the Early Iron Age builders, for its rocky and irregular surface, studded with outcrops and seamed with cliffs and precipices.

Within this class of fort two distinct types can be recognised. The first to be described is that in which the citadel stands freely, and as centrally as the lie of the ground permits, within the protection of the outer defences. The citadel occupies most or all of the highest feature of the chosen hill-top, and the outer works lie lower down. The latter run on more or less regular courses, except that they are designed to include within their fabric any convenient rocky outcrop which may be available and that they make the fullest use of the defensive strength provided by precipitous slopes and cliffs, even though this may mean that an irregular course has to be followed.

The identity of this kind of fort has only recently been established, but judging by certain published plans, such as that of the fort on the Mither Tap of Bennachie, in Aberdeenshire,[1] a good many have yet to be recognised. Among those now on record is the fort at Chatto Craig, near Hownam in Roxburghshire.[2]

An interesting example of this class of fort lies on one of the two

[1] W. D. Simpson (1943), 60–1. [2] RCAMS XIV, 305.

broad shoulders of Dumyat, the most westerly eminence of the Ochil Hills, which stands three miles north-east of Stirling, near the southern limit of the territories of the historical Picts.[1] Here the citadel stands freely on the rocky crag which surmounts the shoulder of the hill, and the outer defences run along comparatively regular but not parallel courses, making use of both outcrops and precipices wherever possible

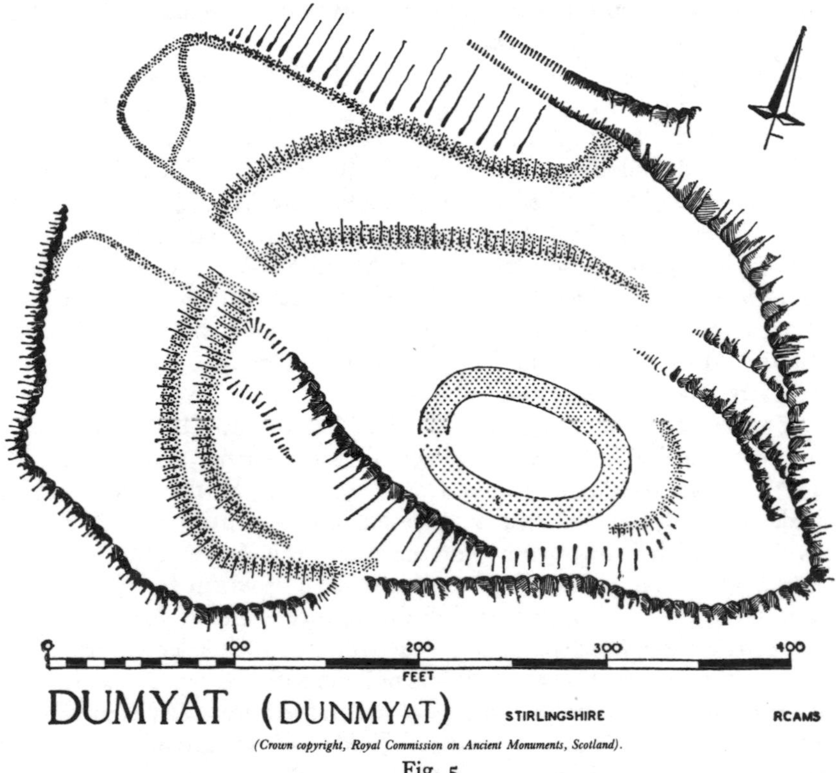

(Crown copyright, Royal Commission on Ancient Monuments, Scotland).

Fig. 5

(Fig. 5). On the north side of the fort, for example, a natural gully originates close by and runs eastward, rapidly becoming deeper and more steep-sided. The outer wall of the fort originates at that point on the southern lip of the gully beyond which, as it runs westward, the gully becomes so slight as to have no defensive value. The wall runs up the slope of the hill from the point where it leaves the gully for some distance before turning westward to take up a course outside the inner wall.

Apart, however, from affording an excellent example of a citadel fort, this structure may well have an added importance in its possible

[1] See above, 24, 34–40, 51.

connexion with the name Dumyat which, it has been suggested, refers to the *Maeatae* (*Miathi*).[1] It is not unreasonable to suppose that, as there must have been numerous forts within the territory of the *Maeatae*, some good reason must have led to one specific fort being distinctively described as "the fortress of the *Maeatae*". And, as the remains shown on the plan in Fig. 5 are the only ones on Dumyat, they might well represent an important stronghold, if not, indeed, the principal centre, of the *Maeatae*.[2]

The same origin has been suggested for the name of Myot Hill, near Denny in Stirlingshire, seven miles south-south-west of Stirling and three and a half miles north of Westerwood Fort on the Antonine Wall. On Myot Hill the extremely denuded remains of a fort which have survived appear to be those of a structure of an Early Iron Age type. This might well have been a pre-Roman structure, and its commanding position so close to the Antonine Wall might well have led to the slighting of its defences by the Romans, which would account for their unusually insignificant nature. The statement of Dio Cassius that the *Maeatae* "live close to the wall that divides the island into two parts" has been discussed above.[3]

The second type of fort in this class has recently been recognised and described by R. B. K. Stevenson under the title of the "nuclear" fort.[4] It can be distinguished from the fort with the free-standing citadel not only by differences in design but also by the shape of the hill upon which it lies. Whether the sites were chosen from necessity or by deliberation, nuclear forts are found on hills which are of elongated form, on the upper slopes of which the surface available for occupation is adequate though attenuated. Moreover, the hills selected are, as in the case of those used by the builders of forts with free-standing citadels, possessed of a considerable number of natural features such as precipices and outcrops which could readily be adapted to provide additional structural and defensive strength.

In his analysis of the nuclear fort at Dalmahoy, Midlothian (Fig. 6), Stevenson emphasised that in this type of fort the citadel was flanked, mainly on two opposing sides along the narrow surfaces of the hill, by series of defensive enclosures. The innermost of these spring directly from the citadel wall, while the more distant ones are attached to each other successively. There was sufficient space on Dalmahoy Hill for the construction of a large fort, and the remains are in fact about 1,200 feet in length. The citadel occupies the highest feature of the hill, a sloping plateau surrounded on all sides by rocky slopes and

[1] W. J. Watson (1926), 58–9. And see above, pp. 6, 24, 40, 51.
[2] For an alternative suggestion see above, p. 24.
[3] See above, pp. 50–53.
[4] R. B. K. Stevenson (1949*b*).

low but mural precipices, and measures internally about 140 feet by 90 feet within a wall about 12 feet in thickness.

An example of a nuclear fort which has been created by augmenting and altering an earlier structure can be seen in the work known as Moredun, on the summit of Moncreiffe Hill, two miles south-east of Perth (Fig. 7). Observations from a ground survey of this impressive structure suggest that the earliest defensive works on the hill consisted of a stone wall which ran round the contour some way below the top of the hill and a slight outer line, possibly originally a

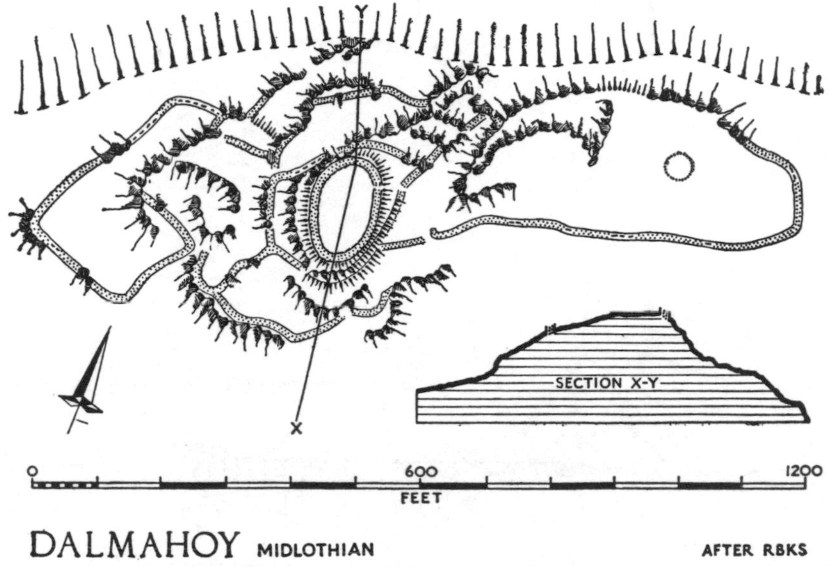

Fig. 6

staked rampart, which ran at a distance of between 40 feet and 80 feet outside it. The area enclosed measures about 560 feet by about 330 feet, and the structure can be described as a contour fort.

A second period of work seems to be represented by the oval citadel which crowns the hill. This structure measures about 160 feet in length by about 120 feet in width internally. The walls of the citadel and of the inner line of the contour fort are extremely ruinous and have been systematically robbed of the majority of their facing stones; but it appears certain that the south sector of the citadel wall overrode a length of the inner defence of the contour fort which, in this sector, runs along the crest of some crags and is not accompanied by the outer rampart. It would be unlikely that the relationship between the citadel wall and the inner wall of the fort could result from anything but successive periods of construction.

In addition, however, a large court, the nature of which recalls the outer enclosures of a nuclear fort, is formed by a now ruined wall which encloses an area to the north of the structures already described. The two extremes of this wall run through the outer line of defence of the contour fort to meet the inner line, which suggests very strongly that this court, like the citadel, was built in the course of a reconstruction. In all probability, the court and the citadel were con-

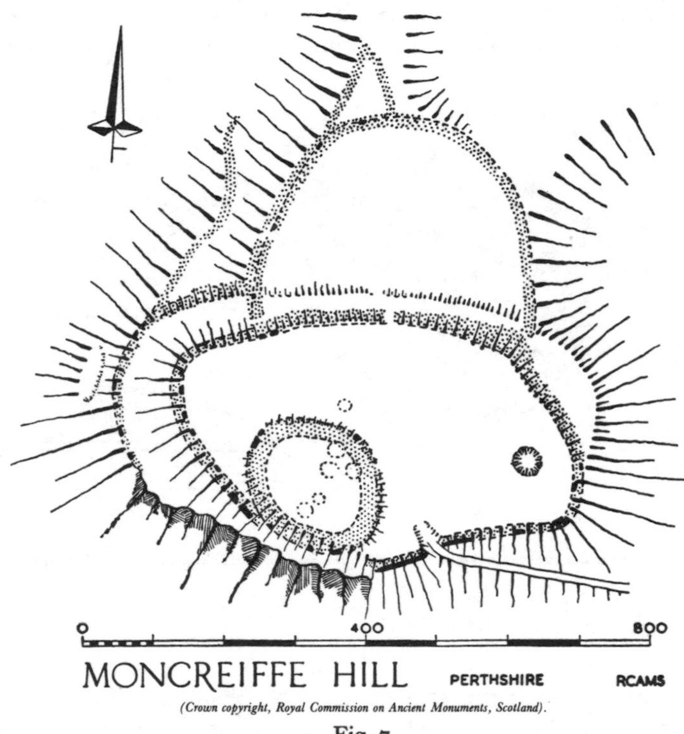

(Crown copyright, Royal Commission on Ancient Monuments, Scotland).

Fig. 7

temporary. The whole combined structure, in the form of a nuclear fort, was evidently disused before the occupation of Moncreiffe Hill finally came to an end, as is testified by the remains of several round huts, some of which lie upon the spread of the ruin of the citadel wall.

In addition, however, to the interest provided by the structural details of this fort, it acquires an added importance in that the name Moncreiffe is considered quite possibly to be that *Monad Croib* referred to as the scene of a battle in the year 729.[1] It is possible that this fort, lying well within the main Pictish area, was a stronghold of the historical Picts, built (or rebuilt) and used by them.

[1] W. J. Watson (1926), 400–1. And see above, p. 23.

Two other forts which can claim the distinction of literary reference lie one within the territory of the Scots of Dalriada and the other towards the western limit of the main Pictish area. What may be a late, and perhaps a final, development of the nuclear fort is to be found in the famous structures at Dunadd in Argyllshire and at Dundurn in Perthshire. Both these forts are situated, not on hills, but on prominent isolated rocks standing in level land. The rock of Dunadd dominates access to Knapdale and Kintyre across the Crinan isthmus, and that of Dundurn commands the passage of upper Strathearn.

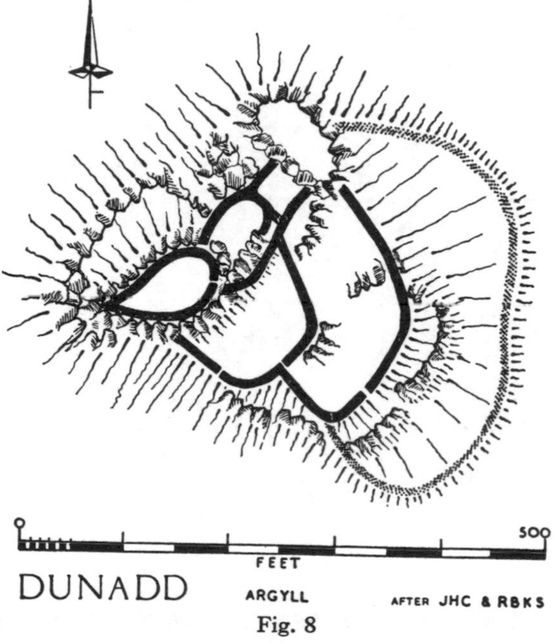

Fig. 8

Dunadd (Fig. 8), which may well have been a main stronghold of the Dalriadic Scots, or at least one of their more important centres, was the scene of excavations in 1904 and in 1929, and these are mentioned here, although the fort was certainly not Pictish, as the only source as yet extant from which information about such structures can be obtained.[1] Numerous relics were recovered, from which it was deduced that the fort at Dunadd was occupied intermittently from the beginning of the sixth century to the middle of the ninth. Among the items listed there are three fragments of wattle and daub.[2] Neither of the excavations provided evidence of the former presence within

[1] D. Christison (1905); J. H. Craw (1930).
[2] J. H. Craw (1930), 123, Fig. 8, no. 6.

the fortified area of internal structures in the form of post-holes or trenches, but it is certain that buildings of wood with wattle walls, and possibly wattle roofs, once stood within the massive stone defences here, as in other stone forts of the same period inside and outside the main Pictish area. Literary evidence of these, and of their destruction by fire, has been fully set forth by Graham,[1] who writes that houses were universally of wood eked out with wattling.

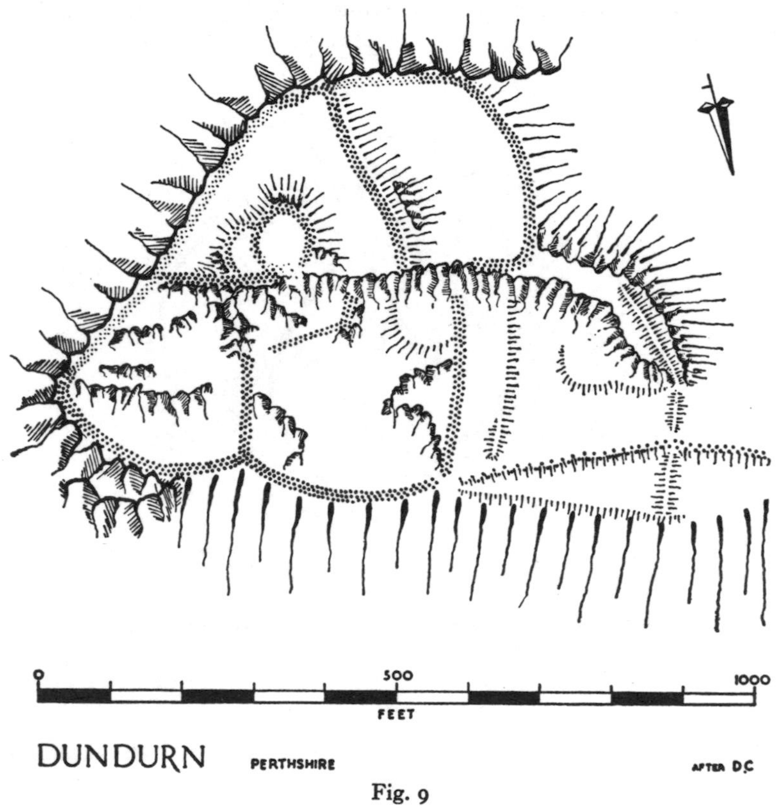

Fig. 9

Dundurn has not been disturbed, as far as is known. The plan (Fig. 9) shows the citadel, occupying the topmost part of the rock, as an enclosure about 70 feet in internal diameter bounded by lengths of stone walling which link outcrops of rock. All round the citadel there is an angular succession of walls, each of which encloses the limits of one of the natural terraces which form the surface of the rock. Dundurn was identified by Skene as that Dundurn which is mentioned in the *Annals of Ulster* as being under siege in the year 683

[1] A. Graham (1951), 72, 78.

(*Obsessio . . . Duinduirn*).[1] Skene went so far as to suggest that Dundurn may have been the principal stronghold of the Picts of Fortrinn; but, whether this was so or not, its position so far to the west of the main Pictish area must not be overlooked.

In addition to the ring-forts and to the citadel forts, certain other classes of fortified structures are found within the main Pictish area. One well-defined type consists essentially of a strong stone wall which runs round the edge of a steep-sided and comparatively flat isolated eminence of suitable size. The enclosure thus formed is shaped accord-

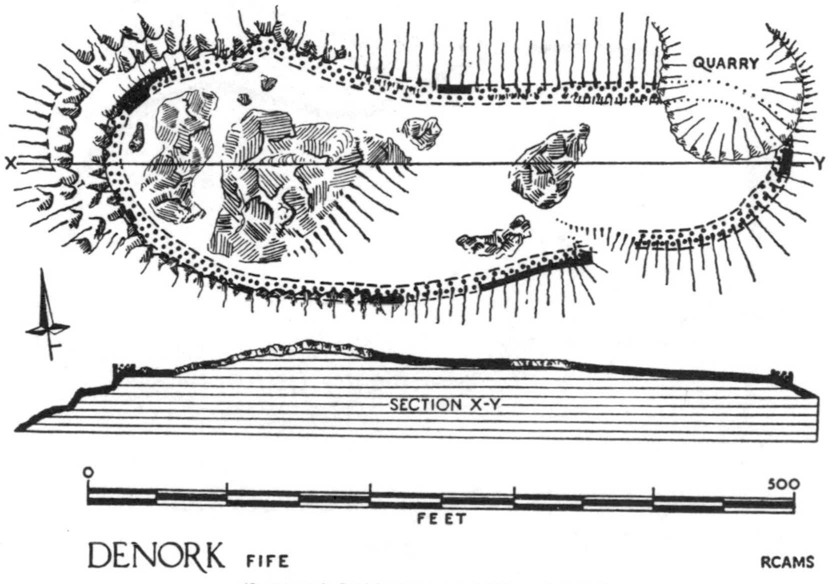

(*Crown copyright, Royal Commission on Ancient Monuments, Scotland*).

Fig. 10

ing to the irregular limit of the site and therefore defies classification within ordinary geometrical terms. The sites chosen for this class of structure were usually much longer along one axis than the other, and the name "long dun" may be used to distinguish the class. The example shown in Fig. 10 is at Denork in Fife. Internally it measures 450 feet in length by a maximum of 150 feet in width. The wall follows closely round the top of the steep sides of the rocky hill, making full use of outcrops and cliffs, and the lower courses of outer facing stones lie well over the edge. The name Denork was the subject of a reference by Watson,[2] in which he suggested that it contained a tribal name *Orcoi*, "boars". At the time when Watson wrote the presence of the fort was not suspected.

[1] W. F. Skene (1876), I.264. [2] W. J. Watson (1926), 29–30.

The long dun at Peniel Heugh in Roxburghshire (Fig. 11) is a valuable example of this class of structure, as it overlies the half-obliterated remains of an Early Iron Age contour fort. The earlier fort occupied the summit of the hill, its twin ramparts following the contour some distance below the highest point. The long dun was built along the crest of a series of cliffs and steep rocky slopes which border three sides of the hill-top, and its wall twice crosses the line of the earlier defences with complete disregard. As Peniel Heugh,

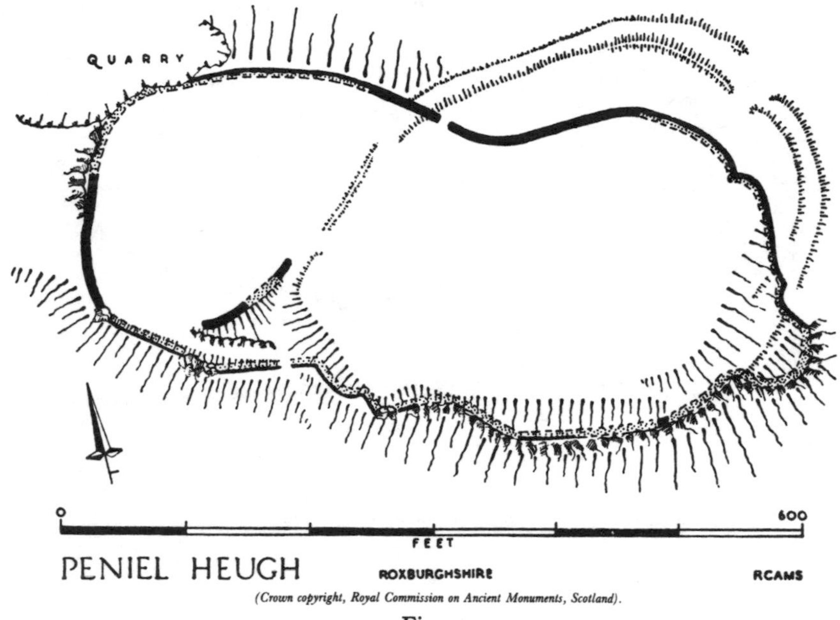

(Crown copyright, Royal Commission on Ancient Monuments, Scotland).

Fig. 11

only seven miles from Newstead, lies in an area where the Roman occupation was as vigorous as anywhere else in Scotland, any structure secondary to a pre-Roman fort is very likely to be post-Roman in date. Among other examples of long duns may be cited the structure known as Dun Mor near Beauly in Inverness-shire,[1] which measures internally about 180 feet by 100 feet.

Finally, small oval or D-shaped structures of the class often referred to simply as "duns" appear in the Pictish area although, as far as is known at present, only marginally. Six of these structures lie close together in the upper reaches of the valley of the Bannock Burn in eastern Stirlingshire, south of the Forth but north of the natural boundary between the Highlands and the Lowlands, which is de-

[1] National Grid Reference NH 534428.

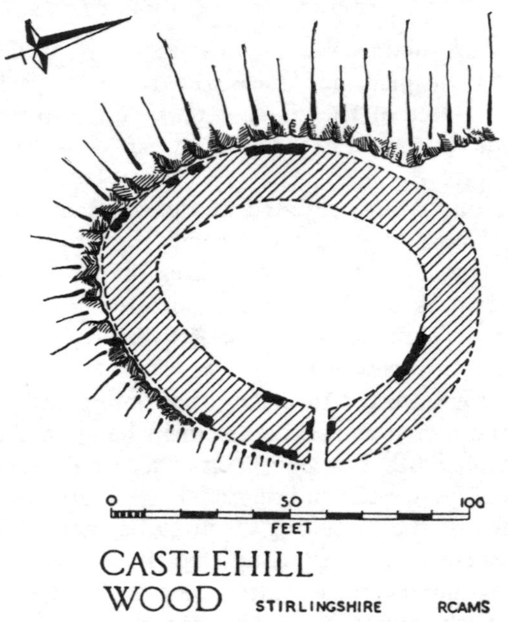

(Crown copyright, Royal Commission on Ancient Monuments, Scotland).

Fig. 12

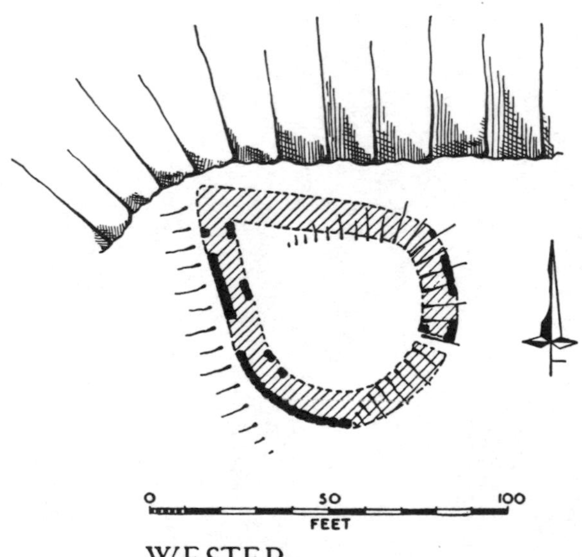

WESTER
CRAIGEND STIRLINGSHIRE RCAMS

Based on Crown copyright plans by permission of the Controller of H. M. Stationery Office

Fig. 13

lineated by the Antonine Wall. One of these, at Castlehill Wood (Fig. 12), is oval on plan, and measures internally 75 feet by 55 feet within a wall 15 feet in thickness. This dun is placed on a rocky bluff, and gains defensive strength from the cliffs which border the west and south sectors.

Another of this group, situated at the brink of the steep descent of the Sauchie Craigs at Wester Craigend (Fig. 13), resembles on plan the citadel at Dunadd. Other structures of this class are found in the district known as the Aird, at the north-eastern end of the Great Glen, and further examples occur in Argyllshire,[1] Ayrshire and elsewhere on the western seaboard.

It will be clear from the foregoing that until a wide and systematic survey of all the monuments which remain between the Moray Firth and the Firth of Forth has been completed, no attempt to prepare a basis for identifying and studying such structures as may represent the fortifications of the Picts can claim to be more than exploratory. When such a survey has been completed, it will be possible to select sites for a programme of excavation, and so at last to bring about conditions in which some positive knowledge may be obtained.

[1] For references to these and other duns and forts see R.W. Feachem: *Guide to Prehistoric Scotland* (1977).

Chapter IV

HOUSES AND GRAVES

F.T. Wainwright

A STUDY of Pictish dwellings and their contents would throw much light on the Picts. From it we should be able to imagine them in the domestic context of their day-to-day life, we should be able to assess their skills and techniques in building, and we should get a clearer impression of their arts and crafts, their occupations and their economy, their weapons, their tools, their pottery and their personal ornaments. The examination of even a single Pictish village should give us a firm picture of their social and economic arrangements. A study of Pictish burials, especially those of the pagan period, would throw light on their mental attitudes, on their religious rites and customs and, if we were fortunate, on their artistic and cultural achievements. From such studies, also, we might hope to isolate features which would help us to solve the problem of Pictish origins. As the Picts were apparently a heterogeneous people, we should not expect to find a cultural uniformity among them; but the very differences displayed in their material equipment might help us to distinguish and trace backwards into prehistory the various elements that coalesced to form the historical Picts.

Conclusions that we might build upon evidence of this kind, however, lie entirely in the future. It is a sad, if somewhat surprising, fact that we cannot with confidence affix the label "Pictish" to a single dwelling or to a single burial. The attractive prospect outlined above is no more than a prospect. The immediate problem is one of identification. Which houses and which graves are Pictish? Where can we find them? And how can we recognise them? Only when the basic work of identification has been done shall we be able to draw upon the evidence at present buried with the structures which the Picts built to shelter their bodies in life and after death. We must find these abodes of the Pictish living and the Pictish dead before we can study them.

It is a reasonable assumption that many Pictish graves have been discovered and have been seen by archaeologists and others. Many, indeed, have been described as "Pictish" in the reports and records of an earlier age, but the fact remains that we cannot today point to a single burial and say with certainty that it is Pictish. The reason for our doubt and hesitation arises chiefly from the nature of the burials themselves. When the Picts adopted Christianity they would tend to adopt Christian rites and forms of burial, and these present a uniformity which is not helpful to the archaeologist who is seeking to distinguish different peoples by their different burial customs or by the objects found in their graves. The pagan Pictish period offers a more promising diversity of burial practices, but here we run into a difficulty which arises from the nature of the people whom we call the Picts. That they were an agglomeration of once separate peoples seems to be sufficiently proved,[1] and the elements of which they may have been composed stretch far back into antiquity.[2] Political unity came late to them, and it is highly unlikely that there was anything approaching cultural uniformity in pagan Pictland. Therefore there is no reason to suppose that there ever was a single pagan Pictish type of burial; there could have been, and probably were, several different types. When the component elements of the historical Picts are clearer, their possibly divergent burial customs may help to identify or confirm the separate elements, but at present they confuse us, especially if we are blindly looking for a single kind of burial all over Pictland in the pagan period.

It is even more difficult to attach the label "Pictish" to dwellings. Basic similarities are dictated by conservatism and imitation, but house-types are seldom as distinctive as burial customs, for they are likely to be influenced more by the modifying demands of practical convenience and less by the binding force of tradition. Houses, more than graves, tend to be modified by such factors as household requirements and availability of material. Also houses are not so permanent as graves; they are pulled down and rebuilt frequently, and they leave fewer traces for the archaeologist. Compared with graves they are temporary and ephemeral structures, often obliterated by successive phases of occupation which have continued to the present day. A deserted fortress dominates the landscape for centuries; a grave is not as a matter of course either dismantled or used a second time; but houses tend to be built on or near the sites of other houses so long as there is no fundamental change in the basic social and economic order. Therefore many Pictish houses will survive, if at all, only as faint boulder-impressions or post-holes, and many will lie buried beneath the farms, the villages and even the towns of modern Scotland. All of which makes the archaeologist's task exceedingly difficult.

What are the possibilities? It may be that a Pictish settlement site will soon be discovered and recognised, but where to look for such a

[1] See above, Chapter I. [2] See above, Chapter II.

site is a problem. It is always worth while to keep an eye on demolitions and deep excavations in places known or suspected to be ancient. It is doubtful if even a trained observer would recognise traces of a Pictish hut in a narrow trench cut to receive a drain, but stray finds may turn up to indicate early settlement in the area or to locate it more precisely. There are many places where, on historical or archaeological grounds, the existence of Pictish settlements may be presumed, and these especially should be watched. Often formal excavation is out of the question, and at such places investigation is mainly a matter of waiting and watching.

More positive action may be taken at sites which are deserted and therefore available for examination by excavation. The sites of deserted villages in England are now receiving much attention,[1] and it may be expected that they will greatly increase our knowledge of the social, economic and domestic background of peoples who were contemporaries of the Picts. In Scotland very little has been done in this not unpromising field. The excavation of a deserted village site in Pictland deserves to be undertaken for its own sake, but it would be a large-scale operation and only the optimist would count on finding a recognisably Pictish level of occupation. Such an excavation should perhaps be directed by an archaeologist who is interested primarily in a particular site, or in medieval and early modern villages generally, rather than by one whose chief concern is to investigate Pictish dwellings. But the approach offers possibilities, and attention may be drawn to deserted villages like Pitroddie, Pitmiddle and Pitalpin in the Carse of Gowrie. We do not know the age of these sites as settlements, but it is obviously desirable that we should have thoroughly excavated at least one site which preserves in its name the presumably Pictish element *pett*.

At best, however, the above investigations would be little more than excavational shots in the dark from the point of view of the student of Pictish dwellings. Results are more likely to be obtained at present from sites which, though not primarily domestic, were occupied by the Picts—from sites, that is, which as sites and not merely as names belong or are thought to belong to the Pictish period. Into this class fall the Pictish or potentially Pictish fortresses surveyed by R. W. Feachem in Chapter III. Until we find Pictish sites that were primarily village sites, if such existed among the Picts (which we have no reason to doubt), we cannot do better than look for traces of Pictish dwellings in or near ring-forts, "nuclear forts", "citadel forts" and the

[1] See, for example, H. M. Colvin (1952), M. W. Beresford (1953), J. Golson (1953), and the references provided in these articles.

like. Ring-forts present excellent opportunities to the modern excavator; we do not yet know for certain whether they are Pictish or Scottish, and the excavation of even a single example by modern methods would greatly increase our knowledge and would probably produce an instructive array of occupation material. Hut-circles may be seen on Moncreiffe Hill (Perthshire),[1] some of them overlying the citadel wall and therefore in a chronologically significant relationship to the "nuclear fort"; another group of hut-circles overlies and is therefore later than the walls of the fortress on Norman's Law (Fife)[2]; at Green Craig (Fife) there is a small settlement which Professor Bersu thinks may belong to the early centuries of the Christian era[3]; and circular farm-like structures within small enclosures are being noticed at many sites. Possibilities are numerous, but there is no point in listing them here, for they cannot contribute much to our study until their age and their nature are revealed by excavation. Some may be later than the Pictish period; some may be earlier; all should be kept in mind until positive evidence becomes available.

In the centuries before the Pictish period material for a study of habitation sites is much more abundant. It can be demonstrated[4] that the souterrain-builders, or some of them, were definitely proto-Picts, i.e. that the descendants of the men who built the souterrains formed one element in that complex of peoples which from A.D. 297 is known to historians as the Picts. It is inherently probable that the broch-builders were also proto-Picts in this sense of the term, but the probability, though very strong, falls short of proof. Nevertheless, the student who wishes to study the habitation sites and the domestic arrangements of peoples who were ancestral to the historical Picts cannot afford to ignore the structures of any potentially proto-Pictish people, least of all those of the souterrain-builders and the broch-builders.

Brochs have been considered above in two separate contexts—as fortifications (Chapter III) and as part of a cultural complex (Chapter II). Stuart Piggott and R. W. Feachem both draw attention to them in a third context—as structures which, though defensive, are essentially houses.[5] From the excavation of brochs and of secondary structures often associated with them we may expect a mass of occupation material and a wealth of information about an archaeologically important people of the pre-Pictish period. Souterrains, too, were

[1] See above, p. 80.
[2] See above, p. 30. The hut-circles are not mentioned in RCAMS XI.
[3] It is later than the hill-fort on the top of Green Craig. See G. Bersu (1948*b*), 264–75.
[4] See below, pp. 91–2.
[5] See above, pp. 59, 67–8.

sometimes dwellings ; sometimes they may have been built for another purpose ; but always they were either used as dwellings or closely associated with dwellings. Souterrains do not all fall into a single undivided class—they may vary in age and in function from one area to another [1]—but so far as one can see a souterrain site, as distinct from the souterrain itself, was always a habitation site, a place where people lived and carried out their normal day-to-day work. A large body of evidence has accumulated for the study of the economic and domestic arrangements of the souterrain-builders. If this evidence is not further considered here, that is partly because it is too voluminous for discussion and partly because our immediate concern is with the dwellings of the historical Picts, not with those of proto-Pictish peoples. In a few cases it can be shown that broch sites and souterrain sites continued to be occupied in the Pictish period, but on the evidence at present available it would seem that the broch-builders and the souterrain-builders themselves lived in the pre-Pictish period.

Souterrains stand closer than brochs to the Picts. Their distribution covers in a remarkable way the known extent of Pictland and almost duplicates the distribution of symbol stones. The largest concentrations are in Aberdeenshire and Angus, but variant forms stretch northwards to Shetland and westwards to the Hebrides. Very few are found south of the Antonine Wall, and it is clear that examples in Midlothian (Castle Law and Crichton Mains) and in Roxburghshire (Newstead) represent a few wandering colonists from the main souterrain areas, which lie farther north in Pictland proper.[2] The souterrains of Aberdeenshire and Angus, at least, belong chronologically to the two or three centuries which preceded the Pictish period, and their occupation can be brought without difficulty to within a hundred years of A.D. 297.[3] It is possible that some of them may have been built after A.D. 297, in which case we could properly describe their builders as Picts. But no example has yet been proved to have been in use (as a souterrain) in the Pictish period, and it seems probable that most souterrains had fallen out of use before the fourth century. On the whole it is safer to regard the souterrain-builders of the main Pictish area as a people or peoples who lived in the period immediately preceding that which we call Pictish.

One aspect of souterrain studies is especially relevant to our problem. Excavations carried out in 1949–51 at Ardestie and Carlungie in Angus revealed two souterrain complexes, each consisting of a great souterrain

[1] F. T. Wainwright (1953*b*), 228-32.

[2] See F. T. Wainwright (1953*b*) where it is suggested that the various groups of souterrains may represent separate, though not necessarily unrelated, peoples.

[3] F. T. Wainwright (1953*a*), 70–1.

and an array of associated surface dwellings.[1] At both sites it was observed that at a certain point in time the souterrain structures were systematically dismantled and filled in. But the sites continued to be used—without a break in the sequence of occupation and, so far as can be seen, by the same people who had earlier used the souterrains. This post-souterrain occupation of souterrain sites, by the souterrain-builders and their descendants, apparently continued well into the Pictish period.

Two important conclusions follow. One is that the "post-souterrain people" of Ardestie and Carlungie, and presumably of other sites in the area,[2] can be fairly and accurately described as Picts. Therefore the souterrain-builders of Angus are brought into direct relation with the historical Picts, and are themselves proved to be proto-Picts. They are one of the elements for which we have been seeking, one of the several archaeological elements which combined to form the heterogeneous Pictish people of history. The same is probably true, though yet unproved, of souterrain-builders in other parts of Pictland. And it is probably true, though again not specifically proved, of the broch-builders and of other known archaeological peoples of the pre-Pictish period.

The second important conclusion is that in the post-souterrain phase at Ardestie and Carlungie we have before us at last the houses and domestic arrangements of a people who were Picts. The approach is perhaps more important than the evidence, for the latter is unfortunately slight. The post-souterrain level of occupation was so near the modern ground surface that most of it had been effectively removed by ploughing and agricultural cleaning. Traces of huts were found, but only at Carlungie was there sufficient evidence to allow plans of them to be drawn. The post-souterrain huts, however, were not very different from those used in the souterrain period—some of the huts used in the post-souterrain period, indeed, had belonged to the original souterrain complex. These were strongly-built circular or ovoid structures, without central posts, carefully paved with stone slabs, and apparently roofed in wigwam fashion by boughs wedged into the walls and then covered with bracken and turf. The lowest course of their

[1] See Ardestie and Carlungie Excavation Reports (forthcoming). Much of what is said here (pp. 91–3) is based upon evidence which will be made available in these reports. See list of References and Abbreviations under "Ardestie and Carlungie Reports".

[2] A similar sequence of souterrain and post-souterrain occupation may be foreshadowed by a preliminary excavation carried out at a third site, Carlungie II. Here a brooch, attributed to a period which centres on A.D. 200, was apparently in the possession of the souterrain people before the souterrain was dismantled. The post-souterrain period at Carlungie II was therefore later, perhaps considerably later, than A.D. 200. See F. T. Wainwright (1953*a*), 65–71.

walls consisted of huge glacially worn boulders of the kind used in the souterrain itself. The huts that were added in the post-souterrain phase were perhaps not so substantially built; they lacked the massive course of boulders, and they seem to have had double walls of smaller stones. There was also an open paved yard or court, and that at Ardestie extended over the dismantled souterrain. Finds, which were few, suggest that the "post-souterrain people" had much the same standards, economy and material culture as their predecessors, the souterrain-builders. They were farmers and hunters, they kept cattle, they ground corn, and they used a crude coarse pottery which was not a credit to peoples familiar, as they were, with the products of the Roman Empire. Full details of their structures and their culture will be published elsewhere.[1]

The chief importance of the "post-souterrain people" is that they bring into a definite association the archaeological souterrain-builders and the historical Picts. The method is the old one by which an advance is made, backwards or forwards, from the known to the unknown. Brochs offer similar possibilities to this approach. Some of them are known to have been occupied in Pictish or post-broch times; the question which we want to have settled is whether or not there is any break in the sequence of occupation, whether the broch-builders became a "post-broch people", as the souterrain-builders became a "post-souterrain people", or whether the "post-broch people" were unrelated to the broch-builders. If it could be proved that the broch-builders became a "post-broch people" in the Pictish period, it would be proved that the broch-builders are proto-Picts. It may be fairly safe to assume that some of them are, but in the interests of accuracy it should be stressed again that even a strong probability falls short of a proof.

It may be that another opportunity of advancing from the known to the unknown will be provided by the excavations recently completed by the Ministry of Works at Jarlshof in Shetland. Jarlshof has produced an impressive series of sites, the occupation of which stretches from early prehistoric times into the Middle Ages. Our immediate concern is with those phases which fall chronologically into the historical Pictish period. Mr J. R. C. Hamilton, who has supervised the work carried out at Jarlshof since the war, has identified several pre-Viking huts which he calls "Pictish"; he has also identified at least three post-broch phases of occupation, one of which has yielded pottery identical with pottery obtained from the so-called "Pictish huts".[2]

[1] Ardestie and Carlungie Reports.
[2] J. R. C. Hamilton (1952), 159–60. See also ANL IV. No. 8 (1952), 123.

Now a "pre-Viking people" and/or a "post-broch people" in Shetland are inherently likely to be Picts. Whether or not these peoples can be proved to be Picts, stratigraphically or otherwise, is one reason why we await so eagerly the publication of Mr Hamilton's report.[1] It is also important for us to know definitely whether the "post-broch people" of Jarlshof are the descendants of the broch-builders or newcomers to the site. If they are the descendants of the broch-builders, but only if they are, it may be possible to use them to prove beyond the need for assumption that the broch-builders in Shetland are proto-Picts. The high interest of Jarlshof is as a Viking settlement, the most complete yet found in Britain, but we may expect that the report of the excavation will throw a powerful beam of light on the Pictish problem in an area remote from the historical centres of the Pictish kingdom.

Pictish burials present a more difficult problem than Pictish houses, for we cannot yet see so clearly what approaches or lines of investigation are likely to identify them for us. Most of the Picts who were Christian were probably buried in what are still kirkyards. Burial grounds are levelled and re-used from time to time, not always intentionally, and it is unlikely that we should find undisturbed Pictish burials in a kirkyard which, however ancient, has been in use for more than a thousand years. Therefore it matters little that such sites are not available for excavation. Burial grounds attached to long-deserted chapels are much more likely to contain the undisturbed remains of Picts, and there is no reason why we should not find and examine Christian Pictish burials at such sites. But it is doubtful if they would tell us much more than that the Christian Picts were Christian, a fact which scarcely needs to be confirmed by excavation. Early Christian sites in Pictland, especially sites of chapels and monasteries, may be expected to throw much new light on ecclesiastical developments among the Picts, an important problem not discussed in this volume, and the need for a programme of excavation directed towards this end may be described as urgent. But there seems to be no good reason why at this stage we should excavate Christian Pictish burials for their own sake.

As for the more interesting pagan Pictish and proto-Pictish burials, it has been suggested above that there are likely to be not one type but several.[2] It ought to be possible to discover and label some of them. But how? The burials of the souterrain-builders suggest a line of approach parallel to that which led to the conclusion that post-souterrain

[1] Jarlshof Report, for which see list of References and Abbreviations.
[2] See above, p. 88.

houses are Pictish. But it is seldom easy to associate a group of burials with a particular settlement. People do not usually bury their dead in the immediate vicinity of their houses, and even when burials are only a short distance from a settlement it can be extraordinarily difficult to prove that they belong to it, unless there are recognisable affinities between the grave-goods and the general culture of the settlement.

In 1859 a souterrain was discovered at West Grange of Conon (Angus), and within a few yards of it there was a cluster of six extended burials in coffins "of rude stone slabs . . . much the shape of the wooden coffins of modern times".[1] Andrew Jervise, who supervised the excavation, provides a short but useful description of these graves and their contents. It seems almost certain that they belonged to the souterrain-builders of Conon, but the report of the excavation offers neither proof nor evidence that this was the case. Jervise, naturally enough, did not doubt it, and perhaps it would be unduly sceptical to doubt it now. A considerable number of burials, both long cists and short cists, have been found at Carlungie within the last hundred years, but it is not clear which, if any, belonged to the men who built the souterrains there. The burials at Conon remain the only burials that can reasonably be associated with a souterrain site, and we must be grateful to Jervise for providing a description of them. It is obviously important that other burials of the souterrain-builders should be identified, as well as burials of the broch-builders and of all other potentially proto-Pictish peoples.

The problem of pagan Pictish and proto-Pictish burials is part of the wider problem of when and under what circumstances the rites of cremation and inhumation respectively were practised in Scotland. It would appear that either might be found among the peoples who became the Picts.[2] There is also the problem of long-cist and short-cist burials. From reports scattered throughout the *Proceedings of the Society of Antiquaries of Scotland* it seems clear that short cists were still used in post-Roman times in Scotland. Therefore some of our Pictish and proto-Pictish peoples may have been buried in short cists; others will certainly be found in long cists, for by the historical Pictish period it seems probable that long cists were normally used for inhumations. These are fundamental questions in Scottish archaeology, but upon their solution depends the problem of Pictish burials.

Symbol stones may also contribute to the solution of the problem. Many burials have been reported either under or in the vicinity of symbol stones; in most cases the association is fortuitous, though it may not be so in every case. Where we can rely upon the observations

[1] A. Jervise (1862), 497. [2] See above, p. 65.

of earlier investigators we cannot always rely upon their interpretations. At Meigle, for example, an extended skeleton was found with its head to the west and with its feet under a symbol stone,[1] but the case for associating the burial with the stone is greatly weakened when it is realised that the stone stood in the churchyard and that we do not know that this was its original position. A high archaeological priority exists for the competent excavation of areas around two or three symbol stones which have not been moved, as so many have, from where they were originally set up. There was no burial in the immediate vicinity of the stone at Kinblethmont (Angus), the most recently discovered example, but no firm conclusion can be drawn from this, for it has been demonstrated that the stone, though once erect at the spot where it was found buried, nevertheless had been moved from its original position.[2] We do not know to what extent, if at all, symbol stones were erected over burials; they may have been simply monuments and not normally associated with burials. The problem urgently requires attention. If burials are found in proved association with symbol stones, a study of them will undoubtedly increase our knowledge of the Picts. We shall see clearly for the first time how they buried their dead, and we may obtain clues that will help us to understand the purpose of symbol stones and to disentangle their chronology. But it is necessary first to find out if burials accompanied the erection of symbol stones and, if they did, to identify indisputable examples.

It will be clear that the questions raised by Pictish houses and graves range far beyond our ability to answer them. Even when we see, dimly, how associations and equations may be established ultimately, we are rarely able to do more than indicate possibilities. It is clear that these two classes of archaeological remains are vital to our understanding of the economy and way of life of the Pictish peoples. Their evidence will also help us to isolate the various elements that combined to form the Pictish kingdom and, perhaps, to relate archaeological distributions with historical divisions, such as the provinces of Pictland, and with proto-Pictish divisions such as those of the peoples listed by Ptolemy. Advances cannot be made until we are able to recognise archaeologically the various Pictish and proto-Pictish elements known or suspected. That is why, as emphasised above, the immediate problems presented by Pictish houses and graves are problems of recognition and identification.

[1] J. Stuart (1856), I.xxiv, 23–4.

[2] F. T. Wainwright (1951), 180–2.

Chapter V

PICTISH ART

R.B.K. Stevenson

PICTISH art is in the first place identified by the presence of certain symbols, carved on many stone monuments, and almost all found in parts of the country known to have had Pictish rulers about the time to which the monuments can be dated. To stand in front of one of these sculptured stones is to come as close as is now possible to the Picts. For not only are they vivid works of art, but they are what chiefly survives of Pictish culture. Most of them, complete or fragmentary, have been fully published, as have the few other known remains of Pictish craftsmanship. The purpose of this chapter is to indicate what has been written about their characteristics and artistic development as a whole; and by examining certain details to attempt to take a step further the problems of the origin and sequence of their styles. Aesthetic judgments are for the most part left to the readers to make for themselves.

It is nearly a century since the first attempt at an illustrated *corpus* was published,[1] but the first writer thoroughly to assess, classify and date the symbol stones was Joseph Anderson,[2] whose still most valuable Rhind Lectures for 1892 were published in 1903 as an extensive introduction to *The Early Christian Monuments of Scotland*.[3] Anderson's classification is as follows:

Class I	Symbols incised on more or less undressed stones, seventh and eighth centuries A.D.
Class II	Symbols in relief, usually accompanied by a cross on a carefully shaped monument, ninth and tenth centuries.
Class III	All monuments without symbols, overlapping with Class II and continuing to the twelfth century.

The major part of the work is a very well illustrated catalogue by J. Romilly Allen, with exhaustive lists of the location and combinations of symbols, of all types of patterns on the stones, and so on. It is an inexhaustible storehouse of information for later workers to reshuffle. The symbols on Fig. 14 are arranged in Romilly Allen's order of frequency, and all the monuments cited in this chapter will be found in *Early Christian Monuments* unless another reference is given.

[1] J. Stuart (1856–67). [2] J. Anderson (1881), II. [3] ECM I. iii–cxiii.

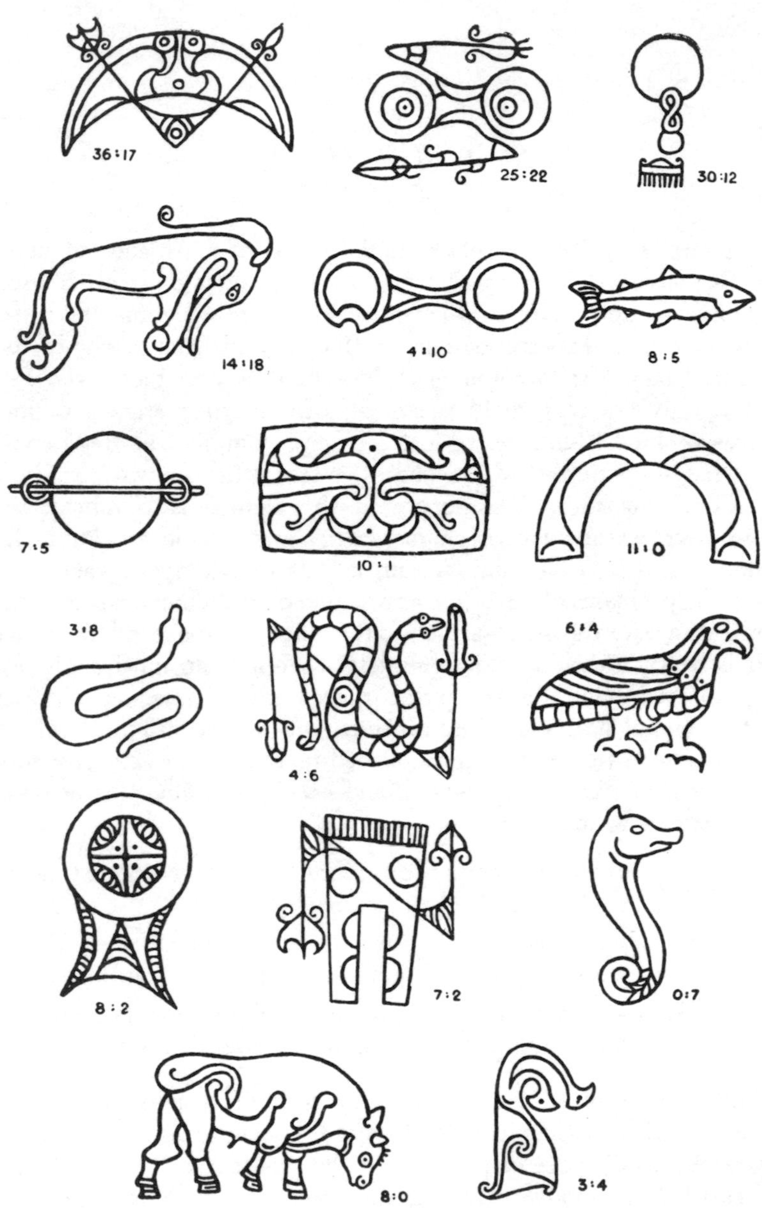

Fig. 14

Pictish Symbols; with number of occurrences incised and relief, as shown in *Early Christian Monuments*

A generation passed before a full-scale attempt was made, by Mrs Curle,[1] to break down Anderson's periods, each two or three centuries long, into styles and phases. This was possible and necessary because of the amount of recent study, and controversy, on the Irish, English and Continental art of those times. The artistic originality, powers of adaptation and tenacity of the Picts, the extent and importance of their cultural contacts, can only be measured by comparison with the neighbouring peoples. In this comparison relative chronology is an essential factor. Mrs Curle advanced the study greatly, but has been severely criticised, particularly by Mr Radford.[2] While following her in much, the conclusions now reached differ considerably from those of either writer, particularly in the case of the monuments in relief.

Symbols and Incised Sculpture

The various symbols are virtually stereotyped in form though not in details or decoration.[3] The bull has conventional scrolls at the joints but is triumphantly natural. On the other hand the animal referred to as the "Elephant" is imaginary; it has a curved snout and its ear is elongated to be a lappet. The Mirror-and-comb is obvious, but the "Spectacles" and the Crescent, crossed by floriated rods, resemble nothing real. It might be wise to discard the Hippocamp (Fig. 14, 0:7) and other creatures only found in relief monuments, as not being symbols in the same sense as the rest.[4] All the early decorative patterns are curvilinear. The masterly drawing of some of the incised animals is unparalleled in Dark Age art elsewhere. Taken together, the symbols define for us by their distribution (Map 3) the boundaries of Pictland. They embrace mostly arable or good pasture towards the east coast from the Forth to Orkney. Some outliers, all simply incised, probably mark transitory occupation or, in the west, areas lost before later fashions reached there. It is interesting that animals by themselves, all incised, are not common except round the Moray Firth. Orkney, occupied by the Norse about the beginning of the ninth century, has one transitional stone but none fully in relief. There is not sufficient difference in number between incised and relief symbol stones to suggest that the former cover a longer period, particularly as not a few fragmentary stones in relief cannot be included on the map because they have lost all trace of the symbols they once no doubt had. On the south-west the Ochil Hills seem to form the boundary. Silver chains found farther

[1] Cecil L. Curle (1940). [2] C. A. R. Radford (1942). [3] And see below, pp. 122–3.
[4] The discussion of the Hippocamps by N. Åberg (1943), 70–5, is confused by a failure to realise the limits of Pictland.

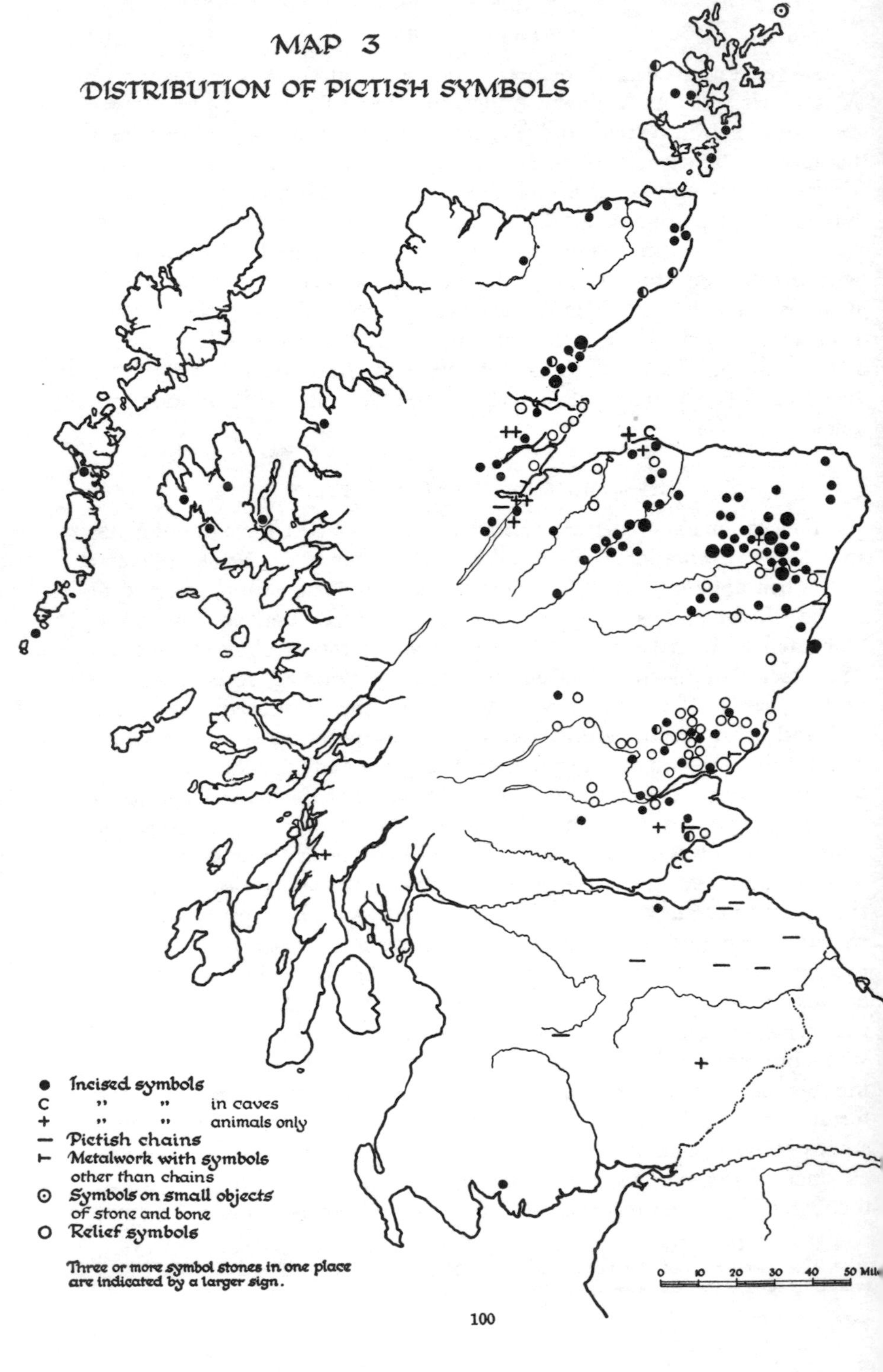
MAP 3
DISTRIBUTION OF PICTISH SYMBOLS
Incised symbols
C " " in caves
+ " " animals only
Pictish chains
Metalwork with symbols other than chains
Symbols on small objects of stone and bone
Relief symbols
Three or more symbol stones in one place are indicated by a larger sign.
0 10 20 30 40 50 Mil

south than that will be considered later; they must have been lost to raiders or invaders. The fort of Dundurn,[1] if really Pictish and not Dalriadic, must have been on the western frontier as it lies beyond the symbol stone area. The north-east corner and Kincardineshire are curiously bare. There are thick clusters of early stones in the valleys of the Don, Urie, Spey and Ness, and in the neighbourhood of Golspie in Sutherland, while Perthshire, Angus and the north-west shore of the Moray Firth predominate later.

For this southward shift a historical explanation has been suggested, though it does not help to date the shift closely; it is known that St Columba visited an important Pictish king near Inverness in the second half of the sixth century, and that a couple of centuries later dynasties in Angus and Gowrie were prominent. But at what period exactly does our map begin, and what are the origins of Pictish art? A closer consideration of separate features provides material for the answers. It involves frequent reference to works of art in England and Ireland, which are fortunately illustrated and discussed fully in readily accessible books.[2]

Curvilinear Patterns

In England, remains of about seventy bronze hanging-bowls have been found in the Lowland Zone, often in pagan Saxon graves.[3] Where these bowls were made is one of the major unsolved problems of post-Roman archaeology. The makers of most shared, or inherited, as can be seen from enamelled escutcheons on them, the taste for swelling curves and spirals that marked pre-Roman Celtic art. The bowls seem to range from the fifth to the seventh century in date, with a correspondingly long stylistic development. The finest and most elaborate of them was already old when buried at Sutton Hoo about 650.[4] An Irish origin for the series has been claimed, but from Ireland no work of comparable complexity can be produced at the dates in question. Irish metal-work, such as pins and brooches, has spirals (often with bird-head terminals), pelta or palmette shapes and red enamel, but not fat trumpet spirals or yellow enamel. Kendrick suggests rather the southern Midlands as the source of the most developed trumpet-spiral group.

[1] See above, p. 82. [2] T. D. Kendrick (1938); Françoise Henry (1940).
[3] See also Françoise Henry (1936); T. D. Kendrick (1932); E. T. Leeds (1933); H. E. Kilbride-Jones (1937).
[4] BM (1947); P. Grierson (1952).

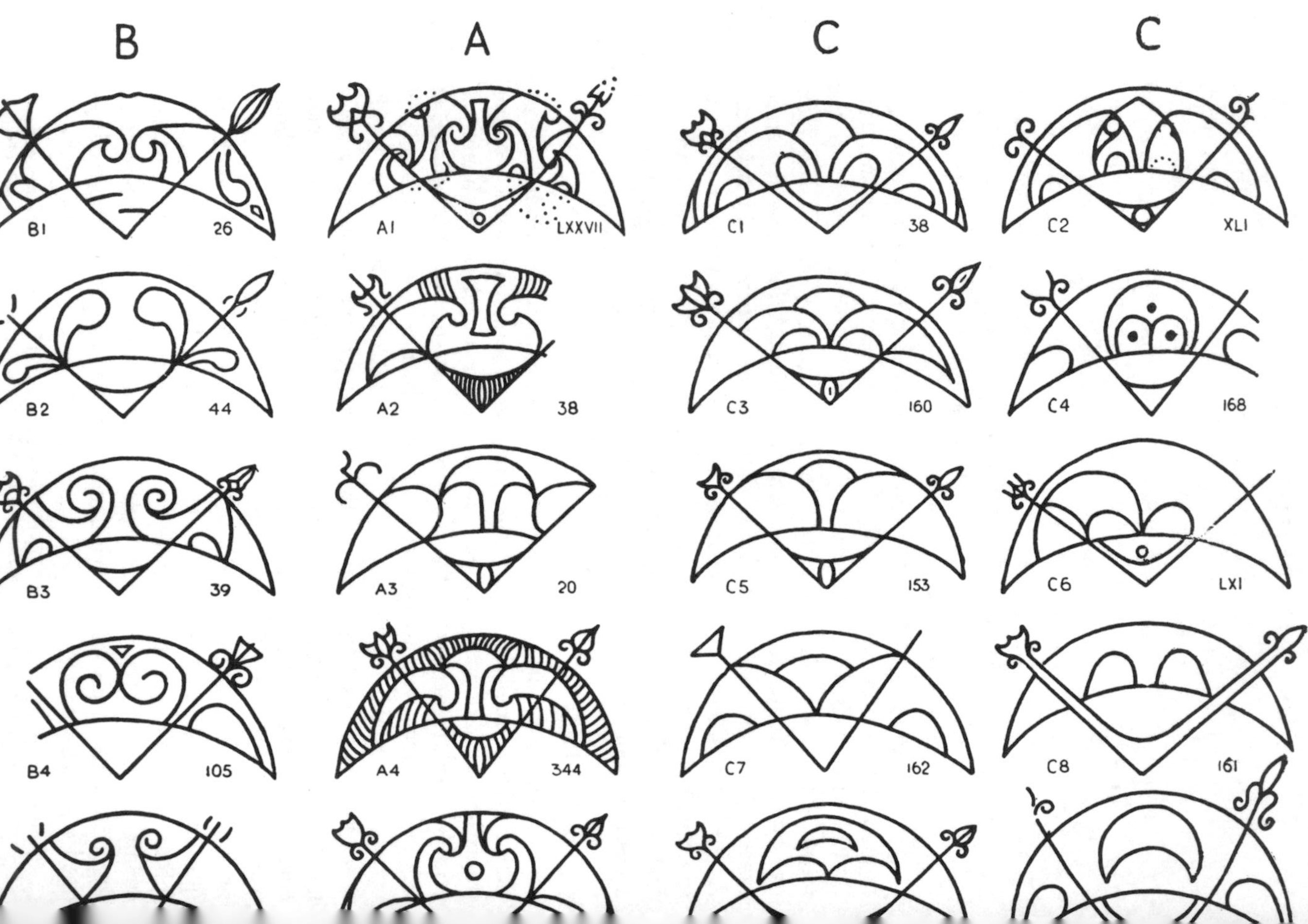
B
A
C
C
B1
26
A1
LXXVII
C1
38
C2
XLI
B2
44
A2
38
C3
160
C4
168
B3
39
A3
20
C5
153
C6
LXI
B4
105
A4
344
C7
162
C8
161

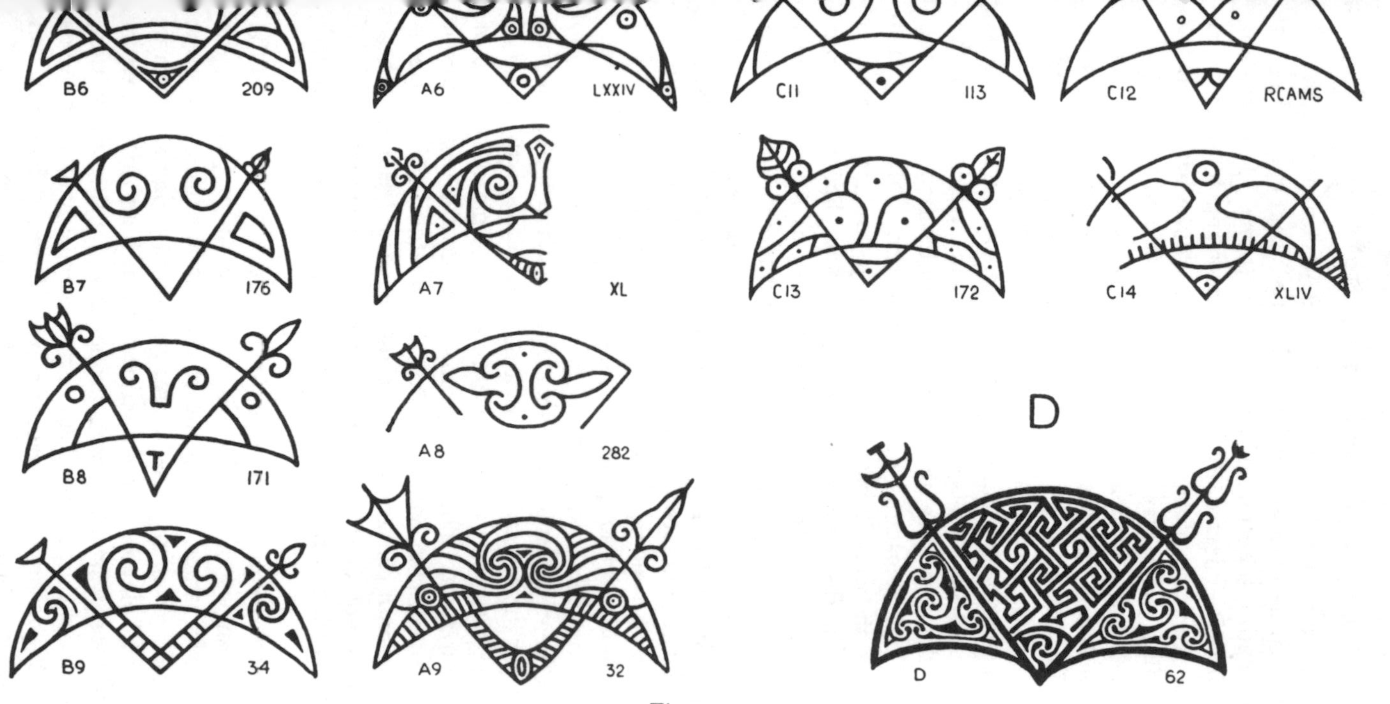

Fig. 15

Patterns on the "Crescent and V-rod" Symbol, all incised unless otherwise stated. Arabic numerals refer to pages of *Early Christian Monuments*; Roman to subsequent vols. of PSAS.

A, *Peltas*: 1—Golspie, Sutherland. 2—Clynekirkton, Sutherland. 3—Redland, Firth, Orkney. 4—Lindores, Fife. 5—Greens, Orkney. 6—Garth, Orkney. 7—Advie, Banff. 8—Abernethy, Perthshire. 9 (part relief)—Skinnet, Caithness. See also Fig. 14 (36:17)—St Peter's, S. Ronaldsay. **B**, *Spirals or scrolls*: 1 (on bone)—Burrian, N. Ronaldsay, Orkney. 2—Kintradwell, Sutherland. 3—Clynemilton, Sutherland. 4—Lynchurn, Inverness-shire. 5—Logie Elphinstone, Aberdeenshire. 6—Strathmartine, Angus. 7—Logie Elphinstone, Aberdeenshire. 8—Kinnellar, Aberdeenshire. 9 (part relief)—Ulbster, Caithness. **C**, "*Dome and Wing*": 1—Clynekirkton, Sutherland. 2—Raasay. 3—Crichie, Aberdeenshire. 4—Inverurie, Aberdeenshire. 5—Inveravon, Banff. 6—Fiskavaig, Skye. 7—Old Deer, Aberdeenshire. 8—Daviot, Aberdeenshire. 9—Moy, Inverness-shire. 10—Knockando, Moray. 11—Pabbay, nr Barra. 12—Dun Osdale, Skye. 13—Kintore, Aberdeenshire. 14—Tote, Skye. **D**, Hilton of Cadboll, Ross (part relief) *cf.* No. A 9.

Now, the only common Pictish symbol that is normally decorated at all elaborately is the Crescent and V-rod. The diagrams in Fig. 15 show a representative selection of its incised patterns. It is evident that they can be divided into three classes, according to their main features: those with two spirals (Fig. 15, col. B), those with a central pelta-shaped figure either way up (Fig. 15, col. A), and those with a central dome and wing-shapes at the sides (Fig. 15, cols. C). But these classes merge into one another and placing is sometimes uncertain. This strongly suggests a common origin, for example the dome design (No. C5) from which could have come the simplest pelta (No. A3). But it seems to the writer that the most convincing starting-point is the most complex pelta (No. A1). For it contains a majority of the details found in the others, details which it would be hard to combine, but which could have separated during simplification. Moreover, this complex figure is an over-all pattern of double peltas not adapted to the Crescent at all, the semi-circles along the base line being ends cut off, as indicated in the diagram; Mrs Curle was surely mistaken in the detail of seeing birds' heads in No. A6, and another from Orkney when she started this line of investigation. If the complex figure which is from Golspie (Sutherland) [1] is accepted as nearest the prototype, it follows that all the decorated Crescents are later than a design of that type, which is a poor relation of the hanging-bowl patterns. The curves remain slightly asymmetrical or lop-sided. A parallel development from the normal bowl patterns is on the unique bowl from Lullingstone in Kent. It, too, has a simple linear pattern, but one that continues to stress the spirals. Kendrick dates it to the sixth century; others prefer the early or the mid-seventh century, partly because of the presence of interlace. There is a symmetrical double-pelta without spirals on the Sutton Hoo hanging-bowl. Symmetrical pelta patterns also occur on seventh-century incised cross-slabs in Ireland. These analogies, though not close, indicate a date hardly earlier than the seventh century for our pattern, and other features of it help to confirm this.

Thus the lenses, frequently widened into circles, which occur in the spandrel-shaped angles of the V-rods resemble in proportions the Lullingstone bowl's rather curious use of the lens-like inserts frequent in trumpet spirals. Similarly used lenses are found in initial letters in the *Cathach* of St Columba, a manuscript for which an early seventh- or even sixth-century date has been proposed.[2] Further decoration, got by adding straight or, more often, curved parallel hatchings, seems to be about half-way in the Crescent series. Straight hatching can

[1] J. M. Davidson (1943). [2] C. Nordenfalk (1947), 151–9.

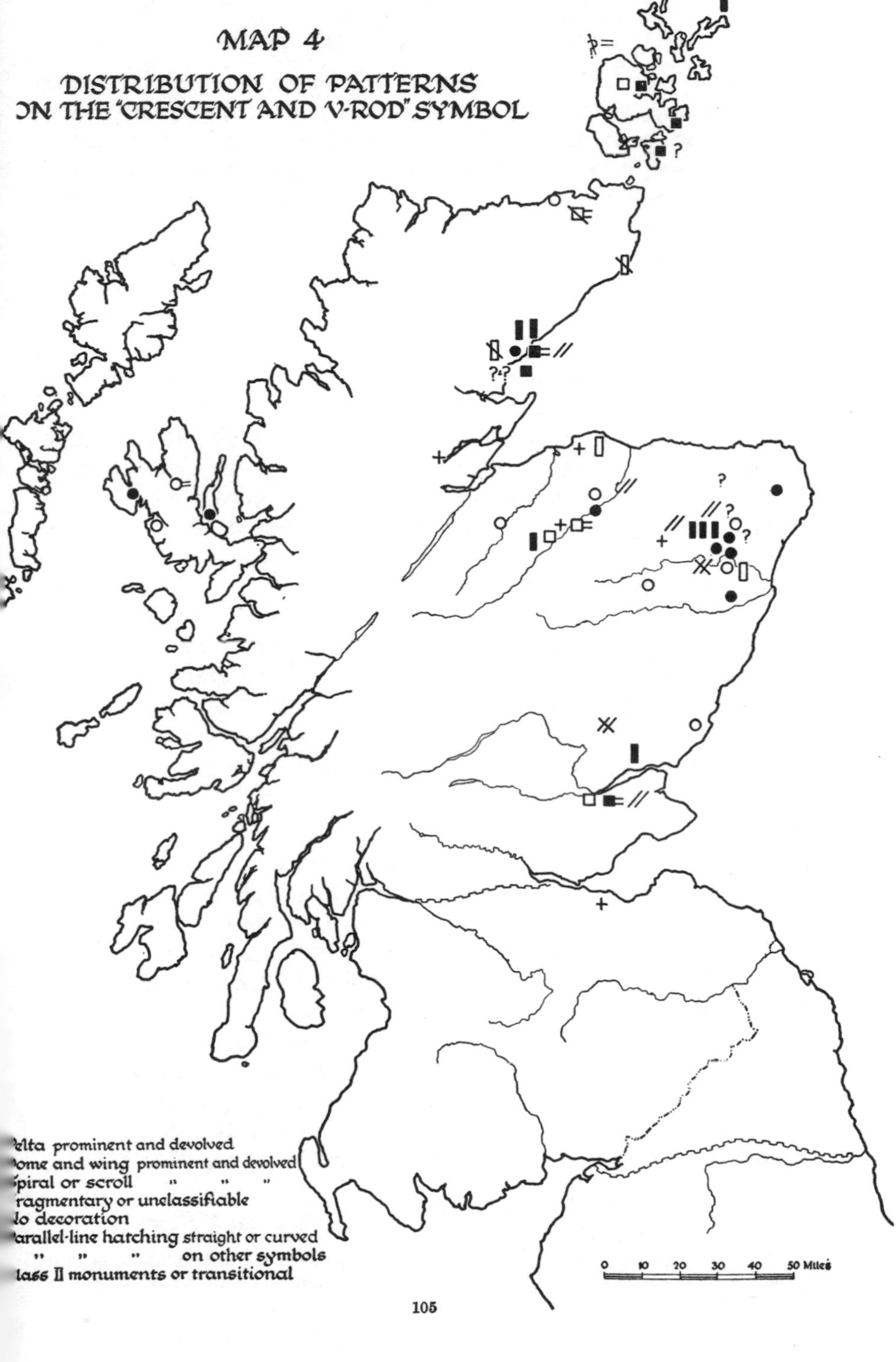
MAP 4
DISTRIBUTION OF PATTERNS
ON THE "CRESCENT AND V-ROD" SYMBOL
elta prominent and devolved
ome and wing prominent and devolved
piral or scroll " " "
ragmentary or unclassifiable
lo decoration
arallel-line hatching straight or curved
" " " on other symbols
lass II monuments or transitional
0 10 20 30 40 50 Miles

be seen on the Tara brooch and other Irish metal-work of the early eighth century, and curved hatching in a mid-eighth-century manuscript.[1] Two pelta designs with the latter feature, and notably similar to one another, have been found at Clynekirkton (No. A2), Sutherland, and at Lindores (No. A4), Fife. Abernethy, near Lindores, has a very simple double-pelta (No. A8).

Spiral designs are widespread; the simplest are found in Aberdeenshire (Nos. B5 and B7), as are some very obviously degenerate patterns (Nos. C13 and B8). A simple wing-shaped design comes from the Outer Hebrides (No. C11), while a more elaborate one on Raasay near Skye (No. C2)[2] is associated with an incised *Chi-Rho* cross for which Mrs Curle indicates a late-seventh-century date.

Map 4 sums up the distribution of these patterns. It is apparent that undecorated Crescents are relatively few. The best pelta patterns are found in Sutherland, Orkney and Fife; devolved ones in what might be loosely called the Spey-Don area, where there are the probably equally devolved good dome and spiral patterns. Dome patterns go across Scotland in a belt and there is one good one in Sutherland (Fig. 15, No. C1). Parallel hatching is centred in Aberdeenshire, and is found, though not solely by any means, on devolved patterns. It occurs on a semi-relief slab from Brough of Birsay (Orkney).[3] Several devolved or unclassifiable patterns are on stones that combine relief with incision. Crescents purely in relief (Fig. 15, D) break away entirely from the basic patterns and are not included in the map.

Animals

Animals and hunting scenes were extremely popular in late Roman art, and poor echoes are to be found later, for example on south French Merovingian sarcophagi.[4] This tradition, or objects such as the Coptic bowl with vigorous animals engraved on it buried at Sutton Hoo, may have inspired the animals on the Lullingstone hanging-bowl, which Kendrick considers to be Kentish-made[5] but with features derived from Merovingian work. The craftsman who made roundels, which we have considered already, apparently decided to put a similar spiral on his little stags; had he perhaps seen one of the pre-Roman Celtic objects that have such joint spirals? He also made fish and birds. A fine fish modelled in the round swims in the Sutton Hoo hanging-

[1] T. D. Kendrick (1938), PL. LV (Echternach).
[2] J. S. Richardson (1907).
[3] Cecil L. Curle (1940), PL. XXI.
[4] L. Coutil (1930), 23–6.
[5] T. D. Kendrick (1938), 58*n*; H. O'N. Hencken (1935), 201, while apparently accepting this, suggests for the bowl a position intermediate between British and Irish work.

bowl, and on the magnificent clasp and purse are very recognisable boars and rather more stylised birds and lions.[1]

Thus naturalistic art as opposed to the Germanic interlaced animals was not unknown in southern England in the first half of the seventh century. But the Book of Durrow of the middle or third quarter of the century brings us closer to the Picts. For its Lion of St Mark, derived inevitably from Mediterranean iconography, is decorated with joint scrolls. Note that these are not spirals like those of the Lullingstone stags, or the lion's own ear, but are scrolls as on the majority of Pictish animals. Some have neither, but only the lion on the Papil stone has spirals.

Various writers have shown how the Book of Durrow is an amalgam of styles and motifs. The text is palaeographically Northumbrian. There appear to be Coptic or Syrian manuscript influences, and the ribbon interlacing also comes from the Mediterranean world. On the other hand ribbon-like interlaced animals on folio 174*b* are purely Anglo-Saxon. Points to notice are their relatively short ears, straight jaws and fringe-like feet. The focus of that page is a tiny "maltese" cross. Metal-work has clearly inspired much of the ornament, and the symbolic figure of St Matthew (folio 245*b*) is decorated to imitate millefiori glass inlay. The whole style is described as Hiberno-Saxon, for wherever the book was actually illuminated, there is no doubt that the artistic impulses at work amalgamated in Northumbria, which included the monasteries at Melrose and Lindisfarne, the latter founded from Iona in 635 but not officially connected with Ireland after the Synod of Whitby in 664. If the hanging-bowls were Irish, the spiral page of the Book of Durrow (folio 111*a*) indicates a strong Hibernian contribution; but if they were English, or rather "British", as most recent writers believe, then the Irish element in Hiberno-Saxon art has often been greatly overstressed.[2] The important thing, however, for the present study, is that we must look south at least as much as west for a "Celtic" art that might have influenced Pictland. And if this is the case with illuminated manuscripts, then equally there are grounds for not assuming all related metal-work with interlace and spirals and animals to be Irish wherever it may be found, which is chiefly in Viking graves in Norway.[3] Pictland and Northumbria were also raided by the Scandinavians from the late eighth century.

Hiberno-Saxon art developed swiftly, and a generation or two after the Book of Durrow—at any rate before 721—the Lindisfarne Gospels were penned only sixty miles from Pictish shores. Their precise and

[1] BM (1947), PLS. 18, 23, and Fig. 16.
[2] A. W. Clapham (1934). [3] J. Petersen (1940).

fantastically complex beauty is superb, and it is not surprising that their artistic repercussions lasted long; the Book of Kells a century later is full of echoes of Lindisfarne. Kendrick emphasises that the Gospels were illuminated at least thirty years after the departure of the last Irish abbot. But to return to animals, these are now much more naturalistic despite the fantasy. Dog-like heads are characteristic. Noticeable features for our purpose are that the ears are often prolonged so as to form lappets, that there are now joint spirals, and that the forepaws have a ball and projecting claw. Birds, probably gannets and cormorants, are an unusual feature of the Lindisfarne Gospels, and sometimes have spirals and lappets.

This exquisite early eighth-century Hiberno-Saxon style is found in metal too, for Mlle Henry says of the so-called Tara Brooch, and the Ardagh Chalice, that the spiral and animal ornamentation are as near as possible to the Lindisfarne Gospels. A similar brooch, less fine but still outstanding, comes from Hunterston in Ayrshire.[1] Fig. 16 is based on illustrations by a recent German writer.[2] Two of the Hunterston brooch animals are at the bottom (Nos. 9 and 10), drawn without the obscuring effect of the granulated filigree of the original, and their pedigree is set out above. First comes the maximum stylisation on the great gold clasps from Sutton Hoo (No. 1), then the same Anglo-Saxon animal as drawn on the Faversham Brooch (No. 2) from Kent and claimed by Åberg as Irish.[3] No. 3, from the Durham Gospels, is ascribed to a date perhaps just before A.D. 700.[4] It has joint spirals, an interlaced tail here omitted, and ball-and-claw feet. No. 8 comes from the Lindisfarne Gospels and has one true ear, a lappet and a ball-and-claw foot. The two animals Nos. 5 and 6 are not in Haseloff, but are drawn from the front of the famous Monymusk Reliquary or *Brecbennoch* of St Columba[5] for which a date between Durrow and Lindisfarne has been suggested by Mlle Henry[6]; they certainly resemble beast No. 3 and have the same foot but sometimes lappets and also occasional joint spirals. In passing it may be noticed that the Reliquary's strap-hinge is partly in the hanging-bowl style and seems to be about the last object combining red and yellow enamel, and Mlle Henry points out that the mounts on the front of the Reliquary are a very early instance of the cast interlaced work that superseded the earlier style. The wide-open mouths and curling snouts of the Monymusk beasts

[1] J. Anderson (1881), II.1–6; ECM I.xcvii.
[2] G. Haseloff (1951), Figs. 10, 11, 17.
[3] N. Åberg (1943), 54. [4] G. Haseloff (1951), 25.
[5] J. Anderson (1881), I.241–50; ECM I.lxxxviii–lxxxix; F. C. Eeles (1934). No really satisfactory illustration of the interlaced animals has yet been made.
[6] Françoise Henry (1940), 70.

Fig. 16

Pedigree of the Pictish "Elephant". 1—Sutton Hoo clasp. 2—Faversham brooch. 3—Durham Gospels. 4—Tara brooch. 5–6—Monymusk reliquary. 7—Tara brooch. 8—Lindisfarne Gospels. 9–10—Hunterston brooch (*after Haseloff except* 5–6) are repeated on a brooch fragment from Dunbeath (Sutherland).[1] The Tara Brooch beasts (No. 7) are sterner, and some are more contorted (No. 4). None approach the gay abandon of the Hunterston animals which have closed but still curling snouts. Turn their heads round and straighten out the hindquarters, and you have a Pictish "Elephant" (Fig. 14, No. 4).

Two deductions may thus be drawn from this pedigree. First, that the Monymusk Reliquary and the Hunterston and Dunbeath brooches are linked in more than in just having their location in Scotland. They may have originated in a Hiberno-Saxon school working east of the North Channel and conveniently situated to suggest to the Picts their fourth most frequent symbol. Second, that this "Elephant" originated about the beginning of the eighth century.[2] This does not mean, of course, that even a majority of the symbols must have commenced as late as that; the "Elephant" is as common in relief as incised, whereas the Crescent is twice as common incised, which suggests that it started earlier. Moreover, the Crescent has a distinctly northern distribution, while the "Elephant," though reaching Orkney, is most common in Aberdeenshire; south of Aberdeenshire it is commoner in relief than the Crescent is. It is, however, found on the Golspie stone beside the Crescent whose decoration seems to be closest to the prototype.

Silver Objects

The dog's-head symbol on the pair of silver plaques from the hoard found at Norrie's Law in Fife[3] is typologically very close to the Lindisfarne dogs, though like the "Elephant" it is a kindly animal. A date about A.D. 700 or later is therefore suggested, on the supposition that the Lindisfarne artist was the originator, but the perhaps less likely alternative that the Lindisfarne animals are due to Pictish influence would affect the dating little. The triple spirals in the "Spectacle" symbol may be a sign of relative lateness since few incised "Spectacles" on the stones are decorated other than with concentric circles, though there is one at Dunnichen which has running spirals rather like early hanging-bowls. Two "hand-pins" also from Norrie's Law, decorated with simple spirals, are of a type commoner in Ireland than Scotland and bear on the central "finger" a "maltese" cross reminiscent of that already mentioned in the Book of Durrow. On the back of one there

[1] J. Anderson (1881), II.16; ECM I.xciv.
[2] Cecil L. Curle (1940), 75, first pointed this out. The Lindisfarne Gospels, however, had nothing directly to do with it, as they are typologically later.
[3] J. Anderson (1881), II.34–42; ECM I.lxxxiii–lxxxiv.

is engraved a single circle and Z-rod. The engraving on the front of the plaques and pins was filled with red enamel. Other silver articles in the hoard might be of earlier dates. Coins said to come from the spot are worthless for dating; the earliest goes back to Mark Antony, and the latest is Byzantine of the late sixth century, not late seventh as often repeated from a misprint.[1] Another large silver hand-pin, with elaborate spiral ornament but without symbols, was found with a light silver chain and other objects at Gaulcross (Banffshire).[2]

These are not the only silver objects definitely ascribable to the Picts. There are massive silver chains, over eighteen inches long, which have been found at various places from Inverness to Lanarkshire,[3] as shown in Map 3. The Lanarkshire example and one from Aberdeenshire have typical symbols engraved and enamelled on a broad open ring that may have fastened the two ends to form a choker neck-ornament. The "Spectacles" on one are ornamented with a simple spiral pattern.[4]

Conclusions

Summing up, we have found that some of the incised Pictish symbols correspond in various stylistic details to Hiberno-Saxon styles from the seventh to the mid-eighth century; that the decoration on the Crescent suggests that the elaborate decoration of no earlier than seventh century date came before any simpler versions; that Mediterranean animal art of the sixth-seventh centuries could, especially at the time when increasingly natural animal forms were being developed in Northumbria,[5] have inspired the more natural Pictish animals, which quickly developed on highly individual lines; and, lastly, that one of Northumbria's semi-natural beasts, immediately preceding the Lindisfarne Gospels, was adapted as a Pictish symbol. No artistic developments definitely earlier than the mid-seventh century can so far be ascribed to Pictland. Not only, therefore, as the relief monuments will show us, was there not anything incompatible between the symbols and Christianity, but the evidence all points to their being devised after the Picts became Christian. The suggestion that they derive from a scheme of pagan tattooing must be put aside, even if regretfully.[6] Similarly there is no support for Clapham's theory that the Picts kept La Tène art alive during the Roman and immediately post-Roman

[1] PSAS XVIII (1883–4), 246–7: 682 for 582.
[2] J. Stuart (1867), II.75 and PL. 9. [3] A. J. H. Edwards (1939).
[4] J. Anderson (1881), II.44; ECM I.lxxxvi–lxxxvii.
[5] So, too, Cecil L. Curle (1940), 66, who, however, refers to Hiberno-Saxon manuscripts as Irish.
[6] F. C. Diack (1944), 28.

period, and transmitted it to the southern makers of the hanging-bowls [1]; he did not suppose that any were made in Scotland. One of his chief arguments for a pre-fifth-century beginning for the symbols was the similarity of the Mirror to late La Tène ones. However, what seems to be an actual metal mirror handle of this kind in a context datable to the late seventh or early eighth century has recently been found in Ireland.[2] It has also been suggested that some rare potsherds from the Hebrides, incised with animals, might be forerunners of the sculptured stones,[3] but their date is very uncertain. Whatever early Pictish art existed is still unknown.

Early Relief Sculpture

Besides Hiberno-Saxon art there were in Northumbria at the end of the seventh century strong impulses direct from the classical Mediterranean world, which led to one of the earliest and finest "Saxo-Romanesque" monuments being erected at Ruthwell in Dumfriesshire.[4] The Ruthwell cross is typologically older than that at Bewcastle, now generally acknowledged to be dated by its inscription to not later than 709. For our purposes we note that except for one in Kent (Reculver), there are no earlier free-standing crosses in Britain; some supposed seventh-century Irish crosses [5] the writer believes to be several centuries later. The figures at Ruthwell, such as the impressive Christ and Mary Magdalene scene, are evidently copies from southern designs, and so is the symbolic vine growing up the sides, inhabited by birds and beasts. At Bewcastle panels of interlace are rendered in stone. From such early crosses grew the great series of Northumbrian and Anglian crosses in succeeding centuries of which a good eighth-century example is to be found at Abercorn on the Forth.[6] There seems no reason to connect any of the Abercorn stones with the short-lived bishopric of 681, and another fragment there, described as eighth century by Kendrick,[7] may indeed be tenth century like a Durham cross for which he revised his earlier date.[8]

North of the Forth the Picts, when they came to emulate sculpture in relief, did not care to copy the free-standing cross, but devised instead a new form of monument, the cross-slab with a raised cross on one face. Perhaps they simply wished to retain something of the form

[1] A. W. Clapham (1934), 44–7; his main thesis, that Hiberno-Saxon art owed little to Ireland, is not affected.
[2] Françoise Henry (1952).
[3] V. G. Childe (1935), 243 and PL. XVI.
[4] T. D. Kendrick (1938); RCAMS VII.219–86.
[5] Cecil L. Curle (1940), 77.
[6] C. S. T. Calder (1938), 217–23.
[7] T. D. Kendrick (1938), 136.
[8] T. D. Kendrick (1949), 95n.

of their previous monuments, but the decision had the important consequence of giving them the scope of a larger surface to decorate. Like the Ruthwell cross, the earliest cross-slabs appear fully fledged—the design may have been worked out entirely "on paper", as Kilbride-Jones suggested for the Tara Brooch form. They are all in the heart of southern Pictland, Angus and east Perthshire. That near the church at Glamis, 8¾ feet high, has a bold cross and characteristic shape, though the top is damaged. It is covered with varied interlace, an innovation in Pictland, but altered from imported models and elaborated particularly in the close-knit central roundel. The back is an undressed surface with incised symbols, probably an earlier monument re-used, as was quite often done within the period of incised symbols.[1] Beside the cross are two symbols which are a compromise between incision and relief. Other figures include a centaur, from classical sources, and two men fighting with axes, all in low flat relief. The lion (as it is to judge by its tail) has ball-and-claw paws, which are so common on relief monuments that Mrs Curle calls this the Pictish foot, though as it is not found on incised animals it must be due to Northumbrian influence. At the top of the stone were two animal heads with a human one between. This is another common feature, possibly a Daniel or Jonah motif.

Another cross, in Aberlemno churchyard (ECM No. 2), is one of the most remarkable. It sets a fashion by having deeper hollows in the corners of the cross-arms and more prominent arcs completing the circle and joining the arms. The quadrilobate ring characteristic of this and related crosses is not distinguished in Romilly Allen's list of shapes [2] from the true circular ring of the so-called "Celtic" crosses, but the difference is worth noting. The distinction made between the lower limb of the cross and the shaft is a Lindisfarne inheritance, and it is also characteristic. The relief of the cross is better executed than at Glamis, and the three large circular knots in the shaft together make what is described by Romilly Allen as the most elaborate interlace pattern in sculptured stone-work that has come down to us. To the right are bird-headed beasts interlaced; to the left the animals with long bodies curled through their legs, and each biting the beast above, might have come straight out of the Lindisfarne Gospels (folio *26b*). The mannerism of a central line on the beasts is, however, a mark of this Angus school of sculpture.

The scene on the back of this same cross-slab brings us to one of the most original achievements of Pictish art. For the stone has been used as a great page (7½ feet high and 3 to 4 feet broad) to portray scenes

[1] E.g. Inchyra (Perth Museum, unpublished), Easterton, Logie-Elphinstone, South Ronaldsay, etc. [2] ECM II.52.

on a scale and of a kind unknown in stone in western Europe at that time. The inspiration may have come from wall-painting in France [1] or late Roman narrative manuscripts in the tradition of the Sta Maria Maggiore mosaics in Rome, like that copied in the Utrecht Psalter rather later than our monument.[2] A similarly galloping spearman is known from two seventh-century Lombard shields probably made in north Italy.[3] Yet the warriors we see at Aberlemno are surely Picts; their helmets with large nose-pieces are, like that from Sutton Hoo a century or more earlier, part of the sub-Roman culture of the times. The infantry have shields with projecting bosses. The Pictish symbols are very prominent, still part incised and part in relief; some small details of the scene, like spears and a sword, are incised too. The story may be an incident in the life of the person in whose memory the cross was set up, or it may be legendary, as perhaps the man in the lower corner attacked by a bird indicates. Some curiously though not closely similar monuments, but half painted and half in very low relief, are found in Gotland in the Baltic, and are thought to be eighth century in date. Their origin and connexions are obscure, but they appear to depict legends.[4]

On a very fine stone, related to the Aberlemno style, at Rossie Priory, a man holding two birds also suggests a legend, that of Wayland Smith as illustrated on the Franks Casket in the British Museum.[5] Moreover, it has a griffin-headed man attacking a beast and other interesting figures. On the back of the same stone horsemen and hounds bear out Mrs Curle's description of Pictish art as a hunter's art, giving a clue to its naturalistic vigour.

Other monuments belong stylistically to the same early group. A cross-slab from Scoonie in Fife might be earlier than those at Glamis and Aberlemno, for the horsemen are just incised, though the cross is in relief. But it could be the work of an inferior sculptor. A slab at Meigle (No. 1) is later but also not first-class. Another stone at Meigle (No. 9) [6] is not a cross-slab, but a recumbent tombstone. It introduces a simple version of trumpet-spiral; on it, and on a fragment from Monifieth (No. 1) there is a bird and man intertwined. This motif suggests a date closer to the Book of Kells than to the Lindisfarne Gospels in which human figures do not form incidental decoration. On the stones, moreover, the far leg of the bird ends up nearer the

[1] R. Hinks (1935), 100–1. [2] Ibid. 115. [3] J. Werner (1951), 47–50.
[4] S. Lindqvist (1941–2). [5] G. Baldwin Brown (1930), VI.48.
[6] In ECM the monuments found at each site are listed together and are numbered consecutively under the name of the site, e.g. Aberlemno Nos. 1–3, Meigle Nos. 1–30. Consequently the stone referred to here as Meigle No. 9 is the ninth stone to be found under the heading Meigle in ECM, and so on to the end of this chapter.

spectator in a way called by Kendrick the "Anglo-Saxon lock", which he dates from the second half of the eighth century.[1]

On the whole this budding of mature Pictish art is unlikely to have begun before the middle of the century.[2] This still gives time for the not very numerous early monuments and some of their stylistic successors to have been carved before the next major change in the locality. Among the successors may be put the Woodwray stone and an unusual little stone in the important collection at Meigle (No. 5); the latter's peculiar design, deep relief and single rider on the back, mark it as probably well into the ninth century. The other important collection of stones in the same area, that of St Vigeans near Arbroath, includes a very attractive cross-slab (No. 7) with spirals at the corners of the arms, bird-headed and human-headed scrolls, and a base for the cross. It has no fantastic animals at the sides, but elaborately dressed figures, two of them seated as on the related monument at Fowlis Wester (Perthshire), which is remarkable for the preservation of its shallow surface detail.[3] A fully developed circular ring joins the arms. Both may be early ninth century.

Leaving this school in the south—its furthest north is a rather early example, part incised, part relief, at Fordoun (Kincardineshire), with a name inscribed on it—we find in the far north several monuments which Mrs Curle puts much earlier, but which seem to the writer to belong to the same stage and so to the latter half of the eighth century. The symbols on the crossless unshaped slab from the Brough of Birsay (Orkney),[4] are not typologically early; the V-rod has curls at the apex and is in part thickened and hatched, the decoration of the Crescent is unusual, and the Eagle's feet are in relief. Below them the three warriors in relief, particularly the chief with fringed dress and other elaborate details, approach the syle of St Vigeans No. 7. For what it is worth, the oddly pointed noses, remarked on by Mrs Curle, recur at Fowlis Wester.[5] The Papil stone, from Shetland, also partly in relief, has a very sophisticated lion that belies the seventh-century date proposed on the strength of the circular cross-head. Another stone, found more recently at Papil, has in flat relief a cowled rider and monks walking towards a free-standing cross on a base[6]; this suggests an early Iona type, and a date for it only just, if at all, prior to the Norse occupation of Shetland. The cross-slab at Golspie (Sutherland) has on one side incised figures, including a man with an axe, but a relief

[1] T. D. Kendrick (1938), 141
[2] So also, for different reasons, C. A. R. Radford (1942), 16.
[3] J. J. Waddell (1932).
[4] Cecil L. Curle (1940), PL. XXI.
[5] J. J. Waddell (1932).
[6] P. Moar (1944).

cross on the other. The designs on its incised Comb-case and Crescent symbols are highly developed, and an early ninth-century date may be suggested for it, with the Ulbster stone perhaps late eighth. But these last two are aberrations of chiefly local interest as far as stylistic developments are concerned, for the far north had fallen behind.

Hilton of Cadboll

The next great development is found on the north-west shore of the Moray Firth, an area from which no older relief sculpture is known. There is fairly general agreement in placing the Hilton of Cadboll stone about A.D. 800. More like the page of a manuscript than a stone, it is 7¾ feet high and dominated by three Pictish symbols covered with decoration as never before, the Crescent with meander and trumpet-spirals and the pair of roundels with the tight "knitted" knots as seen on the Angus crosses. Below them is a hunting scene. The relief is no longer flat but roundly modelled, and the figures have draperies—the trumpeters at the side in particular, who must represent a fresh borrowing direct from classical Mediterranean art. On the other hand the lady riding side-saddle has a "determinative" symbol in front of her, the Mirror-and-comb, and must surely be the person honoured by the monument. Her husband's nose and beard are in profile to the right of her head, as noted by Mrs Curle but overlooked in *Early Christian Monuments* probably because they balance her hair on the other side. A small square has been rather clumsily recessed for the carving of both. The riders and dogs follow the fashion at home in Angus. Round the scene and symbols there is a broad frame of striking eclecticism. At the sides there is an Anglian "inhabited" vine-scroll of a rather wiry form; the only other inhabited vine-scrolls from Pictland are on the considerably later Sueno Stone and on a small bronze gilt object found at Stromness (Orkney).[1] The bottom panel, which is incomplete, is filled with "Celtic" trumpet-spirals.[2] In Romilly Allen's view it should be twice the present size. This would increase the height of the stone and make the proportions more usual.[3] The whole of the other face, on which there no doubt was a cross, is destroyed. Part of another monument in a similar style comes from Tarbat near by.

[1] ECM I.xcii.
[2] Compare a fragment at South Kyme (Lincolnshire) in G. Baldwin Brown (1937), VI.ii.181.
[3] The tall form and low flat relief of much Pictish sculpture has recently inspired Sir Frank Mears's memorial to the Royal Scots in Princes Street Gardens, Edinburgh.

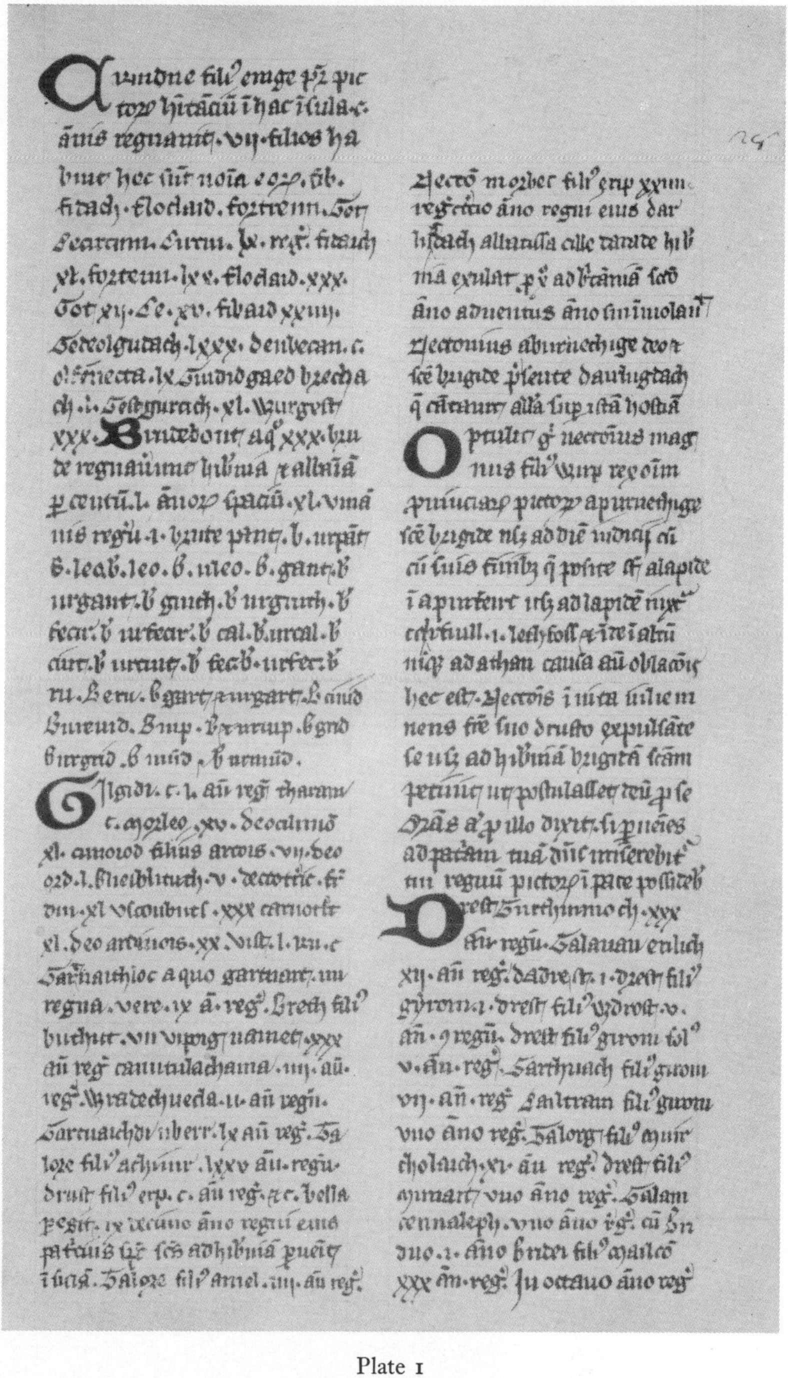

Plate I

The "Pictish Chronicle" (Sections One, Two, and part of Three) from MS A
(*Paris, Bibl. Nat., MS Latin* 4126)

Plate 2

Above Bamburgh Rock, Stronghold of the Angles

(*Photograph : Philipson and Son*)

Right Dumbarton Rock, Stronghold of the Britons

(*Photograph : Aerofilms Ltd.*)

Plate 3

Above Dunadd, Stronghold of the Scots (*Photograph* : *F. T. Wainwright*)
Below Dunollie, Stronghold of the Scots (*Photograph* : *Scotsman Publications*)

Plate 6

Above The Souterrain and Surface Dwellings at Ardestie, Angus
(*Crown Copyright Reserved ; reproduced by permission of the Ministry of Works*)

Below A Model of the Souterrain and Surface Dwellings at Ardestie, Angus
(*Photograph : Hunterian Museum*)

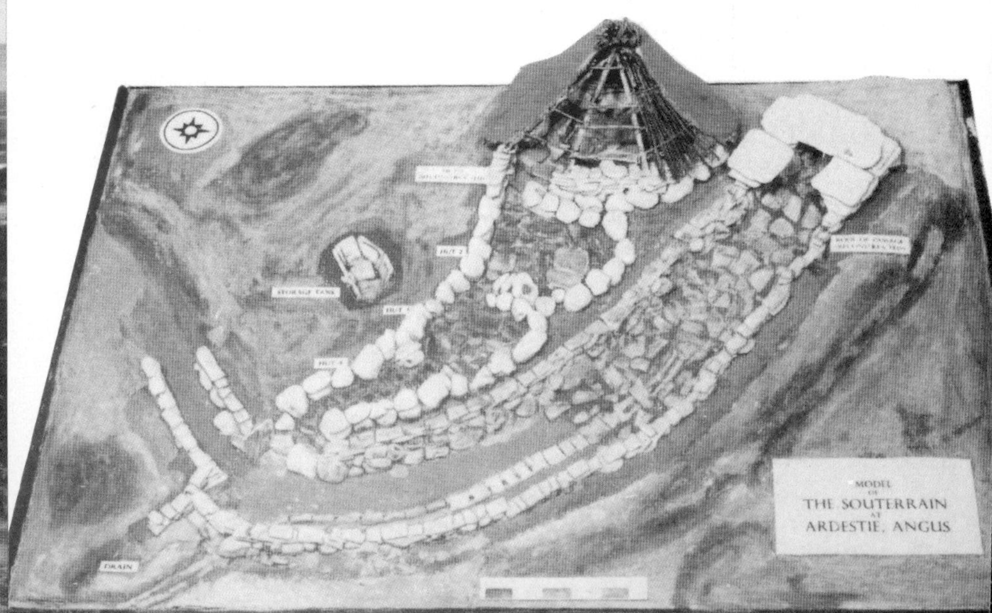

Dunnichen, Angus ($4\frac{2}{3}$ feet)
Photograph : Society of Antiquaries of Scotland)

Knowe of Burrian, Birsay, Orkney ($3\frac{3}{4}$ feet)
(*Photograph : Society of Antiquaries of Scotland*)

Plate 7
Early Incised Symbol Stones

Kinblethmont, Angus ($2\frac{2}{3}$ feet)
(*Photograph : F. T. Wainwright*)

Newbigging Leslie, Aberdeenshire ($2\frac{1}{12}$ feet)
(*Photograph : O. G. S. Crawford*)

Plate 8

Cross-slab (No. 2) at Aberlemno, Angus ($7\frac{1}{2}$ feet)

Front
(*Photograph : O. G. S. Crawford*)

Back (*Photograph : F. A. Ferguson*)

Hilton of Cadboll, Ross-shire ($7\frac{3}{4}$ feet)
(*Photograph : National Museum of Antiquities*)

Plate 9
Cross-slabs sculptured in Relief

Nigg, Ross-shire ($7\frac{1}{4}$ feet)
(*Photograph : Society of Antiquaries of Scotland*)

Plate 10

Fragments of a tomb-shrine at St Andrews, Fife ($2\frac{1}{3}$ feet)

(*Photograph from casts : National Museum of Antiquities*)

Plate 11

Opposite page. Later Sculptured Stones

Meigle (No. 11), Perthshire (5½ feet)

Meigle (No. 26), Perthshire (5¼ feet)

Inchbrayock, Perthshire (2½ feet)

(*Photographs : Society of Antiquaries of Scotland*)

Plate 12 Incised Symbols and Inscriptions

A vaguely contemporary object, a Crescent-and-V-rod symbol of bronze, seemingly with part at least of its decoration in low relief, is known only from an eighteenth-century drawing.[1] The overall coffering pattern on one side is closer in spirit to the Cadboll and later meanders than to the curvilinear designs of the incised symbol stones. On the other side are a "Spectacles-and-Z-rod" and a ram's head related to the Norrie's Law plaque.

EARLY BOSS STYLE [2]

The Cadboll stone is the only stone on which rounded relief and motifs of varied origin are combined with the serene uncramped feeling of the cross-slabs at Glamis (No. 2) and Aberlemno (No. 2). It forms a brief stage of perfection between those earlier classics and the full flower of the art, as represented by the higher relief and more restless complexity of three monuments, that at Nigg, a smaller but most important work at St Andrews, and the great roadside stone at Aberlemno (No. 3). The latter, over 120 travelling miles to the south, repeats remarkably in a fuller version the Cadboll hunting scene with the two trumpeters,[3] the close interlace, the Crescent's meander ornament, and the spirals forming incipient bosses on the "Spectacles". The main rider, however, is astride and has no Mirror-and-comb. There is no vine-scroll, but southern sources have inspired figures symbolic of Christianity, angels with bowed heads on the front and on the back David rending the lion, his harp placed above him as a "determinative". The whole cross-head is a translation from metalwork that had projecting amber or enamel inlays, to the round bosses of which a close mesh has been applied as if they were the Cadboll flat roundels, while the rectangular ones were given a meander pattern.

St Andrews

We now come to the chronological crux of the whole sequence. A first-hand copy of southern art with David again prominent is evident in the main panel of the tomb-shrine at St Andrews. Mrs Curle already before her main paper argued that a Byzantine ivory with oriental features was the prototype, and proposed a late eighth-century date.[4] Radford, on the other hand, prefers a western continental manuscript

[1] J. Anderson (1881), II.45 ; ECM I.xxxv.
[2] Not to be confused with Mrs Curle's *ronde bosse*.
[3] It is conceivable that though typologically later this Aberlemno stone was carved before the one at Cadboll.
[4] Cecil L. Mowbray (1936).

source and strongly favours the first half the tenth century.[1] Yet the plastic rendering of the figures is as much a novelty in the art of Pictland as are the iconography and foliage on the front or the monkeys at the side, and a three-dimensional model must have been followed—not slavishly, for the notched shield seems local, to judge by a similar one at Ardchattan, though Mrs Curle cites foreign parallels for David's sword. The tenth-century date was chosen partly to coincide with the time when St Andrews became paramount as an ecclesiastical centre, but an equally historically-founded date would be about 820–34, if we identify the Angus MacFergus who reigned then[2] with the king who brought St Andrew's relics to Scotland. St Andrew, not being a Pict, would not be entitled to symbols on his monument, nor would St Regulus if it was his shrine; the old Class I, II and III terminology is misleading in this and other aspects. The main reason, however, for Radford's late date is because on Irish analogies he ascribes the crosses at Iona to the tenth century, and the similarity between the bosses on them and on the end panel of the St Andrews shrine is universally admitted. Now while it is no doubt the case that the Iona crosses could have been erected later than the first flight of the monks from the Norse raiders in 806, contrary to Mrs Curle's supposition, and probably were, it is arguable that the artists of Iona inspired the Irish ninth-century crosses and not vice-versa. Such an authority on Irish sculpture as Mlle Henry, who would not go as far as that, treats the Iona crosses in her chapter on the eighth and early ninth centuries, and speaks of their style as produced by the same bold modelling as the St Andrews and Nigg stones.[3] Moreover writhing snake-like animals, very horrid to our eyes, are one of the striking features of the St Andrews shrine, for which Mrs Curle notes a close parallel on a Northumbrian cross at Rothbury, that has been stylistically dated by Kendrick as Carolingian and "vaguely centred on the year 800".[4] Lastly, six small crosses sunk in the overall interlace pattern on one of the shrine's corner stones are closely paralleled in a late-eighth-century Northumbrian manuscript (Leningrad Gospels, folio 18*a*), where Kendrick notes it as a typical convention of the Book of Kells period.[5] So there is as much agreement as possible on a date not later than about 825 for the St Andrews shrine.

At St Andrews some of the intertwined beasts have escaped and turned into snakes crawling round the bosses, which are more pro-

[1] C. A. R. Radford (1942), 6–11.
[2] Another king of the same name reigned 729–47. Cf. A. O. Anderson (1922), I.267.
[3] Françoise Henry (1940), 111.
[4] T. D. Kendrick (1938), 157–8. [5] Ibid. 148.

nounced than those at Aberlemno. There is a spread of close-mesh interlace, but small spirals surround the central boss on the square side-panel, and it has also been covered with them though this is not clear in illustration.

North and West

Bosses with mesh and spiral decoration, snakes in maximum profusion, and three or four pairs of interlaced snake-like beasts on each arm of the cross are found on a monument at Nigg on the Cromarty Firth, not far from Cadboll, which is 7¼ feet high despite the known loss of one row of bosses. It brings to a climax the love of intricacy. Besides those features repeating the St Andrews style, the very plastic modelling on the shrine's main panel has a counterpart at Nigg in a scene of St Paul and St Anthony in the desert,[1] which is squeezed rather barbarously into the Pictish triangular top.

Large-scale Eagle and "Elephant" symbols were carved on the upper quarter of the back, where the relief is lower than on the front and perhaps by a different sculptor. The "Elephant" was unique in being covered with a meander pattern, rather like that on the Cadboll Crescent. The only other decorated "Elephants" are at Brodie and Glenferness.[2] The lower figures include David, with harp, lion and sheep once more. Curiously unfinished-looking incised-interlace panels are paralleled at Aberlemno (No. 3) and Tarbat. They may correspond to the dotted single-line interlace on some manuscripts such as the Leningrad Gospels (folio 78*a*).

One of the most remarkable features at Nigg, particularly compared with the staid nearly two-dimensional trumpet-spirals of Hilton of Cadboll, is the presence in some of the front panels of a whirl of spirals that spring up into bosses of various sizes. They reappear on the crosses at Iona and Kildalton (Islay) at the other end of the Great Glen, on which snakes and large bulbous bosses covered with closely "knitted" interlace are also prominent. Close interlace, as already noted, has an earlier history in Angus ; but it has not in Ireland, which is one reason for deriving the Iona boss style from Fife and Angus via Ross and Cromarty. On the other hand it is true that a possibly earlier flat whirl of spirals is found in the west at Kilnave (Islay). An indirect tribute to the significance of Pictish art is paid by Mlle Henry when she observes [3] that the Iona spiral-boss panels are practically identical with parts of the most intricate pages of the Book of Kells, that supreme

[1] Cecil L. Curle (1940), 101.
[2] See below, p. 121.
[3] Françoise Henry (1940), 148 and PL. 65.

achievement of Hiberno-Saxon art. She follows Mrs Curle in noting that the work of another of the several illuminators of the book has affinities with Pictish animal art,[1] and she uses this comparison along with that of the spiral bosses to point towards Iona as the place where at least part of the illumination of the Book of Kells was made. The date for the book she gives as between 760 and 820, which corresponds with Kendrick's *c.*800. We might wish for a few years' extension at most.

Metal-work

There is some metal-work that should be related to sculpture in high relief. Two bronze objects found in Norway, one in a ninth-century grave,[2] have large bosses, snaky beasts raising their heads in a way not possible in stone sculpture, and not intertwined but appealing to the same phase of taste as Early Boss sculpture, a phase which from its very exaggeration one would envisage to be fairly short. Their place of origin, Ireland or possibly some part of Scotland, is of course not known. More restrained, but much more readily claimed as Pictish, are two silver gilt or gold-mounted brooches of penannular "Irish" type, with birds' heads in high relief placed as if drinking out of the disk on each terminal.[3] One was found at Rogart (Sutherland), and one near Perth. They may be assigned to the first half of the ninth century or to the end of the eighth.

Late Boss Style

North

A number of monuments round the Moray Firth show what happened to the Pictish Boss Style. On the front of the fantastic cross-slab at Shandwick near Nigg the style has run to seed; small bosses cover the cross, which rises from four large bosses surrounded by heavy serpents. The back is all in relatively low relief, its panels including a large remarkably clumsy "Elephant" with a T-pattern on its lappet, a crowded hunting and duel scene, and an elaborate panel of C-shaped spirals, with little trefoil ornaments such as were used more sparingly in the Book of Kells and at Hilton of Cadboll.

Roughly contemporary is probably the monument at Rosemarkie, which harks back to a manuscript page in its low relief, in its whole

[1] Cecil L. Curle (1940), PL. XIX.
[2] J. Petersen (1940), Nos. 84 and 108; Françoise Henry (1940), PL. 44.
[3] J. Anderson (1881), II, Figs. 4, 14; E.C.M., I.xcv–xcvi.

composition, and in portions such as the panels containing crosses. The symbols are once more very prominent and their decoration is overdone. Two animals above the Crescent have simply twisted bodies but tails forming a background interlace, a novel feature probably derived from Northumbria. Ordinary zoomorphic interlace covers half the front. On the sides there are curious animal and animal-headed interlace designs, of which that on the middle left-side panel foreshadows tenth-century taste. A date about the third quarter of the ninth century may be suggested. The evident need for simplifying the Boss Style, after elaboration had gone as far as can be imagined, is met another way at Brodie, near Forres, unfortunately in parts defaced. The "Spectacles" there might be early in style, but lateness suggested by a peppering of very small bosses is confirmed by decoration on the "Elephant" and the clumsy squaring of its curving snout. The prominent position on this late stone of a pair of hippocamps is the best evidence for Romilly Allen's inclusion of this animal among the symbols.[1]

South

The southern developments were much more restrained; indeed there is a striking absence of first-class close successors to the Early Boss Style monuments. The 8-feet-high cross-slab at Meigle (No. 2) is the chief claimant; it is connected with one at Aberlemno (No. 3) by its size, its general arrangement, and the hunting scene ranging across part of the back in relief, now weathered but evidently rounded and well modelled. On the front much of the relief is very high. The centaur with axes and a branch occurs only here and at Aberlemno (No. 3). An important novelty is that, perhaps for the first time on the cross-slabs, there are no Pictish symbols; for though the Centaur was listed as such in *Early Christian Monuments*, it does not occur on the incised stones, and Baldwin Brown has pointed it out with its branch on late-eighth-century Anglo-Saxon coins (*sceattas*).[2] The Old Testament scene representing Daniel in the lions' den is now very prominent at the expense of the hunters. On the front an unusually shaped cross seems to be trying to free itself from the background. The decoration includes small bosses, some on a meander field which is less appropriate than the spiral field at Nigg. The animals on the shaft are surely Anglian "Twin-Beasts", paired and *affrontés*, from the free-standing

[1] Of the northern boss-style stones not discussed the finest is at Glenferness (Nairnshire).

[2] G. Baldwin Brown (1915), III.87, cited by Cecil L. Curle (1940), 89.

cross-shafts of ninth-century Northumbria,[1] as noted by Radford, though Mrs Curle points vaguely to Ireland. The tangled background of interlace, which grows from them, is rather exaggerated—the two Rosemarkie animals came closer in this to the Anglian model—and the suckling young or hunting dogs are a Pictish touch. A recumbent tombstone at Meigle (No. 11) is closely connected with this cross-slab by its spiral bosses, animals and riders in spirited relief. On the other hand a large but incomplete cross-slab at Meigle (No. 4) is probably rather earlier than either. Another recumbent monument (No. 26) is sculptured in the boss-style on top, but has flat relief on its sides, which foreshadows later developments. Some of the animals on the latter retain their Pictish joint-scrolls.

Though there is thus a continuation of the flow of Mediterranean ideas, with the Anglo-Saxons indicated as intermediaries, the absence of symbols on a cross-slab of such evident importance in its own time as Meigle No. 2 presumably denotes the subjection of independent Pictish rulers at the hands of Kenneth mac Alpin about 850, after which, to quote Mrs Curle, "Pictish culture must have been merged with that of the Scots, and all that was most characteristic gradually disappeared". Her statement, however, needs qualifying to the extent that the later sculpture continues to show Northumbrian influence and not Scoto-Irish; there are no Irish or Iona crosses, for example, in eastern Scotland.

Before consideration is given to the monuments which indicate the gradual disappearance of Pictish identity by the much reduced space and importance allowed to the symbols, the suggestion may be hazarded that the over-elaboration of the symbols in the northern late Boss Style, was a deliberate flaunting, and indicates an area in which an already important community—the Cadboll stone was carved say fifty years earlier—resided as Free Picts longer than further south, and then was suppressed completely. There are no small symbols in the Moray Firth area such as are seen farther south.

At Dunfallandy[2](Perthshire), actually from Killiecrankie, there is a delightful cross-slab reminding us of the classic churchyard stone at Aberlemno (No. 2); but, while evidently in that tradition, it has later features. There are small bosses, rather formally grouped on backgrounds of dull C-spirals and on meanders comparable to those on Meigle No. 2. The figures beside the cross stand on a separating line or strip of ground and the animals are not interlaced. Three human figures, widely spaced, occupy most of the back, and beside each there

[1] T. D. Kendrick (1938), 198.

[2] The Dunfallandy stone's supposed move is a mistake by Romilly Allen.

are one or two small symbols. A small free-standing cross is represented in the middle. Radford has stressed that Pictish sculptures, the later ones at least, were memorials and secular, in contrast to the Irish crosses, which were essentially monastic [1]; and the symbols at Dunfallandy surely refer to the adjacent figures, as though they were the persons commemorated and the symbols told something about them, perhaps their rank or office. The Mirror-and-Comb of the lady at Cadboll was a similar "determinative", for which Anderson cites the analogy of the mirror-and-comb clearly denoting a woman in the case of late medieval west Highland grave-stones, as of a Prioress at Iona. His exhaustive discussion on the meaning of the symbols, however, reaches no positive conclusions.[2]

Though quite different from the stone at Meigle (No. 2), the tall cross-slab at Fowlis Wester (No. 1) has the same cluster of small bosses in the centre of the cross-head, and again the cross is trying to get free —the ends of the arms project from the rather narrow slab. Otherwise the sculpture is fully in the Pictish tradition, but the two symbols present are both rather small. Another cross-slab with bosses and reduced symbols is at St Madoes. Its horsemen, each in a separate panel, are badly proportioned (a foretaste of things to come), but the other face is very good with bold animals. Those, unfortunately now headless, on the top of the stone are particularly three-dimensional and derive from the St Andrews shrine type of *ronde bosse*.

Something of the same quality of animal is found on a slab at St Vigeans (No. 1), which is important because of its Drosten inscription. It has rather coarsely decorated though prominent symbols, and a scene like that at Shandwick. A kneeling archer occurs on both these, at Glenferness, and at Meigle (No. 10). Up the side is a poor vine-scroll without animals. A mid-ninth-century date seems to fit these features best, though there are no relief bosses; the writer's choice of bosses as a useful guide to style and date does not imply that all sculptors of the period favoured them.

Small spiral bosses are, however, found on one finely carved fragment of great interest discovered recently at Edzell. It is not from a cross-slab, but is the centre and one arm of a free-standing cross, ringless like those of Northumbria. This confirms the impression given by the stones at Meigle (No. 2) and Fowlis Wester (No. 1) that these were coming into fashion in Pictland. Moreover a sadly decayed fragment of ringed cross-head at St Vigeans has a curious large conical boss on the arm; it was clearer in Stuart's day.[3]

[1] C. A. R. Radford (1940), 18.
[2] ECM I.xxxii–xlvii, cx–cxi.
[3] J. Stuart (1867), II, PL. XIII.

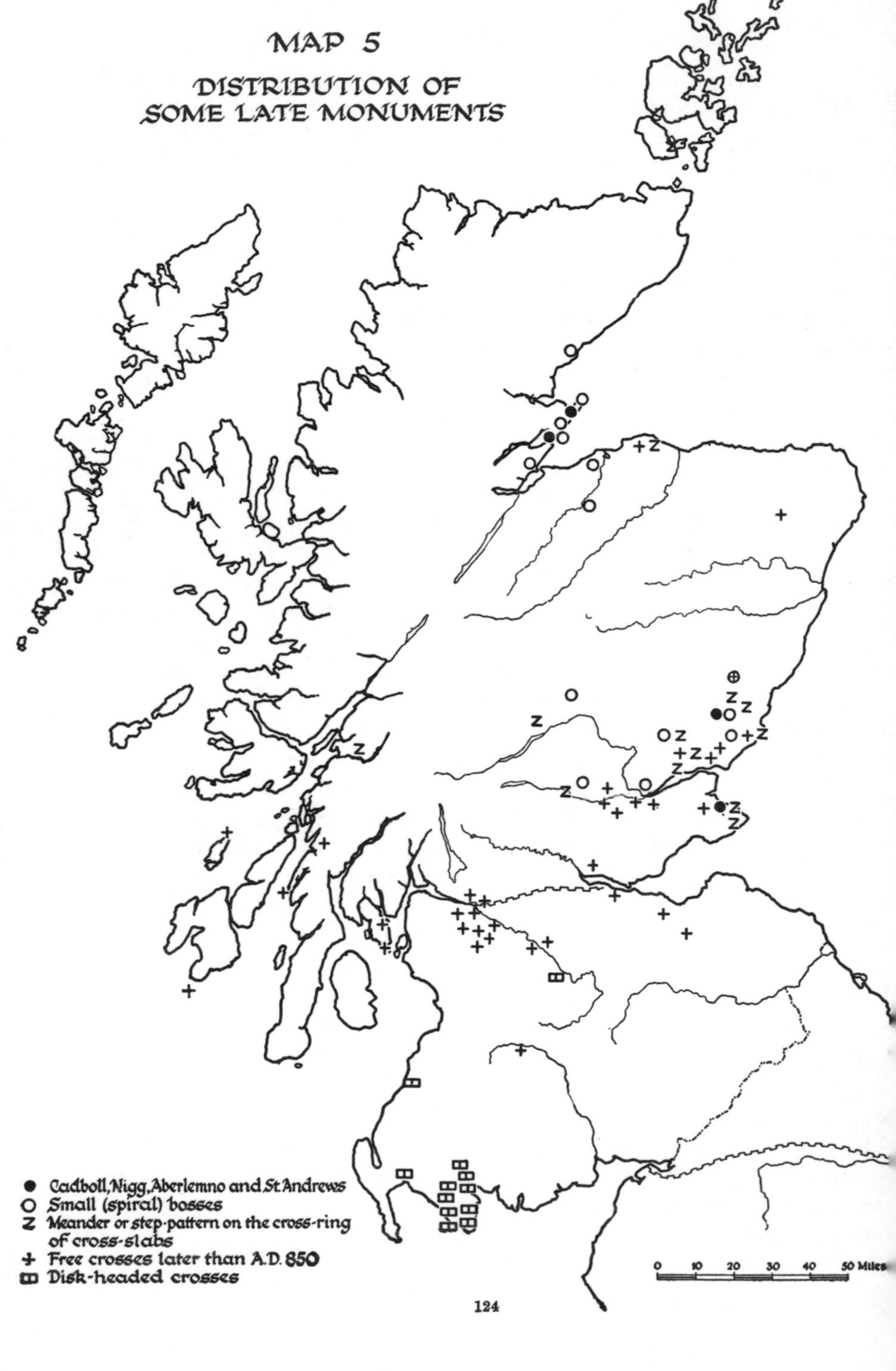
MAP 5
DISTRIBUTION OF
SOME LATE MONUMENTS
Cadboll, Nigg, Aberlemno and St Andrews
Small (spiral) bosses
Meander or step-pattern on the cross-ring of cross-slabs
Free crosses later than A.D. 850
Disk-headed crosses
0 10 20 30 40 50 Miles

Free-crosses and Latest Slabs

Though the separate Pictish state came to an end about 850, the Picts inevitably remained. By continuing to follow the course of their art we can see how they merged into a wider Scotland. Map 5 looks back and forward from the point we have reached. It shows the massing of important monuments north-west of the Moray Firth, the sites of Cadboll and Nigg and of their parallels at Aberlemno and St Andrews, and the distribution of stones with small bosses, the degenerate cross-slab at Dunblane omitted as hardly in the tradition. Out of the mass of later sculpture two features have been chosen rather arbitrarily for the map, the first being Anglian crosses after 850 with their derivatives outside Northumbria. At first sight most bear no relation to this survey, since they are outside Pictish borders. But it is surely significant that the warriors and hunters, so characteristic of Pictish monuments hitherto, but quite foreign to Northumbrian art, are frequently found on the later sculpture not only of the east coast, but of Clydeside, which previously had no sculpture; and from there the figures, no longer Pictish, and the cross-slab form had spread to the Isle of Man by about the middle of the tenth century. Furthermore, the degree of barbarisation which we shall see in Pictland was universal over the whole area, and so probably is to be attributed to a wider cause than the loss of Pictish independence. Incidentally it provides a measure of the unlikeliness of a tenth-century date for the St Andrews shrine. The other factor mapped, meander or step decoration on the rings or haloes of the crosses of cross-slabs, seems for some reason or other to show the extent to which Pictland survived as a distinct region. The one northern site, also prominent for the number of stones found there, is Kineddar (Drainie), where the Cathedral of Moray was situated before Spynie and Elgin.

The absence from Aberdeenshire of the Boss Style and also of almost all symbol-less monuments,[1] suggests that the earlier scarcity of relief symbols, compared with incised ones, was not entirely due to the longer persistence of the latter here suggested, for they can scarcely have still been in fashion far into the ninth century. The intractable granite and whinstone, which the sculptors of the area for the most part seem to have had to use, is a possible explanation. Yet some difference in population or social structure from Angus or Moray should perhaps be sought. The original site of the monastery of Old Deer,

[1] The cross mapped is the problematical but evidently late shaft-like stone at Fyvie.

when located, may however alter the emphasis. On the Maiden Stone near Chapel of Garioch there are prominent symbols in separate panels, flat relief and two-ply interlace; a date about the middle of the century may be proposed. Quite different in style is the relief cross-slab at Dyce (No. 2). It has medium-sized symbols decorated with S and C curves for which a mid- or late-ninth-century date may be suggested. The cross is covered with interlace and has spirals projecting from the corners of the arms and shaft. Other examples of the same features are the very fine, probably earlier though symbol-less, slab from Loch Kinnord and the Ogam-inscribed symbol stone from Formaston, both now at Aboyne. The badly drawn cross flanked by small symbols at Migvie marks the end of that series. In Caithness the fine cross-slab from Skinnet may be contemporary with the Boss Style, while in Sutherland the remarkable symbol-less slab at Farr and the precisely carved fragment from Collieburn are not likely to be much later.

To the second half of the ninth century may be dated the fine free-standing cross at Dupplin, west of Perth. Anglian Beasts and grapeless vine-scrolls are imported like the cross-form. Local taste has produced the human figures, including a very poor David with the lion, and warriors. But we have not seen before the close setting of the foot soldiers, or the horseman's long moustache. Was he a Scot rather than a Pict? The men on the early tenth-century Muiredach's Cross at Monasterboice (Co. Louth) have similar moustaches. Four characteristics of later ninth- and tenth-century taste in our area are to be noted in the decoration at Dupplin: the prominence of key and step patterns, C-scrolls set horizontally and vertically with a lack of imagination, and two-ply interlace. It is not that these motifs are now introduced but that they now become very fashionable.

A tall cross-slab at Crieff has no figures but reproduces the Dupplin patterns badly in poor relief, and has a meander on the cross-ring. The mustachioed warrior recurs at Benvie (Angus) on a cross-slab just 3 feet high, which is a barbarous production compared with, say, the warriors in Aberlemno churchyard, though the front of the slab is interestingly and skilfully designed. At St Andrews the very many small cross-slabs have mostly no figures, but the motifs just mentioned as characteristic are very prominent, which makes it impossible to ascribe them to the eighth and ninth centuries rather than at earliest the late ninth and early tenth, when indeed the site became so important ecclesiastically. Though most of the St Andrews slabs have ringless crosses, several are closely similar to one from Invergowrie, near Dundee, which has a ring and, on the back, three men full-face whose draperies are in a flat corrugated style, probably based on a Northumbrian manner, seen for example at St Andrew Auckland (County Durham), already in the late eighth century. On a larger scale are draped figures on the huge arch stone from a building at Forteviot (Perthshire); its greater flatness may be due to the scale rather than a sign of later date. A suggestion by J. S. Richardson, that the shepherds watching their flocks are represented, may not suit the curled hair of one and the long moustaches, which perhaps indicate a warrior chief.

It is curious that, though full-face figures are found in seventh- and eighth-century Hiberno-Saxon manuscripts, and on the Ruthwell cross and its successors in Northumbria, only David on the St Andrews shrine and, inevitably, the lady riding side-saddle at Cadboll, face us on Pictish sculpture till the latter half of the ninth century, Daniel at Meigle (No. 2) being then the earliest. A new fashion is to be seen at Elgin on a tall boss-less slab that has on the back a hunting scene and prominent but coarsely decorated symbols on which C-spirals are conspicuous. On the front the four Evangelists stand full-face round the cross, and below this there is an interlace of straplike animals which Mrs Curle compares with those at Colerne (Wiltshire), dated by Kendrick to 850–75.[1] Such Evangelist figures recur on very ugly slabs, no doubt tenth-century, at Aldbar and St Vigeans (No. 11). With these may be classed the slab at Kirriemuir (No. 1) which is the last of the Mirror-and-Comb series, and probably of all the symbols. The "Spectacles" and Crescent had appeared on small slabs not very long before, at Monifieth (Nos. 1 and 2) and at Kingoldrum, in Angus like the foregoing.

There is an entertaining slab from Inchbrayock, Montrose, which, as Mrs Curle says, is hard to date. What may be a "Two-disc" symbol occurs on it, but the general appearance of the cross-design on the front resembles the late ninth- and tenth-century slabs, and a confirmation is provided by the very disorganised spiral panels. The scenes on the back include what Joseph Anderson recognised as Samson slaying a Philistine with the jawbone of an ass. The Philistine wears a hood, which is a useful reminder that the "cowled figures" on the cross-slabs are not invariably ecclesiastics. The greatest difficulty about this slab however, is that Kendrick has noted quite a number of detailed resemblances to the Franks Casket,[2] philologically ascribed from its inscription in Anglian runes to early eighth-century Northumbria; and we may add Mrs Curle's comparison of the bows on the casket and on a stone at St Vigeans (No. 1).[3] One answer may be that much

[1] T. D. Kendrick (1938), 190.
[2] Ibid. 123*n*; see also G. Baldwin Brown (1930), VI.18–51.
[3] Cecil L. Curle (1940), 91–2. The Inchbrayock sword-hilt seems too simple to be used for any dating.

that we have been treating as Pictish in the narrative art of our stones was really copied from small-scale Northumbrian carving in a style otherwise unknown in Northumbria; another is that there is a strong Pictish strain in the casket, but that it has been dated a century or two too early.[1]

We must not spend too much time on these dregs of Pictish tradition, yet we must consider the possibility that the Ogam-inscribed Bressay stone from Shetland is a late ninth-century or tenth-century copy of the Papil stone, characterised by a haphazard scatter of decoration and a marked clumsiness of drawing. Rings appear not only in the little ornaments on the circular cross-head (as already at Papil) but also in the two-strand ring-twist* on the back, a pattern typical of the Norse-influenced sculpture of Clydeside, south-west Scotland, Wales and elsewhere. Though its beginning is to be found in manuscript decoration of the eighth century and earlier,[2] it is not found in Pictland.[3] Moreover the ring-twist has "split-bands", a late eighth-century Norse invention that was common in the Viking period.[4]

A cross-shaft from Monifieth (No. 4) has flat closely placed figures, including a rather grotesque Crucifixion, and thick repetitive but well-cut interlace with curling animals at the bottom double-outlined in the Anglo-Danish style of tenth-century Northumbria. Sueno's Stone at Forres, though over 20 feet high and skilfully carved, bears in its design the stamp of the same late period—the monotonous interlacing and more particularly the rows of tightly packed figures such as are found on Irish crosses of the time and on an uncertain cross-slab at Dunkeld.

Finally the "hog-back" at Meigle, which would be almost entirely at home in northern England, and a terribly barbarous coped stone at Brechin, bring us to about A.D. 1000, to judge from the latter's beasts and tendrils of Anglo-Danish derivation.[5] The continuing stream of art influences from beyond the Forth had long been degenerating in quality owing to wars and invasion, and the Picts, themselves impoverished by the same causes, had no stimulating contacts with the further south. They had lost their power to adapt incoming styles, and had indeed lost all trace of their individuality.

[1] See also above, p. 114.
[2] V. E. Nash-Williams (1950), 204*n*.
[3] References given in ECM II (below Fig. 574) are errors not repeated in ECM III.
[4] H. Shetelig (1948), 81.
[5] T. D. Kendrick (1949), 98–9.
* Ring-twist occurs also on St. Vigeans No.10.

Chapter VI

THE PICTISH LANGUAGE

K.H. Jackson

ALMOST everything connected with the Picts has formed the subject of controversy at some time or other, and perhaps nothing has been so controversial as the question of what language they spoke. There are various reasons for this. One of them is the fact that the available evidence is scanty and difficult to interpret. Another is the way in which language is commonly regarded as a function of "race" and as an infallible index of origin. Race and racial origins are matters which are obscure in their very nature, but always arouse considerable interest and sometimes even feeling, and hence may lead to violent argument, as has been the case notably with the "Pictish problem". In general the policy adopted in this book is to avoid undue speculation about the origin of the Picts and their more remote background. Nevertheless, any consideration of the history of the Pictish language must involve a consideration of its wider linguistic affinities; and this in turn makes it essential to pay at least some attention to the question who the Picts were and where they came from. This problem is touched upon, therefore, in the present chapter in an attempt to show how the conclusions arrived at on purely philological grounds corroborate and especially are corroborated by what we know or suspect about the background of the proto-Pictish peoples.

Before entering on a sketch of the controversy over the Pictish language it is necessary to define two or three linguistic terms. The *Common Celtic* branch of the parent Indo-European stem is divided into two great families, *Q-Celtic* and *P-Celtic*. The most important of a number of distinguishing marks of Q-Celtic is the fact that it preserves the original Indo-European *qu* unaltered; and one of the chief characteristics of P-Celtic is that it turned this *qu* into *p*, a change which took place also in some Greek and Italic dialects. This is by no means the only difference between the two families, but these names make a convenient shorthand for distinguishing them. The Q-Celtic group is represented by the *Goedelic* or *Goidelic* languages, namely Irish, Scottish Gaelic and Manx; and "Goedelic" is commonly used not only of these but also of the hypothetical ancestor sub-dialect of Common Celtic from which they all descend. The P-Celtic branch covers a wide conglomeration of dialects which comprise the *Gaulish* of the Continental Gauls of history, and the *British* spoken by the people of Roman Britain, by their immediate descendants for about a century, and by their ancestors in this island as far back as our direct information in classical sources reaches. The later offspring of British are Welsh, Cornish, and Breton; and all these, together with the parent British, are called the *Brittonic* or *Brythonic* sub-group of the P-Celtic family. There must have been a stage in the history of P-Celtic, before the migrations of the Brittonic-speaking peoples to Britain, when Gaulish and Brittonic were not yet differentiated, or were only beginning to be differentiated; and this stage will be referred to as *Gallo-Brittonic.* Whether a Brittonic language or dialect proper was ever spoken in northern Scotland is one of the subjects which have to be discussed in this chapter; and to avoid begging any questions now, the term "British" will be used only in the strict sense of the language of the people living in what became the province of Roman Britain, south of the Antonine Wall. This language is no problem, as its nature is pretty well known from later literary remains as well as from contemporary classical ones, and it seems to have been remarkably homogeneous.

Now, how about Pictish? Was it a Celtic language? If Celtic, was it Goedelic, or a Brittonic dialect more or less identical with British ("Northern British", as it were), or was it an independent offshoot from the Gallo-Brittonic stage not immediately connected with British? If Goedelic, was it a separate dialect, a sister to Irish and Scottish Gaelic and Manx, or was it actually Scottish Gaelic itself in its most archaic form? If not Celtic, was it some other Indo-European tongue, or was it not even Indo-European at all but "non-Aryan", to use an old phrase? All these theories have had their advocates, some less reputable and authoritative than others.

The view that Pictish was not Indo-European was proposed by Sir John Rhys,[1] who thought at first that it was an Iberian language allied to Basque, though he abandoned this later. His chief evidence was the unintelligible inscriptions which will be discussed below, and he undertook at one time to translate them with the help of Basque. Zimmer[2] likewise considered the Pictish nation fundamentally "non-Aryan", though overlaid in historical times with Celtic elements both Goedelic and Brittonic. He drew his arguments mainly from the Pictish customs of tattooing and matrilinear succession, both of which he held to be not proper to an Indo-European people, so that his arguments were chiefly not linguistic. The Irish historian MacNeill revived this theory a generation later,[3] though he allowed a considerable

[1] J. Rhys (1892, 1898). [2] H. Zimmer (1898).
[3] E. MacNeill (1933, 1939).

Brittonic element in the population of the east of Scotland as far north as the Moray Firth. He relied principally on the names in the document known as the *Pictish Chronicle*. Lastly, the Irish archaeologist Macalister,[1] dealing solely with the inscriptions, also asserted that Pictish was not Indo-European, and he was so sure that he could interpret these mysterious inscriptions that he wrote a grammar of the language, correcting the engravers when their Pictish was ungrammatical.

Next we have the opinion that Pictish was Goedelic. In its more extreme form this is expressed as follows: Goedelic was brought to the British Isles by a race of Celtic invaders who settled not only in Ireland but also independently in Scotland; the Scottish branch was the Picts, and Pictish developed in due course directly into the Scottish Gaelic which we know. This was popularised by Skene as early as 1836,[2] and it was widely accepted in Scotland, where it had the advantage of making the Gaelic language appear to be indigenous and not an importation from Ireland. Skene's arguments are now quite out of date, and need not be recapitulated. Even in his lifetime they were regarded as wild by scholars competent to judge, though accepted without question by the public; so much so that Macbain indignantly complained: "This plausible but revolutionary theory has completely captivated the popular historians. . . . In fact they do not seem to know that Skene's theories are revolutionary".[3] Not a single philologist of standing has supported Skene's opinion, and the voice of Celtic scholars has been unanimous in condemning it.[4] Subsequent writers who have adopted it [5] have only succeeded in discrediting it by the unsound nature of their arguments. In point of fact, the idea that Scottish Gaelic is descended from an independent Goedelic dialect, and not from the Gaelic brought to Scotland by the Irish settlers of Dalriada, is easily disproved in the light of our modern knowledge of historical Gaelic philology.[6]

A less extreme form of the Goedelic hypothesis has been advanced, rather tentatively, by one good Celticist and one only, John Fraser.[7] This is that the Picts were indeed Goedels, closely related to but not the same as those other Goedels who occupied Ireland, and that their language was Goedelic; but that this speech was later superseded all over Pictland by the Gaelic of the Dalriadic colony from Ireland, which alone is the parent of present-day Scottish Gaelic. Fraser made this

[1] R. A. S. Macalister (1940).
[2] W. F. Skene (1836).
[3] A. Macbain (1897), 192.
[4] Cf. Macbain's criticisms (1897); (1902), 387–8.
[5] E.g. E. W. B. Nicholson (1896, 1904); F. C. Diack (1944).
[6] Cf. K. H. Jackson (1951).
[7] J. Fraser (1923, 1927).

last point clear, as a Celtic scholar is bound to do, saying: "Whatever the language of Pictland may have been at the commencement of this period [sixth to ninth centuries], it is quite certain that a few centuries later it was a Goedelic language which had been gradually introduced from Ireland".[1] His arguments, which are put forward with an attempt at impartiality, are not only very doubtful but are to some extent tendentious. The chief of them will be examined below.

As to the view that Pictish was Indo-European though not Celtic, there is no need to linger over old Pinkerton's idea that the Picts were "Goths" from whom the Lowland Scots are descended. A more serious proposal is contained in Julius Pokorny's well-known hypothesis of the Indo-European people he called Illyrians, who migrated widely over Europe, including Britain, and appear in Scotland as the Picts.[2] This has not been well received among philologists, who consider it ill-founded and too ingenious, and so far as Pictish at any rate is concerned it rests on nothing very solid. Nevertheless one should not lose sight of the general possibility that some place-names in Britain which have an Indo-European look but are not clearly either Celtic or Germanic may be due to non-Celtic Indo-European elements among the prehistoric immigrants to these islands.

The opinion held almost universally among Celtic scholars from at least the time of Stokes [3] has been that Pictish was a P-Celtic language. One form of this hypothesis, well argued by Watson,[4] is that Pictish was simply a northern Brittonic offshoot of British. The other expression of it is that Pictish was a separate speech of Gallo-Brittonic origin, allied both to Gaulish and to British but distinct from both. This was the view of Stokes and Macbain [5]; indeed Macbain was so positive that he concluded by saying, "We may now claim, despite the cranky theories and objections of certain people, that the Pictish question is settled".[6] Macbain was an optimist! Quite recently the opinion held by Stokes and Macbain has been restated by T. F. O'Rahilly, who gives detailed refutations of other theories [7]; and there for the present the matter rests.

It certainly does look as if Fraser was not exaggerating when he said: "Arguments in favour of the views that the language of the Picts was Goedelic, that it was Brythonic, that it was not a Celtic or even an Indo-Germanic language, seem to have made little impression

[1] J. Fraser (1927), 201.
[2] J. Pokorny (1938).
[3] W. Stokes (1890), 392.
[4] W. J. Watson (1926), particularly 70–2 and 126–7.
[5] W. Stokes (1890); A. Macbain (1892), 287–8; (1897), 211; (1902), 389–401.
[6] A. Macbain (1892), 288.
[7] T. F. O'Rahilly (1946), 353–84, 529–38.

on any but their authors".[1] The evidence on the problem, now to be discussed, falls into five distinct classes. They are: (1) direct or indirect statements on Pictish by medieval writers while the language was still alive; (2) northern Scottish names in classical sources; (3) the inscriptions of Pictland; (4) names in medieval works such as Adamnan's *Life of St Columba*, Bede's *Ecclesiastical History*, and the *Pictish Chronicle*; and (5) the modern place-names of the Pictish area.

Adamnan mentions in two places in the *Life of St Columba*,[2] completed between A.D. 692 and 697, that Columba made use of an interpreter in conversing with the Picts. This has led to controversy. On the one hand it is argued, rightly we may well think, that this means the Picts spoke a language different from Columba's,[3] whose native tongue was Gaelic; while on the other hand it has been asserted that a mere difference of dialect would be enough to make an interpreter necessary. Thus Fraser says this does not mean that the speech of the Picts and that of Columba differed from each other any more than Perthshire Gaelic does from Lewis Gaelic at the present day.[4] If this is meant to imply that a Perthshire man cannot understand a Lewis man without an interpreter, it is untrue and misleading. MacNeill on the contrary believed that these passages prove Pictish to be distinct from Gaelic,[5] since even at the present day Gaelic speakers from Pictland and from Columba's own country of Donegal can talk together,[6] and how much more therefore in Columba's time. It seems reasonable to think that this use of interpreters shows that Pictish and Gaelic differed considerably, though admittedly it does not of itself prove that Pictish was not an ancient Goedelic dialect. Bede's *Ecclesiastical History* was finished in 731, when the Pictish nation was still very much alive, and in two passages [7] he speaks quite unequivocally of Pictish as a fourth language distinct from Gaelic, Brittonic and English. Since Bede's own monastery of Jarrow had been in very close touch with the Picts in his own lifetime, he should have been in a position to know; and he would know also, from the numerous contacts of Jarrow with the church of Iona, and doubtless indirectly from sources among the Britons of Strathclyde, that Pictish was different both from the Gaelic of Scotland and from Brittonic. Bede says elsewhere,[8] of the place now called Kinneil at the eastern end of the Antonine Wall, that the name *in the Pictish language* was *Peanfahel*. Discussion of this must be postponed at present; but for the moment it is further evidence that

[1] J. Fraser (1923), 10.
[2] Adamnan I.27, II.33.
[3] So T. F. O'Rahilly (1946), 355.
[4] J. Fraser (1927), 185.
[5] E. MacNeill (1939), 7–8.
[6] This is doubtful.
[7] Bede I.1, III.6.
[8] Bede I.12.

Pictish was a language on its own. Again, Cormac the king and bishop of Cashel mentions in his Glossary, composed about A.D. 900, not long after the extinction of Pictish independence, a word *catait* or *cartait* meaning a "thorn" or "pin", which he says is a Pictish expression, *berla Cruithnech.*[1] It is certainly neither Gaelic nor Welsh. So far, then, we seem to find it implied or clearly stated by contemporary and almost contemporary writers that Pictish was a separate speech of its own, identical neither with the Gaelic of Ireland and Scotland nor with Brittonic.

Next is the evidence of northern Scottish names in classical writers; that is to say, north of the Forth-Clyde isthmus, since south of that line is admitted on all hands to have been British territory, not Pictish, in the Roman period, so that the names there are relevant to Pictish only so far as they parallel forms which occur in Pictland. The opportunity may be taken to remark here that the tribe-name *Epidii* and the place-name *Epidion Akron* (Epidion Headland), given by Ptolemy in Kintyre, have been regarded as Pictish, and have been used as evidence that Pictish was P-Celtic.[2] They would certainly supply an exceedingly strong argument for that view if there were any reason to suppose that the Epidii were Picts. Unfortunately there is not. It has been assumed, without discussion, that they were, presumably on the following unspoken line of argument: Kintyre is now part of the Highlands; the Highlands lie beyond the Forth-Clyde line; Pictland was north of the Forth-Clyde line; therefore Kintyre was in Pictland. Actually of course we have absolutely no warrant for supposing that Kintyre formed part of the territory of the Picts, or of their ancestors in Ptolemy's day, rather than of the Britons; indeed since the Epidion Headland, the Mull of Kintyre, lies some fifty miles south of the latitude of the northern British capital at Dumbarton, it is quite probable that the Epidii were Britons. Hence the name proves nothing about Pictish.

The first relevant information we possess is the statements attributed to the Greek voyager Pytheas, who sailed round Britain about 325 B.C., that the British Isles were called the Pretanic Islands and that the cape facing the Orkneys was Cape Orcas. Whether these statements really derive from Pytheas is uncertain, but at least they are as old as Diodorus Siculus (first century B.C.). *Pretanic* derives from the name of the people, the Pritani or Priteni, who would appear to

[1] J. Fraser (1927), 185, suggests this refers to the Cruithni of Ireland, but see below, p. 159. He is wrong to imply that Pictish did not survive in Scotland as late as Cormac's lifetime.

[2] J. Fraser's treatment of the name (1927), 189–90, is too wide of the mark to be worth discussing.

have been one of the earliest Celtic tribes to reach this island. We shall see presently that they were afterwards identified with the Picts, but at the moment it is enough to note that the name as it stands is probably Celtic; and if so, it is P-Celtic. As for *Orcas*, it is a form with a Greek termination derived from the name of the tribe inhabiting the Orkneys, which must have been **Orci*, unquestionably a Celtic name meaning "The Young Pigs", doubtless a totemistic appellation. The word *orc* exists only in medieval Irish, not in medieval Brittonic, but this by no means proves that it was an exclusively Goedelic one, since other Celtic words which were known in early Brittonic failed to survive into the medieval period in Britain though they did survive in Ireland. In any case, here is clear proof of the presence of a Celtic people in the far north of Scotland as early as the first century B.C., if not the fourth.

Next there is Tacitus, writing in A.D. 97, who in Chapter 29 of the *Agricola* tells of the heroic Caledonian leader Calgacus, and of the battle of Mons Graupius against the Romans in A.D. 84. *Calgacus* is certainly Celtic, meaning "The Swordsman"; but the name *Caledonia*, which was synonymous with Scotland to the Romans, and is still seen in Dunkeld, Schiehallion, and Rohallion, all in Perthshire, where Ptolemy put his Caledonii, cannot be proved to be Celtic and may therefore very possibly be pre-Celtic. The same is true of *Graupius*; if Celtic, it would be P-Celtic.

The most important source for the toponymy of Roman Scotland is Ptolemy's map, drawn up from information acquired from various sources at the end of the first century so far as Scotland is concerned. He gives us thirty-eight different names of tribes, towns, rivers, bays, capes, and islands in Scotland north of the British country of the Damnonii and Votadini, plus a few others which are Latin or Greek and may therefore be disregarded here. These names have naturally always formed a key point in arguments about the Picts. For instance, Macbain asserts [1] that only three or four cannot be accounted for as Celtic; that one quarter are paralleled on Gaulish or British ground and are therefore Brittonic; and that Ptolemy's names are not Goedelic. Macbain was rather over-enthusiastic in favour of Celtic, and a more cautious examination reveals a rather different picture. In the writer's opinion, sixteen of the thirty-eight names, or 42 per cent, are clearly or probably Celtic, and the remainder are not certainly Celtic at all. Two of the sixteen belong philologically to the P-Celtic group, and none can be shown to be Q-Celtic. We ought to remember, however, that names of natural features always tend to contain a higher proportion

[1] A. Macbain (1892), 287–8.

of forms handed down from older populations than do names of tribes and towns. Twenty-three of the thirty-eight names are those of rivers, bays, capes, and islands; of these, eight,[1] that is only 35 per cent, are clearly or probably Celtic, the rest being not demonstrably Celtic at all.[2] The remaining fifteen are names of tribes or towns, and here eight,[3] that is 53 per cent, are clearly or probably Celtic, two [4] of them being certainly of the P-Celtic branch philologically speaking, and two others [5] having associations which suggest the same. It is remarkable that in the case of one of these last two, *Smertae*, the associations in question seem to be Gaulish.[6] Of the nine native tribe- and town-names of what we may call the Pictish heartland, that is the eastern parts of Scotland between the Firth of Forth and the Moray Firth, only *one*, the town-name *Bannatia*, is fairly certainly Celtic, or two if we include *Devana*, which is really a river-name applied to a town. On the other hand the four chief tribes, the Caledonii, Vacomagi, Taixali, and Venicones,[7] have names which cannot be said to be Celtic with any confidence. This high proportion of what may be non-Celtic tribe- and town-names in the Pictish heartland is remarkable.

Before leaving Ptolemy it is necessary to say a word on four names whose history has been used in the attempt to prove that the inhabitants of the North-East were Goedels all through the Pictish period. These are: *Varar*, the Beauly Firth, which survives in the river Farrar; *Devana* and *Deva*, really the names of the rivers Don and Dee; and *Loxa*, the river Lossie in Moray, which is probably related to the Greek λοξός, "crooked". Fraser believed in 1923 that the modern forms of these names proved that they had developed in a Goedelic context between the second and sixth centuries,[8] but in 1928 he had rightly changed his mind and abandoned all but *Loxa*.[9] It is unnecessary to enter into detail here [10] (Fraser was mistaken in most of his datings of Brittonic linguistic changes); but one may remark that one source of error consists in his assuming, in the absence of any evidence, that sound-changes which took place in the British of southern

[1] *Boderia* (if for **Voretia*), *Deva*, *Dumna*, *Lemannonios*, *Longos*, *Loxa*, *Orcades*, *Tarved*[*un*]*um*.

[2] Compare W. J. Watson (1926), 70.

[3] *Bannatia*, *Carnonacae*, *Cornavii*, *Decantae*, *Devana*, *Dve* (*caledonian*) ocean (called after the tribe with the Celtic prefix *dvē-*), *Lugi*, *Smertae*.

[4] *Bannatia* and *Decantae* (Q-Celtic would be **Bennatia* and **Decentae*). The preservation of *nt* here and elsewhere in such early names is no proof of their not being Goedelic; cf. W. J. Watson (1926), 71.

[5] *Cornavii* and *Smertae*.

[6] Cf. W. J. Watson (1926), 16–17.

[7] T. F. O'Rahilly's suggestion (1946), 382, that *Venicones* is a corruption of *Verturiones* is ingenious, but it forgets the inscription *DEAE MINERVAE VENICO* at Ilkley; cf. Holder, III.169.

[8] J. Fraser (1923), 12.

[9] J. Fraser (1927), 187–9.

[10] Cf. T. F. O'Rahilly (1946), 383–4.

Britain or the Goedelic of Ireland must also have occurred in a Brittonic or Goedelic Pictish respectively, and at the same times. On *Loxa*, the argument is that since Celtic *x* became *ch* in Brittonic but *s* in Goedelic, the modern form Lossie shows that it developed in the mouths of speakers of Goedelic. Now, as a matter of fact we have no proof that Celtic *x* would have become *ch* in Moray at all, even in Brittonic. The only hint that it would is the name of the Ochils, which developed from **Ouxelo-* on Brittonic lips. But the Ochils are right on the border of the country of the British Damnonii, not to mention the fact that they were a conspicuous landmark in full view of the semi-Romanised Britons south of the Forth, and the name may well have gained general currency in the post-Roman period from British sources. On the other hand, original Celtic *x* gave *s* in Gaulish exactly as in Goedelic,[1] a fact which previous writers on this point have overlooked; and it is quite impossible therefore to say that it might not have done so in a Pictish of Gallo-Brittonic descent, where the name might well have become something like **Ossel*. Indeed there is positive evidence in support of it. The name *Artcois*, that of the father of one of the prehistoric kings in the *Pictish Chronicle*, looks remarkably as if it contained the Celtic word **coxa*, "leg" or "foot", and meant "Bear's Leg" or "Bear's Paw". If so, it is an additional argument that Pictish agreed with Gaulish rather than with British in its treatment of Celtic *x*,[2] and makes it still clearer that "Lossie" does not prove Pictish to be Goedelic.[3] This possible similarity to Gaulish should be noted.

For other classical sources, one may mention first Dio Cassius, who tells[4] of the Caledonian chief Argentocoxos living about A.D. 210. This name means "Silver Leg", and contains the same **coxa* as perhaps in *Artcois*. The name is certainly Celtic, but there is nothing at this early date to prove that it is either Goedelic or Brittonic.[5] It is true that the *en* instead of *an* looks at first sight Goedelic, but P-Celtic names in **arganto-* are often rendered *argento-* in Greek and Latin under the influence of Latin *argentum*. A little later comes the famous inscription discovered at Colchester,[6] dating from between the years 222 and 235, which tells how a certain Caledonian called Lossio Ueda, nephew or grandson of Uepogenus, made a dedica-

[1] See J. Vendryes (1924), 38–9.

[2] *Cois* appears at first sight very like Welsh *coes* (from Latin *coxa*), but such a Latin loanword in Pictish is not very probable, especially if the name is genuinely early. The *is* may easily be a miscopying of *ss*, which is very similar in the Hiberno-Saxon hand.

[3] In any case the correct reading in Ptolemy may be *loza*. Cf. T. F. O'Rahilly (1946), 382.

[4] Cf. Holder I.211.

[5] On the *nt* see above, p. 136.

[6] BM (1922), 37.

tion. The Latin *nepos* usually means "grandson", but it can also mean "nephew", especially by this period; and in the sense of "sister's son" this agrees very well with the Pictish system of matrilinear succession, under which it would be natural for a man to describe himself as "son of X's sister" instead of "son of Y". In any case Uepogenus was a Caledonian.[1] The name is Celtic, and the *p* in it proves conclusively that it is P-Celtic. The very same name may very possibly be concealed in the corrupt *Uipoig namet* or *Uipo ignauiet*, another of the prehistoric kings in the *Pictish Chronicle*. It may well be that *Lossio* is related to *Loxa* and also means "crooked", but that since it is over a hundred years later than Ptolemy's time it already shows the change of *x* to *s* proposed above for Pictish. It is true that *Argentocoxos* does not do so, but he was earlier than Lossio, and the change in question might well have been taking place in the interval. As for *Ueda*, this may contain the Celtic stem **weid-*, "know", and the whole would then mean "The Knowing Crooked One".

Pictish names in classical writers appear then to point to the following conclusions: (1) there were Celts in the far north as early as the first century B.C., perhaps the fourth; (2) in the first century A.D. there were Celtic peoples, and names of towns and natural features, in various parts of northern Scotland, of which some are clearly of Gallo-Brittonic descent and none can be shown to be Goedelic; (3) a good many names, even those of tribes and towns, appear not to be Celtic at all and would therefore be pre-Celtic; and (4) there are certain points about some of the Celtic names which remind one of Gaulish rather than of British.

The so-called Pictish inscriptions constitute a problem so thorny that many writers who have discussed the Pictish question, however confident they may have been, have carefully avoided attempting to deal with them. Perhaps this was discreet, but it is obviously the duty of anyone investigating the Pictish question not to play safe by ignoring entirely a very material piece of evidence. There are at present about a couple of dozen of these inscriptions known,[2] spread almost equally between Shetland, Orkney, Caithness, and eastern Sutherland in the north, and Moray, Aberdeenshire, Kincardineshire, Angus, Perthshire, and Fife in the south, with an outlier in North Uist. This distribution coincides closely with that of the Pictish symbols described in Chapter V; and indeed some of them are accompanied by these

[1] F. C. Diack's attempt to deny this (1926*b*), 195–202, and to interpret the inscription quite differently, is ill-conceived and unconvincing.

[2] For references and discussion see J. Rhys (1892, 1898); R. A. S. Macalister (1940); F. C. Diack (1944).

symbols on the same stone. The suggestion made above [1] that the western symbols represent areas of Pictish influence which were later lost to the Picts is supported by the almost total absence of inscriptions there; indeed the knife-handle on which the North Uist inscription was cut, being easily carried or stolen, can hardly be said to prove the presence there of any considerable body of Picts at all. It is clear that inscriptions and symbols belong to the same cultural setting.

With two or three exceptions which are written in Latin letters, and one in an unknown script on the Newton Stone (which may be, in any event, a nineteenth-century forgery), the Pictish inscriptions are written in the Ogam alphabet, a sort of linear cypher, which was probably invented by an Irishman in the fourth century [2] and subsequently imported to Scotland by the Dalriadic settlers of Argyll in the fifth. Apart from the Auquhollie stone and perhaps one or two others, none of the Ogams of Pictland can be anything like so early as the fifth century, on epigraphic grounds, and without exception they are likely on historical grounds to be a good deal later. In fact most of them are examples of a special variety of the Ogam script evolved and practised in Ireland probably in the eighth century, and evidently brought to Scotland. These are known as "scholastic Ogams". This late period is confirmed in the case of those of them, about half the total, which have other datable features such as crosses or other decoration, almost all of which belong to the eighth or ninth century according to R. B. K. Stevenson's datings.[3] The two in Roman letters, namely the inscriptions of Fordoun and St Vigeans, are in the script of the eighth and ninth centuries respectively. Thus almost half of the inscriptions of Pictland can actually be shown to belong to the last 150 years of Pictish independence, and most of the rest doubtless do so too.

The reading is full of difficulties. In the first place, some are partly illegible, owing to weathering and similar causes. Then, their Ogam letters were sometimes engraved carelessly, or in other instances were treated in various strange ways peculiar to Pictland, so that though the actual form of a letter may be quite clear it is not always clear how it is to be interpreted. Putting aside those inscriptions or parts of inscriptions which cannot be read with fair certainty, there still remain enough to give us some impression of the language they are written in. One or two names are recognisable as appearing in historical sources. Such is the *Edarnon* of the Scoonie and Brodie stones and probably the *Idarnoin* at Fordoun, which seems to be the same as that of *Ethernan* or *Ithernan* the founder and first bishop of Rathin in

[1] p. 99. [2] See K. H. Jackson (1953), 151-2.
[3] See above, Chapter V.

Buchan, and of the Pict called *Itharnan* who died in 669 according to the *Annals of Ulster*, and who may be the same person. It is apparently not Celtic. The St Vigeans inscription, of the middle or later ninth century according to R. B. K. Stevenson, gives three names, and unlike the other these are Celtic. There is the well-known Pictish name *Drosten* (*Drostan* in manuscript sources), which appears in Brittonic in the Welsh *Trystan* or *Drystan*; possibly another, *Uoret*, which also occurs in Brittonic (Old Breton *Uuoret*) and is perhaps the same name as that of the ninth-century Pictish king *Uurad* and of the fathers of several other kings; and thirdly *Forcus*, which as it stands is certainly Gaelic. Then on the Lunnasting stone in Shetland there is the name *Nechton*, written *Nehhton*, familiar as that of several Pictish kings, and certainly Celtic. Apart from these recognisable names, two other forms occur which are intelligible, both Gaelic. One is the *crroscc* on the Bressay stone in Shetland, dated late ninth or early tenth century by R. B. K. Stevenson, which has a cross on it; it is evidently the Gaelic word for "cross". The other is the *maqq* or *meqq* which is found twice for certain in Shetland (Bressay and St Ninians), twice doubtfully on the far north-east mainland (Latheron in Caithness and Golspie in Sutherland), and once for certain on the Formaston stone at Aboyne in Aberdeenshire. This is presumably the Primitive Gaelic *maqq*, "son", Old Irish *macc*, with late Old Irish genitive *meicc*. *Meqq* may perhaps be an early instance of the *meicc* form of the genitive.

These words *crroscc*, *maqq* or *meqq*, and the name *Forcus*, may perhaps suggest at first sight that the language of the inscriptions is Gaelic (though *Uoret*, *Nehhton* and probably *Drosten* are not Gaelic), and they were used by Nicholson and Diack to argue that very thesis.[1] Their efforts were doomed to failure, partly because of insufficient acquaintance with historical Celtic philology and partly from lack of enough solid material to go upon, though the ingenuity displayed is staggering. In fact the extraordinary thing about the Pictish inscriptions is, as Rhys saw, that apart from the few words just mentioned they would appear to be written in an unknown language, certainly not Celtic, and evidently not Indo-European at all. Thus the St Vigeans stone, in spite of the three Celtic names and what is presumably the Latin *et* (spelt *ett*), has a word *ipe* prefixed to *Uoret*, perhaps also found on the Fordoun stone prefixed to *Idarnoin*, which is quite unknown. From the context it might mean "and", or it might be "son of", "nephew of", or the like, but these are guesses; it would seem to be neither Celtic nor Indo-European.[2] Or let us consider the Lunnasting

[1] E. W. B. Nicholson (1896, 1904); F. C. Diack (1944).
[2] F. C. Diack's "*in pace*" (1944), 75, is not at all probable.

inscription. It is perfectly legible, yet except for the name *Nehton* it is utterly unintelligible. It reads *ettocuhetts ahehhttannn hccvvevv nehhtons*; and it would take superhuman ingenuity to show that that is Celtic or Indo-European at all. So with the Brandsbutt stone, *irataddoarens*; Keiss Bay, *nehtetri*; St Ninians, *besmeqqnanammovvez*; and others. What these things mean nobody knows; doubtless they contain both names and ordinary words. If *meqq* at St Ninians really is "son" *bes* and *nanammovvez* may be names.

Nevertheless the presence of the apparently Gaelic forms and names needs to be explained. Here we must remember two things. First, the Ogam alphabet itself was imported to Scotland by the Irish of Dalriada, and had always belonged essentially to a Gaelic milieu. Secondly, the inscriptions concerned are all very late, belonging to a time when Gaelic influence had already penetrated Pictland deeply, through the Columban Church and otherwise.[1] There is therefore nothing unnatural in the supposition that along with the Gaelic monumental alphabet the Picts also borrowed, at any rate for use on inscriptions, the Gaelic word *maqq*, which was an almost unvarying element in the formulae of the Ogam inscriptions in Ireland. One may compare the way in which we still often use Latin when we set up a monumental inscription, a practice which is of course of Latin origin so far as we are concerned, and call a man *Henricus filius Roberti* instead of "Henry son of Robert". Indeed the wonder is that the engravers did not set out the inscriptions entirely in Gaelic, particularly as Pictish was probably never strictly a written language in the ordinary sense. In these circumstances the use of the Gaelic formula-word *maqq* is only natural. Yet another explanation may be borne in mind. There is reason to think that in the ancient social system of northern Britain it was not of any great importance who a man's father was, as distinct from his mother's relatives, unlike the normal Celtic system of relationship in which the father was all-important; and it may even be that in those primitive times there was no word in regular use which could express "son-of-a-father"—it is significant that Lossio Ueda described himself as *nepos* of Uepogenus. Later, perhaps, under the influence of Gaelic and Christian ideas, the historical Picts may have adopted more and more the concept of the importance of the father, and with the concept the Gaelic practice of naming a man's father in monumental identificatory formulae—and the actual word which was used in Gaelic to express "son" in such a context. In any event, of the four closely datable inscriptions apparently containing this word (Latheron, Golspie, Formaston and Bressay) none is much older than the middle

[1] Cf. F. T. Wainwright, above, pp. 5, 47–8.

of the eighth century; and of these the only certain instances, Formaston and Bressay, are very late indeed, ninth century and late ninth to early tenth century respectively, according to R. B. K. Stevenson.

The other two Gaelic words mentioned are easily accounted for. *Crosc*, "cross", would very naturally be borrowed by the Picts, since Christianity was brought to these northern regions from Gaelic Iona. The Gaels themselves had already taken it from Latin when Christianity reached them. In any case the inscription in which it occurs, Bressay, also appears to contain a Norse word (*dattrr*), and the whole thing seems to point to a very mixed language in Shetland in the late ninth or early tenth century, after the Norse settlements there. Finally, the Irish and Scottish Gaels always made a regular practice of Gaelicising any Pictish names they could. *Forcus* at St Vigeans is the exact Gaelic equivalent of Pictish *Uurguist* [1]; very likely the man who wrote this inscription in Latin letters (itself a Gaelic art) about or soon after the middle of the ninth century was deliberately rendering a Pictish name into Gaelic. But at this date, shortly after the Dalriadic conquest of Pictland, it is probable enough that Forcus was himself a Dalriadic Gael living already in Angus. The conclusion of what has been said is that these Pictish inscriptions are written in an unknown language, not Indo-European,[2] in alphabets derived from the Gaelic west; and that they contain a Gaelic formula-word, a Gaelic or Gaelicised name, and the Gaelic word for "cross", all due to the general influence of Dalriada upon Pictland and to its particular influence in the matter of epigraphy.

The next class of evidence on the Pictish language consists of names in early medieval sources. Adamnan mentions two or three people who were or may have been Picts. Almost all seem to have Celtic names. Emcat or Emchat, baptised by Columba in Glen Urquhart, is not stated to have been a Pict, and may have been a wandering Gael who had penetrated up the Great Glen into Pictland from the nearest Dalriadic country round Fort William. The name has been connected with Gaelic *Imchath* and used as evidence that the Picts were Goedels; but it seems to have been forgotten that there was a P-Celtic cognate (Gaulish *Ambicatus*), which occurs in Britain in the Isle of Man about A.D. 500 as *Ammecatus* [3] and would probably have become **Amcat* in a language of Gallo-Brittonic descent in Columba's day. Adamnan may easily have partly Gaelicised it, accord-

[1] Cf. T. F. O'Rahilly (1946), 368*n*, 370.

[2] Cf. J. Pokorny (1953), 157: "Es kann keinen Zweifel unterliegen, dass wir es hier mit den Resten einer nicht-indogermanischen Sprache zu tun haben, die uns völlig unverständlich sind".

[3] See K. H. Jackson (1950), 209–10.

ing to the common practice, by the alteration of one or two letters. His son Uirolec appears to have the Celtic **wiro-*, "man", in the first half of his name, but what *lec* is is uncertain. *Broichan*, the druid of King Bruide, has been compared by O'Rahilly to the Irish *Froíchán*, older **Vroichān*, of which he thinks *Broichan* a Latinisation [1]; but there is no reason why it should not be the P-Celtic cognate, **Uroican* (with consonantal *u*), Gaelicised by the addition of *h*.[2] *Brude* or *Bruide* itself, in Adamnan, the Irish annals, and other Gaelic sources, seems to represent an early form of what became later in Pictish *Bredei* or *Bridei*; its origin is uncertain, and there is no good reason to think it Celtic. Artbranan, who was converted by Columba in Skye, was apparently a Pict; his name is certainly Celtic, but whether Q-Celtic or P-Celtic cannot be determined. There is also mention of one Iogenan, living in Leinster, and called by Adamnan *Pictus*.[3] The name is Gaelic, but it was used elsewhere to Gaelicise the proper Pictish name *Uuen*,[4] which was itself probably a loan from British; and very likely that was the case here, particularly so since he had settled in Ireland.

The most important name given in Bede's *Ecclesiastical History* [5] is the *Peanfahel* which he tells us was the Pictish name of the place where the Antonine Wall ends near Abercorn. This has caused violent controversy,[6] since it appears to be a peculiar mixture of P-Celtic *penn*, "end", and Gaelic *fál*, genitive *fáil*, "wall". The warring advocates of Q-Celtic and P-Celtic Pictish have struggled to explain away the first and second elements respectively.[7] The simplest and most rational solution, which entirely resolves the controversy, is that proposed by Watson and MacNeill, that the name is a hybrid, just like the *Caerpentaloch* and *Kinpont* quoted by Watson, both of them similarly in the Forth-Clyde lowland (though in these the non-Gaelic elements are Brittonic). The upper Forth had been in Gaelic hands for more than a century by Bede's time, and the presence of Gaelic settlers on the

[1] Dr A. O. Anderson kindly tells me, by letter, that the Schaffhausen MS of Adamnan actually reads *Uroichan* in one place.

[2] On *Uirolec* and *Broichan* cf. W. Stokes (1890), 395, 415; J. Fraser (1927), 191; T. F. O'Rahilly (1946), 533–4; A. O. Anderson (1948), 35. O'Rahilly's *Vroichān* may well be correct, but it hardly makes the name Irish.

[3] Since he lived in Leinster this has been taken to refer to the Irish Cruithni (see p. 159), but like all other early Irish authors writing Latin, Adamnan never uses *Pictus* of the Irish Cruithni.

[4] See *Pictish Chronicle*, and AU *s.a.* 839, for king *Uuen* son of *Unuist*.

[5] Bede I.12.

[6] See W. Stokes (1890), 412; W. J. Watson (1926), 346–8; M. Förster (1922), 231–9; E. MacNeill (1939), 8–9; T. F. O'Rahilly (1946), 356, 381.

[7] O'Rahilly's Anglo-Saxon *f* and Pictish *v* is ingenious but hardly convincing, especially since post-consonantal *f* in Anglo-Saxon can mean *f* just as well as *v*. His theory that Celtic *w* became *v* in Pictish is apparently not borne out by the evidence. See below, p. 163.

lower Forth north of the Wall in the early part of the eighth century is by no means unlikely.

Our most valuable early medieval source for the Pictish language is the document called the *Pictish Chronicle*, or more properly the Pictish king-list.[1] This is a Latin text, possibly first put together out of older materials about the middle of the ninth century; the oldest version of it we have may belong to the end of the tenth century.[2] The original may have been the work of a monk in one of the monasteries of Pictland, possibly Abernethy, the foundation of which it mentions in an excursus, and his sources were doubtless brief written records kept in Latin in the church of Pictland, on the model of the Irish ones, and going back perhaps to the later part of the sixth century. There is another recension of the king-list, which seems to have drawn independently on the same sources, and was probably made by some Gaelic monk, perhaps at Iona, or it may be at Dunkeld or St Andrews —the foundations of both monasteries are referred to in it—after the accession of Kenneth son of Alpin had brought about the final re-Gaelicisation of the Church in Pictland. In this recension the Pictish names are rendered so far as possible by Gaelic translations or equivalents, after the usual fashion of Gaelic scribes, and the fact that they appear in this dress therefore cannot be used as proof that Pictish was Goedelic. The two versions will be referred to here as Recension I and Recension II, and only Recension I will be regarded as evidence on the nature of the Pictish language. As has already been explained by F. T. Wainwright,[3] the names of the kings fall into three groups, of which only the latter half of the third, from the middle of the sixth century, is likely to be historical. The kings here are corroborated in other reliable documents, chiefly the Irish annals, and may be taken as genuine; those in the earlier sections of the list are without doubt legendary, though a few of the latest of them may derive from good oral tradition.

To take first the names from the historical and corroborated part of the list, some of them are not clearly Celtic at all, such as *Bredei*, *Derelei*, *Bargoit* and others, and are quite possibly therefore pre-Celtic.[4]

[1] On this see H. M. Chadwick (1949), 1–25; Marjorie O. Anderson (1949), 35–9, and (1949–50).

[2] Marjorie O. Anderson (1949), 37–8, wishes to separate the "Old Scottish Chronicle" entirely from the king-list, but it seems likely that the compiler of the former prefixed the list to his chronicle himself, so that the list existed before the end of the tenth century.

[3] See above, pp. 16–18.

[4] Cf. C. Marstrander (1932), 308: "La masse majeure des noms propres pictes transmis dans les sources irlandaises me fait l'impression de n'être pas celtique, même pas indo-européenne." Marstrander is thinking primarily of the names of Pictish kings as they appear in the Irish annals, but would no doubt include the *Pictish Chronicle*.

Others are obviously Celtic, as *Talorg* or *Talorgan*, and moreover non-Goedelic Celtic, such as *Drostan*, *Uuen*, *Tarain*, *Lutrin*, and the two famous kings *Onuist* or *Unuist* sons of *Uurguist*, or Angus mac Fergus as their name is often hideously Anglo-Gaelicised.[1] To these one may add two contemporary names of Picts not from the king-list, but also P-Celtic in type, not Goedelic: the *Tolarggan Maphan* of the *Annals of Ulster* A.D. 726, whose title certainly contains the P-Celtic *map*, "son", and the king *Naiton* whose correspondence with Bede's abbot is detailed in the *Ecclesiastical History*.[2] *Naiton* is the same name as what appears elsewhere as *Nechton*, *Nechtan*, and in the Lunnasting inscription as *Nehhton*. It was probably *Nechton* in early Pictish, developing through *Nehton* to **Neiton*, spelt *Naiton* by Bede. The *hh* of *Nehhton* may stand for some kind of weakened *ch* on its way to *i*; if it had been true *ch* it would probably have been rendered with Ogam C, or in scholastic Ogam possibly with CH. The change of *echt* to *eit* is not Goedelic, and though it is not identical with the development to *eith* in Brittonic (compare Old Welsh *Neithon*), the diphthongisation is characteristic of languages of Gallo-Brittonic descent; indeed this treatment of *cht* is closer to what seems to have been the Gaulish one than it is to the Brittonic.[3] The similarity to the well-known name cognate with it in Gaelic, *Nechtan*, is no doubt the reason why the Pictish name appears in documents (of Gaelic provenance) as *Nechton* or *Nechtan* long after it had become *Neiton* in speech.

The names in the non-historical part of the king-list, which are not corroborated by outside sources, have the look of a hodge-podge of all sorts thrown together to fill up a long blank space in history. Some of them, regarded purely as linguistic forms, may be quite spurious and artificial, but others are familiar ones in historical times, such as *Bruide*, *Gartnait*, *Talorg* and *Drust*; and there is no need therefore to suppose that because others are not known elsewhere they must all be merely inventions. Some of these appear to be P-Celtic, like the *Uipoig namet* whose name may possibly be the same as that of *Uepogenus* of the Colchester inscription; but others, if they are genuine, are certainly not Celtic at all, like *Bliesblituth* and *Usconbuts* and *Canutulachama*. Unfortunately the various manuscripts differ so greatly over the readings of these, as of other names, and are often so hopelessly corrupt, that it is generally impossible to know which is correct, if any; for example *Uipoig namet* himself appears as *Uipo ignauiet*, *Poponeuet*, *Uerpempnet*, and *Uumpopual*. Among the unintelligible

[1] The correct Gaelicisation, as in Recension II of the list and the Irish annals, is *Oengus mac Ferguso*, or rather *Forguso*.
[2] Bede V.21.
[3] Cf. K. H. Jackson (1953), §§ 58, 60.

titles of some of the Pictish kings there is one word, an adjective, which is translated for us in Recension II; it is *diuperr*, which is rendered "rich". It may be Celtic, but this is doubtful.

The fifth class of evidence on the Pictish language consists of the medieval and modern place-names of Pictland. Here it is important to make one fact clear at the outset. Goedelic place-names are now found all over Pictland, but they are of no value whatsoever as proof that Pictish was Goedelic, since from the ninth century onwards—and in some parts earlier—Pictland was settled by Goedelic-speaking Dalriadic Scots, who naturally gave Gaelic names to many of the places they occupied. Since none of these names can be shown to be older than the time when the men of Dalriada came there, they prove nothing about the nature of Pictish. On the other hand, any name which is demonstrably P-Celtic in type is proof of P-Celtic elements among the population of Pictland; and these cannot be referred analogously to an immigration of Britons from Strathclyde, since no such immigration took place in historical times. We must remember that many older non-Goedelic names are bound to have been lost when they were replaced by Goedelic ones; and in fact the vast majority of the modern place-names of Pictland are Gaelic, English, or Norse.

We may take first the numerous group of names beginning with *Pit-*, like Pittenweem, Pitlochry and so on. Watson has counted 323 of them,[1] and their distribution (Map 6) is highly interesting and significant.[2] With less than a dozen exceptions they are all concentrated in the eastern part of Scotland between the Antonine Wall and the south-eastern corner of Sutherland round the Dornoch Firth. More particularly, they are found in the lowlands of Fife, Kinross, Angus, Kincardineshire, Aberdeenshire, Banffshire, and Moray; the coastal area round the Beauly, Cromarty, and Dornoch Firths, from the Black Isle to the Tarbat peninsula and Rogart; and the lower and middle valleys of the rivers of Perthshire draining into the Firth of Tay and in Inverness-shire draining into the Moray Firth. Outside this area there are only a few strays: three near the west coast opposite Skye; one in the Great Glen on Loch Lochy; one in Cunningham; and three in the Lothians close to the Firth of Forth. It is perfectly clear that the names in *Pit-* were given by a people living in north-eastern Scotland between the Firth of Forth and south-east Sutherland, whose influence was present at some stage on the west coast facing

[1] W. J. Watson (1926), 407.

[2] So far as they can be identified; for Watson does not name anything like all his instances so far as the eastern mass is concerned. No doubt the map represents the general distribution well enough.

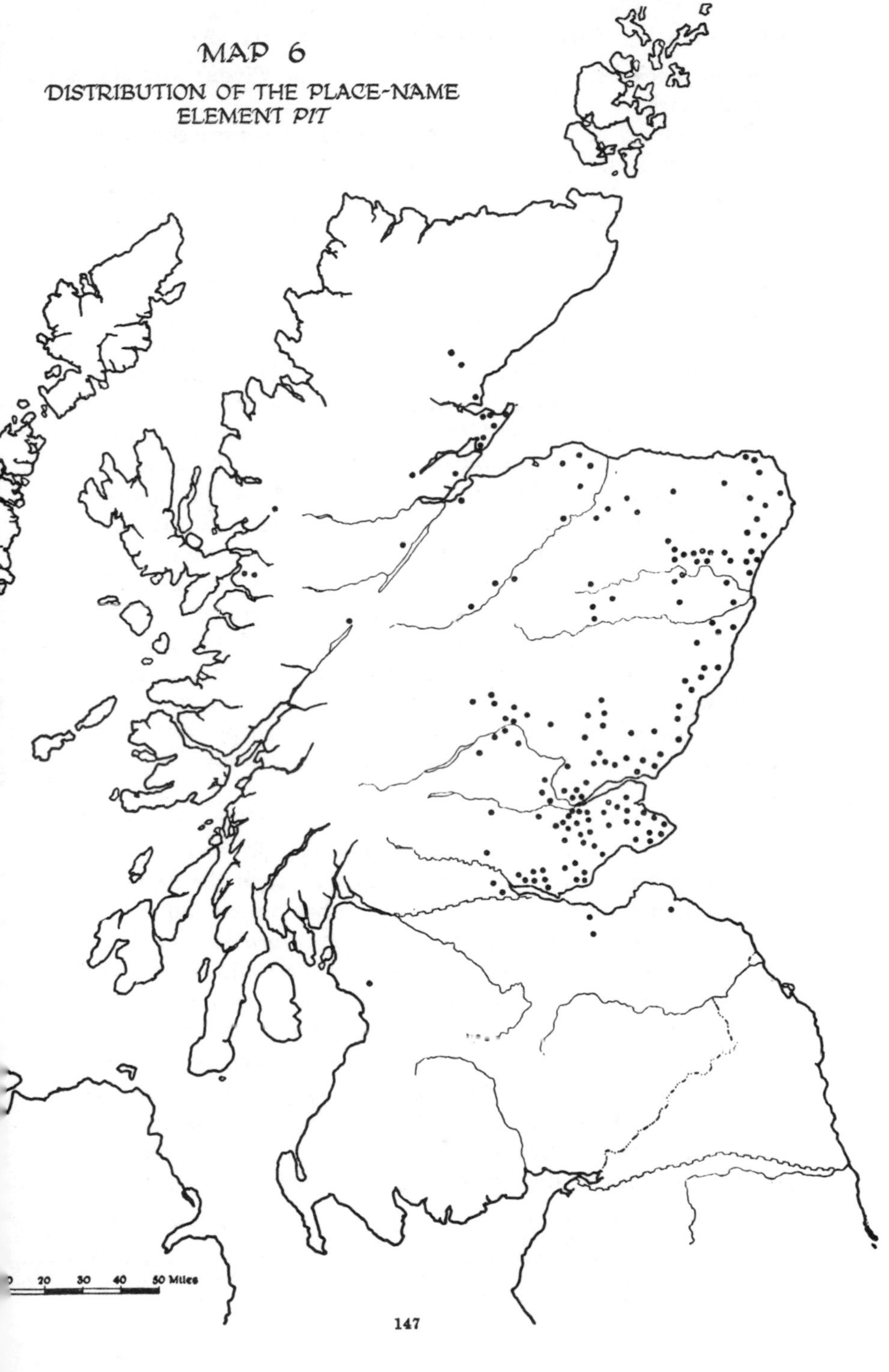
MAP 6
DISTRIBUTION OF THE PLACE-NAME
ELEMENT *PIT*
20 30 40 50 Miles

Skye; in Lochaber; beyond the valley of the Clyde; and across the Firth of Forth.

There is no necessity to enter here into controversy about the etymology and meaning of this place-name element; it has been the subject of acute controversy.[1] Certain facts seem pretty clearly established by now, and they may be summed up as follows: the word was earlier *pett*; it meant a parcel of land or farmland, in which sense it occurs in the *Book of Deer* about A.D. 1150, applied to certain places in Buchan; and it is a P-Celtic word, related to Welsh *peth*, "thing", Breton *pez*, "piece", Gaulish **petia* (whence French *pièce*),[2] and more distantly to Gaelic *cuid*, "portion". The Gaulish word, borrowed into Vulgar Latin in France, occurs there in Latin documents in the phrase *petia terrae*, "a parcel of land", exactly the sense of our *pett*. Now names in *pett* or *peth* are never found in Britain south of the Antonine Wall, that is, in Roman or "British" Britain, except for the four instances already mentioned which are obviously scattered offshoots from the north; and it is quite clear that the Britons of the south did not use it as an element in place-names at all, probably because they had specialised the word in the sense of "thing". A converse development may be seen in the Scots phrase "a wee thing of", meaning "a little bit of". The history of *pett* suggests, then, that it was part of the vocabulary of a P-Celtic people who were distinct from the Brittonic tribes south of the Wall; and it may perhaps hint that their connexions were with the Gauls at least as much as with the Britons.

There are other place-name elements in northern Scotland which appear to be P-Celtic; but unlike *pett* they are found also in the toponymy of the British part of the island, south of the Antonine Wall, and were therefore in use in Brittonic. They are set out by Watson [3] in his Chapters XI and XII. Such are the *carden* seen in Kincardine, Pluscarden, Urquhart (Adamnan's *Airchartdan*) and others; the *pert* in Perth, Logiepert, etc.; the *lanerc* in Lanrick near Callander, Lendrick near Kinross, and so on, as well as in Lanark; and the *pevr* in Innerpeffray, Strathpeffer, and the rest. One of them which is of particular interest is *aber*, as in Aberdeen and Abernethy. This has been another focus of controversy.[4] In spite of attempts to prove the contrary, it is well established that this is not a Goedelic word, and that it is the same as the Welsh *aber*, "confluence" or "estuary", as in

[1] See W. J. Watson (1926), 407; J. Fraser (1927), 192–3, and (1942), 67–71; T. F. O'Rahilly (1946), 356; H. M. Chadwick (1949), 53.

[2] See R. Thurneysen (1884), 70–2.

[3] W. J. Watson (1926), 339–424.

[4] See W. J. Watson (1926), 458; F. C. Diack (1926a), 83–98; J. Fraser (1927), 193–4; T. F. O'Rahilly (1946), 356–7.

Aberystwyth. There are several other words of this sort in north-eastern Scottish place-names, though for one reason or another some of them are less conclusive than these; thus *Car-* and *Ker-* may often be the equivalent of Welsh *caer*, but it is usually not possible to assert of any particular case that it is not Gaelic *cathair* or the like,[1] and names in *trev* and *tom* cannot be distinguished for certain from those with the Gaelic cognates. Again, there are still other P-Celtic words, namely *pres* "thicket", *moniδ* "mountain", *pōr* "pasture", and *dol* "meadow",[2] which were borrowed into Gaelic as common-nouns,[3] not merely place-name elements (these words becoming Scottish Gaelic *preas*, *monadh*, *pòr* and *dail*); and hence no actual instance of one of them can be used as evidence of the presence of a P-Celtic population on that spot, since the name might always have been given by Gaelic speakers in any part of Gaelic Scotland after the word had been borrowed.[4] Nor can we say, of any or all of these four words, that they cannot have got into Scottish Gaelic from the Brittonic speech of Strathclyde. Indeed it is quite probable that *monadh* and *pòr* did so. Leaving aside, then, such doubtful names as these last two classes, and limiting oneself to the more certain ones such as those discussed above and others like them listed by Watson[5] north of the Antonine Wall,[6] the distribution coincides so closely with that of the *Pit-* names (see Map 7), and with the conclusions drawn about the people who used those names, that it is beyond reasonable doubt that they were all given by one single population speaking some sort of P-Celtic language, which inhabited eastern Scotland from the Forth to around the Dornoch Firth, and occupied much more thinly parts of the western mainland from at least Lochaber to Lochcarron and Loch Torridon. The conclusion already drawn from the *Pit-* names that these people may have been a somewhat different family of P-Celts from the Britons south of the Antonine Wall is reinforced by a further consideration: namely, that certain Brittonic place-name elements very common in "British" country, such as *din* "fort", *penn* "head, hill", and *moel* "bare hill", are unknown in Scotland north of the Wall.

Such then in brief are the five classes of evidence on the language of the Picts. They appear at first sight to be extremely contradictory. Starting with early medieval sources and working backwards, the

[1] Cf. W. J. Watson (1926), 365–6.

[2] And *bod*, "dwelling", if this is really the origin of Gaelic *bad*, "clump", with Watson (1926), 423–4, which seems doubtful.

[3] *Pett* is evidently not one of these, *pace* W. J. Watson (1926), 408.

[4] It is through forgetting this that H. M. Chadwick (1949), 55, draws the inference that Brittonic names are found "throughout nearly the whole of the Scottish mainland".

[5] Cf. W. J. Watson (1926), Chapters XI and XII.

[6] There is no need to give instances south of this line, in British territory.

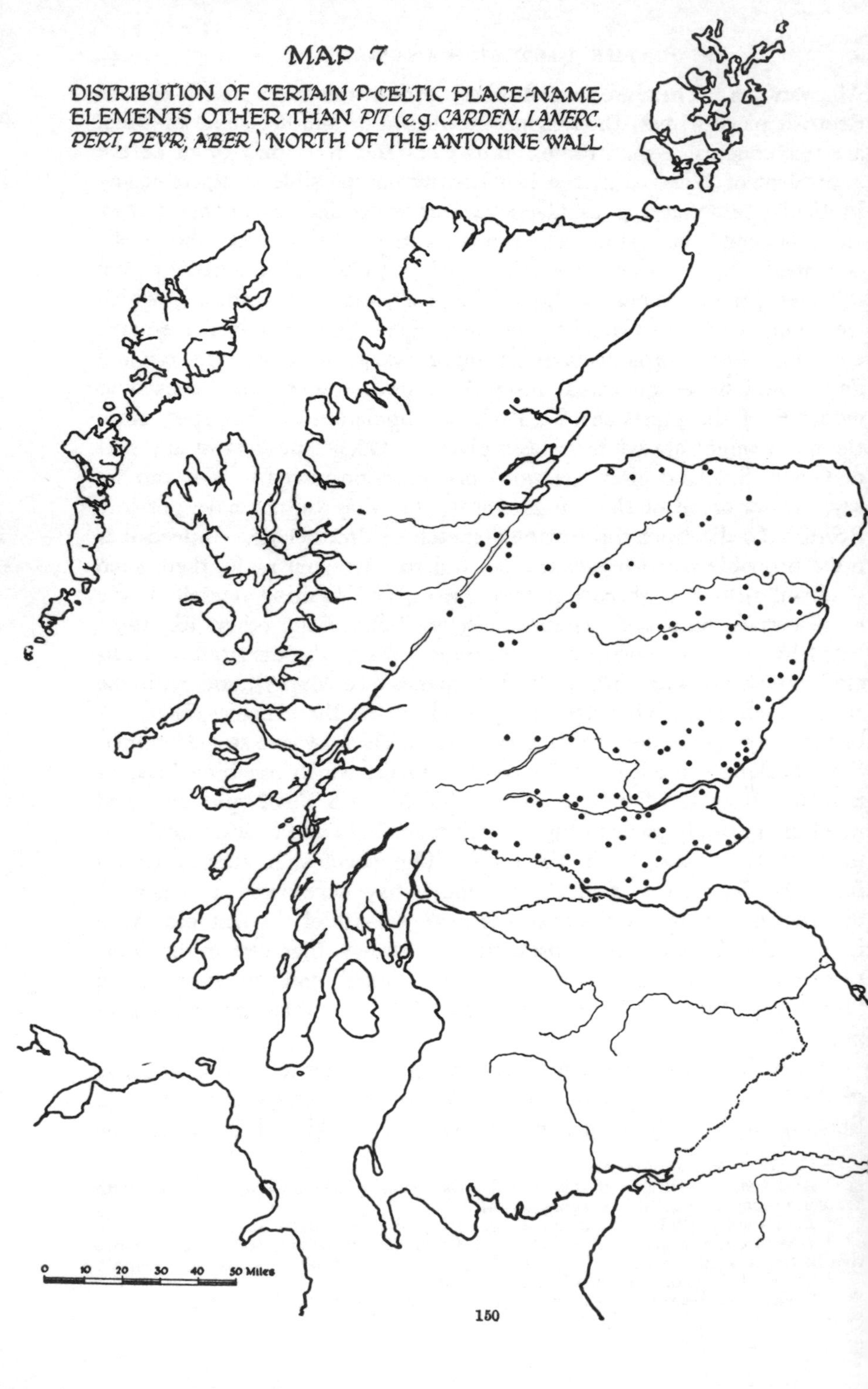
MAP 7
DISTRIBUTION OF CERTAIN P-CELTIC PLACE-NAME ELEMENTS OTHER THAN *PIT* (e.g. *CARDEN, LANERC, PERT, PEVR, ABER*) NORTH OF THE ANTONINE WALL
0 10 20 30 40 50 Miles

personal names in the Pictish king-list are in many cases Celtic, but others, even in its latest section, seem not to be so, and not to be identifiable in any particular language. Of those which are Celtic, some happen to have no special marks by which they can be distinguished, but those which have such marks belong to the P-Celtic group not to the Q-Celtic. The names given in Adamnan as those of Picts, either explicitly or by implication, seem almost all to be Celtic, though on the question of Q-Celtic or P-Celtic their interpretation is uncertain or ambiguous; none *must* be Q-Celtic. The inscriptions, of which some certainly, probably all, date from the late-Pictish period, appear to be written in a quite unknown language, not Celtic and evidently not Indo-European at all; though they contain some Celtic names (both Gaelic and non-Gaelic) and two Gaelic loan-words. Going back into the proto-Pictish period, classical sources show us Celtic tribal- and place-names in various parts of northern Scotland, including Pictland in the narrow sense, by the first century A.D., and in the Orkneys as early as the first century B.C., if not the fourth; and chiefs like Calgacus and Argentocoxos bear Celtic names. In those cases where it is possible to make any distinction, they belong to the P-Celtic group, not the Q-Celtic. Such are *Decantae*, and *Uepogenus* the Caledonian. On the other hand a good number of them seem to be non-Celtic, or at least are not demonstrably Celtic, and these are found even in the heart of what was later the Pictland of history, including such famous names as the river *Tuesis* (Spey) and the tribe *Caledonii*. More or less undatable, because they must be of varying dates, a considerable number of Celtic place-names in Scotland north of the Antonine Wall belong definitely to the P-Celtic family, not to the Q-Celtic; and it is remarkable how these all occur in areas which correspond to the historical Pictland and to the distribution of the inscriptions and the symbol stones discussed in Chapter V, except notably in the far north. Finally there is the clear implication of Bede's words, that in his day the Picts spoke a language which was regarded as distinct both from Gaelic and from Brittonic. In all this accumulated and apparently confusing evidence there is nothing which proves that Pictish was Q-Celtic, Goedelic. The presence of a name like *Forcus*, an element like *-fahel*, and words like *crosc* and *maqq*, all Gaelic, is the very natural consequence of the intimate and growing contact between the Picts and the Gaelic Scots from the fifth to the ninth century, and of the gradual Gaelic infiltration of Pictland mentioned above,[1] in which colonisation, intermarriage (with the resulting exchange of names), and conversion to Christianity can be shown to have played a considerable part. There is no need to

[1] See above, pp. 141–2.

fly in the face of all the facts and suppose, on the evidence of these Gaelic words, that Pictish was Goedelic.

On the other hand, though the Celtic words and names described can often be proved to be P-Celtic, a hint crops up now and then that the language they belonged to was not quite the same as British, not simply a northern form of Brittonic as Watson thought it was. The amount of material is so scanty, and our knowledge of the differences between Gaulish and British which existed in, say, the first centuries B.C. and A.D. is so small, that nothing decisive can be said. Nevertheless there are some slight indications, already mentioned at various points, which may be thought to show that the P-Celtic language of northern Scotland had certain affinities with Gaulish which were lacking in Brittonic, though in most matters it cannot be said to be distinguishable from Brittonic. If so, it would have to be recognised as a third dialect of the P-Celtic family parallel to the other two, neither Gaulish nor Brittonic, though Gallo-Brittonic in descent and closely related to both.

What does it all mean ? Surely it is not too much to suggest that a possible interpretation is as follows. There were at least two languages current in northern Scotland before the coming of the Irish Gaels in the fifth century. One of them was a Gallo-Brittonic dialect not identical with the British spoken south of the Antonine Wall, though related to it. The other was not Celtic at all, nor apparently even Indo-European, but was presumably the speech of some very early set of inhabitants of Scotland. The people of Scotland before the coming of the Celts must, after all, have spoken *some* language, and that language must almost certainly have been a non-Indo-European one. One hesitates to mention the word Basque in this context, and there is not the slightest reason to suppose that it had any connexion with Basque whatsoever (unless through the Iberian element in the population mentioned by Stuart Piggott on p. 55) ; but the parallel of that other ancient non-Indo-European language surviving in another corner of western Europe, and surviving moreover even to the present day, is very striking, and shows that the hypothesis of an analogous survival in Scotland down to the Dark Ages is by no means extravagant. Examples of the co-existence of two different languages in one small country over a period of several centuries can easily be found, for instance in the Balkans, not to mention Ireland and Wales.

We may assume, then, that a people speaking a language of Gallo-Brittonic descent settled in eastern Scotland in prehistoric times, most thickly between the Forth and the south-east corner of Sutherland, where they have left abundant traces of themselves in their place-names. Within this eastern area they must have mingled with the older population, many of whose personal names they adopted and whose language continued to exist side by side with their own. Several considerations suggest that the pre-Celtic element in eastern Pictland must have been fairly strong, in spite of the frequency of Gallo-Brittonic place-names. One is the way in which the Celts evidently took up the aboriginal custom of succession through the mother; for, in spite of attempts which have been made to show that this custom is Celtic or at any rate not inconsistent with Celtic practice, it remains the case that though among the Celtic as among other Indo-European peoples inheritance could pass through the female as well as through the male, anything like what seems to have been the Pictish systematised succession exclusively through the female is quite unknown in Celtic tradition, and quite contrary to it.[1] Another such indication may perhaps be the high proportion of possibly non-Celtic tribe-names in eastern Pictland in Ptolemy's map, though their chiefs, and no doubt therefore much of their aristocracy, would seem to have borne Celtic names, to judge from Calgacus, Argentocoxos, Lossio Ueda and Uepogenus. A third is the very fact, if fact it is, that the language of the aborigines persisted so late in eastern Pictland at all, side by side with that of the Celtic incomers. Pre-Gaelic Celtic peoples certainly settled outside the area where Gallo-Brittonic place-names are thick, as is seen from names in Ptolemy like *Orcas*, *Cornavii*, *Smertae* and *Dumna*, and from modern place-names in Lochaber and on the west coast, but the marked rarity of such names suggests that here the Celtic superstratum was thin. On the other hand, since approximately half the Pictish inscriptions belong to the far north, outside the area of the names in *Pit-* and the rest, we may suppose that the pre-Celtic people were here in at least as great strength as they were further south. No doubt they formed the great bulk of the population.

Two objections may come to mind in considering what has been said. If a people still speaking a pre-Celtic language survived late in Pictland, why have they not left traces among the modern place-names? And if the upper classes in the south-east were Celtic, why did they write their inscriptions in the language of the conquered people? The answer to the first is very likely that they have, but that we have not recognised them. In many parts of Britain there are place-names, especially river-names (which it is well known tend everywhere to preserve remnants of older languages), which are not easily explained

[1] Efforts to prove that the Pictish succession was not exclusively matrilinear, or that alternatively the Celts did practise matrilinear succession, are examples of disingenuous special pleading and distortions of the Irish law of succession, or misinterpretations of Celtic literature, and have completely failed. Cf. T. F. O'Rahilly (1946), 367*n*, for references.

as Celtic or Germanic. Examples are the English rivers Ouse, or the Thames-Teme-Tamar-Teviot series; or in northern Scotland the Isla, Affric, Liver, Nevis and many others. Students of place-names at the present time seem to have quite lost sight of the possibility that pre-Indo-European river-names may have persisted in Britain, and the result is a number of far-fetched struggles to explain away such names as these by recourse to Indo-European "roots" which have nevertheless left no common and unquestionable derivatives in the Celtic languages. It is just as probable that such names are not Indo-European as that they are—indeed more so. As for the other objection, we do not really know which language the aristocracy of Pictland spoke in the last few centuries of their independence—perhaps both. They might actually have adopted the speech of the older population, or some of them might have done so. In that case Columba's interpreter and Bede's separate language would need no further comment. Or, possibly, they took it over in the pagan period for certain ritual or magic purposes, thus consecrating it as the language of learning, and ultimately, when the Ogam script reached Scotland, of epigraphy. A people who gave up their own system of inheritance in favour of that of the aborigines might well have done the same with their ritual, even their whole religion. This is more likely, since the large proportion of Celtic names in late sources like the Pictish king-list do suggest that Gallo-Brittonic Pictish still flourished down to the ninth century. Various other explanations might be found, all equally speculative, but the existence in some form of a pre-Celtic language in historical Pictland seems reasonably clear.

The attempt to identify the language of a people whom we know only as an archaeological culture is a hazardous affair. It is all very well when something can be learned about it from contemporary historical sources; for instance, the Iron Age C people of south-eastern England were certainly speakers of Celtic because their place-, tribal and personal names given by classical writers are Celtic. But when any such direct evidence is lacking one is reduced to comparatively ill-supported inferences. Thus many people would infer that if in prehistoric times a given culture is found in a given area, and no subsequent immigrant culture can be traced there, then the language spoken in that area when it first appears in historical sources was descended directly from that spoken by the people of the culture in question. Such inferences were drawn at one time with the greatest freedom. Nowadays we are more cautious. The enormous progress of archaeology in the last generation has made these inferences not easier but much more difficult; the more archaeological evidence multiplies the harder it may become to relate any one part of it to a broad feature like language. Besides this, one can no longer use with the same happy certainty the words "and no subsequent culture can be traced there". Pre- and proto-historic archaeological studies in Scotland seem to be in a state of flux at present, and the philologist must tread with caution. Hence the speculations offered in the following paragraphs are put forward with the greatest reserve, and it must be made clear that they are purely speculations.

Nevertheless something may be attempted. The linguistic situation sketched above may be thought to be capable of being related significantly, in certain main outlines, to the archaeological one described by Stuart Piggott in Chapter II. He shows us a population of primitive Bronze Age antecedents all over northern Scotland, whose ancestors had settled there by or before the first quarter of the second millennium B.C., at a time when most philologists and archaeologists would agree it is improbable that they could already have been speaking an Indo-European language. They seem to have survived undisturbed until very late, right down to the first century B.C., apart from the hypothetical and at present problematical arrival of some Hallstatt elements in the fifth or sixth century. At the end of the second or during the first century B.C. new cultures, certainly representing immigrant populations, appear in northern Scotland, but scarcely in such force that we should be warranted in concluding that the older peoples were simply wiped out. It hardly seems too rash to suggest that the latter continued for centuries as an important recognisable element in the population, perhaps subjected or largely merged by intermarriage in some places and retaining a good deal of their separate identity in others; and that we have here our speakers of the unknown non-Indo-European language who are directly traceable in widely different parts of Pictland from the time of Ptolemy's map, little more than a century after the arrival of the Iron Age newcomers, down to the end of Pictish independence.

It is generally agreed that both great phases of the Continental and British Iron Age, the Hallstatt and the La Tène, can be said broadly speaking to belong to the people we call the Celts. This is clear, at any rate for the later period, from various types of evidence, such as the place-names and personal names in classical sources of the tribes living in the areas where these cultures are found. This is the stage in archaeological terms to which the name "Gallo-Brittonic" is given in linguistic terms. Now, the present state of archaeological knowledge suggests that in the first century B.C. a people of Hallstatt antecedents, the builders of the oblong vitrified forts, settled in eastern Scotland between the Firth of Forth and the Moray Firth, that is, in the heart of what later became Pictland. So far as one can tell at present, the distribution of these forts would seem in the main to coincide rather strikingly with that of the P-Celtic place-names discussed above, especially in the east. As for the vitrified forts of the west, between Fort William and the Solway, they appear to be of a rather different type, though whether that means a difference of culture is another question. To assert boldly that the builders of the vitrified forts are to be identified with the element in the proto-Pictish population speaking a P-Celtic Gallo-Brittonic language, as already defined, would be unduly rash considering the tentative nature of present archaeological conclusions, but the suggestion may be made[1] as a possible, perhaps even a probable one, and at any rate as a line of thought. It was believed at one time that the vitrified-fort culture reached Scotland overseas directly from Gaul, and this would suit very well the position of Pictish Celtic already proposed, that of a separate Gallo-Brittonic dialect not identical with Brittonic. It now seems more likely that it came, rather, as an offshoot from the Iron Age A (Hallstatt) civilisation of southern England of the last few centuries B.C., but if so the apparently peculiar nature of Pictish Celtic can still be accounted for. The Celtic peoples of the whole of Britain south of the Forth-Clyde line by the first century A.D. belonged predominantly to the Iron Age B or C (La Tène) cultures, though doubtless considerably mixed with the older Hallstatt one, and it is clear that this is the civilisation of the people who became the Brittones—in short it is the Brittonic civilisation, which, so far as language goes, seems to have formed a single linguistic province from Dumbarton and Edinburgh to Cornwall and Kent. But if the Celtic element among the proto-Picts was of older, unmixed Hallstatt origin, the differences which seem to be observed between their speech and that of the Brittones would easily be explained. The Brittonic dialect in England would have overlaid completely the older Hallstatt one, and so for instance no names in *pett* are found south of the Antonine Wall apart from a few obvious strays from the north. Pictish Celtic might be regarded as a P-Celtic dialect of Hallstatt antecedents and Brittonic as one primarily of La Tène antecedents, archaeologically speaking, if we wished to make such equations.

If these tentative assumptions are accepted the conclusion would be that a people speaking a separate dialect of P-Celtic, to be identified with the builders of the vitrified forts and coming ultimately from southern England, settled in Scotland north of the Firth of Forth around the beginning of the first century B.C.; that they there mingled with an older population of a Bronze Age cultural background whose

[1] Already proposed by H. M. Chadwick (1949), 55–65.

language was not an Indo-European one; borrowed some of their personal and tribal names [1]; took over their custom of matrilinear succession; and perhaps even adopted their language to a certain extent, possibly only for religious or ceremonial purposes, though they retained their own Celtic speech to the end. One may add that if the identification with the vitrified-fort people is correct, the distribution of their characteristic place-names may be thought to suggest that they entered Scotland from the east, settled thickly there, and spread in far smaller strength through the passes of Druim Alban towards the west coast, rather than the reverse. But in any case their place-names would be supplanted by Gaelic ones much earlier and perhaps more fully in the Dalriadic area of the west than in the east.

This brings us to the broch-builders. An immigrant population of La Tène antecedents would seem to have arrived in north-western and far northern Scotland (the Hebrides, Sutherland, Caithness, Orkney and Shetland) about or quite soon after the time when the vitrified-fort people were settling further south.[2] Like the latter, these incomers mixed with the Bronze Age people already there, and the fusion resulted in what is called the broch culture. Their archaeological background suggests that the Celtic element was Brittonic, and their Celtic place-names and tribe-names are seen in Ptolemy, such as the Cornavii of Caithness. Nevertheless they seem to have left very few if any traces of P-Celtic names in the post-Roman period or on the modern map. No doubt many names would have been submerged in the later settlements of the Gaelic and Norse peoples, but even so the contrast with the P-Celtic place-names of the east is striking. Perhaps we must conclude that the immigrants of the north-west gave up their Celtic speech almost entirely, adopting that of the Bronze Age natives, who may have constituted the bulk of the population under a Celtic aristocracy. It is significant that the closest concentration of the non-Indo-European inscriptions is in Shetland. Hence, if the broch culture is a mixture of pre-Celtic Bronze Age and Celtic Iron Age antecedents, linguistically it may nevertheless have been almost entirely non-Indo-European.

In any event, we cannot say with Watson [3] simply that the broch-

[1] Compare the way in which the Angles of Northumbria took to themselves the tribe-names *Bernicii* and *Deiri*, which are probably those of the British peoples which they conquered.

[2] See above, pp. 59–60.

[3] W. J. Watson (1926), 61–6. The medieval Irish legend that the Picts first occupied the Orkneys and later raided and settled the mainland is merely legend, based partly on the well-known Pictish raids into (Roman) Britain and partly on what seems to be the fact that in the historical period what had now become the Pictish province of the north was a troublesome one. Besides it is cancelled out by the other Irish legend that the Picts first settled in Fortrinn.

builders *were* the Picts. Rather, they must have been one of the two chief elements among the proto-Picts, and ultimately they seem to have been worsted by the other element. By the fourth or fifth century, when the historical Pictish nation as distinct from its proto-Pictish constituents was already in being, it is probable that southern Pictland had become the chief power in Scotland beyond the Forth, exercising a definite if not undisputed hegemony over northern Pictland. Hence some aspects of the Pictish culture which belong to historical times, such as the symbol stones and the inscriptions, are found fairly evenly distributed between south and north, since it had now become one civilisation. That it was not linguistically homogeneous, however, seems to be our general conclusion. In the south both languages appear to have been current even to historical times, in the north perhaps chiefly the pre-Celtic one; and it is not improbable that when the Gaels and the Norsemen settled in the northern area they found the people still speaking a non-Indo-European language. The resulting linguistic hotch-potch may be reflected for us in the Bressay inscription.

With this summary, it is now possible to tackle one remaining linguistic problem, the names **Priteni* or **Pritani* and *Cruithni*. The British Isles were called the Pritanic islands probably as early as the late fourth century B.C., when Pytheas sailed round them. The name is presumably Celtic, and may mean "the people of the designs", i.e. tattoos; and if it is really as old as Pytheas's time it must first have belonged to the Iron Age A tribes of southern England, who may have borrowed the custom of painting or tattooing from an older population. It had evidently come to be applied, however, to the people of the whole of Britain, which is natural enough, especially in the usage of foreigners like the Gauls who would know the islanders chiefly from the people of the south. There is reason to think that the form **Pritani* was current in southern Britain and the form **Priteni* in the north.[1] Whether the later incoming La Tène Celts ever adopted *Pritani* and applied it to themselves is uncertain; in the Roman period all the natives of the province called themselves *Brittones*, apparently a new formation derived from or influenced by *Britanni*, which is probably a Latin corruption of *Pritani*.[2] In any case they must still have kept the older form to describe the island as a whole, whence Welsh *Prydain* "Britain", from *Pritani*; and they evidently continued

[1] On this point, and on the whole question of *Pritani*, *Priteni*, *Cruithni*, *Prydain*, and *Prydyn* see K. H. Jackson (1954).

[2] There is no necessity to enter into the controversy on this last point; for a discussion and references see T. F. O'Rahilly (1946), 448–52. The doubts which have been expressed (and adequately answered) come from a too rigid application of the letter instead of the spirit in philological theory.

to use *Priteni* of the peoples north of the Antonine Wall, in which sense, and especially as applied to the historical Picts, it survived into the Middle Ages in the Welsh *Prydyn*, "the Picts, Pictland, northern Scotland". The ancient Irish would seem to have known the name as *Priteni* rather than *Pritani*, very likely because they came into contact more with the northern P-Celts than with the southern; and since they had no *p* in their own language they turned the foreign sound by their own *q*, as they often did, making **Quriteni* and **Quritenii*, meaning by this presumably "the people of Britain". No doubt with the rise of the name *Brittones* for the natives of the Roman province the ancient Irish restricted *Quriteni* and *Quritenii* to the peoples north of the Antonine Wall, just as the Britons themselves did *Priteni*; and it would be when the historical Pictish nation as we know it was formed into a single power that these names came to mean at last the Picts, which in a Scottish context is the meaning of their derivatives in Old Irish, *Cruithin* and *Cruithni*.

But the early Irish knew another people whom they called *Quriteni*(*i*), who lived in various parts of Ireland, but were strongest in the north-east; they may perhaps be identified with the immigrants of Iron Age B antecedents from northern England and southern Scotland mentioned in Chapter II. The complicated problem of just who they were, when and whence they came, and what was their relation to the heroes of the ancient Irish epic tales, may be omitted here. In calling them *Quriteni*(*i*) the Irish must have meant "the people from Britain". Hence in the Old Irish period *Cruithin* and *Cruithni* have two senses; one the historical Picts, and the other, in regular use down to the eighth century, these people apparently of British immigrant stock in Ireland. As scholars have repeatedly pointed out, the latter were not Picts, had no connexion with the Picts, linguistic or otherwise, and are never called *Picti* by Irish writers; and it is a gross confusion to speak of "Irish Picts", as is nevertheless still often done. There is no reason to suppose that they spoke a language other than Irish in historical times,[1] or practised matrilinear succession; indeed the evidence is to the contrary. They would seem to be simply immigrants from Britain, as their name, being interpreted, naturally shows.

As for the Romans, from the late third century on, if not before, they came to use a single undistinguishing term for all the tribes north of the Antonine Wall, *Picti*. Whether this was ever really some native word or not, the Romans who used it obviously understood it to mean "the Painted People", a reference to the custom of painting and tattoo-

[1] So that Cormac must have meant the Picts of Scotland by his *berla Cruithnech*; see above, p. 134.

ing, which had survived among these remote northern tribes long after it had died out farther south. The probability is that it was always simply the Latin verbal adjective *picti*, and it is not impossible that it was first used as a translation of *Priteni*. Since there is good reason to think that the Gallo-Brittonic element among the proto-Picts were Priteni, and since it is desirable to find a convenient name for them to distinguish them from the composite Picts of history, one may suggest that they might in future be called *Priteni* (not *Pritani*) and their language and culture *Pritenic*. We do not know what they called themselves, nor do we know what name the historical Picts used of themselves either.

APPENDIX I

K.H. Jackson

BY way of an appendix, it might be of interest to analyse briefly the chief special characteristics of the Celtic language of Pictland so far as we can observe them. For our earliest sources we can say that there is adequate evidence for its being a P-Celtic language in the name *Uepogenus*; and the fact that it descends from the Gallo-Brittonic group is shown by *Bannatia* and *Decantae*. As to subsequent linguistic developments, that is to say post-Roman ones, the following may be noted [1]:

(i) *Celtic Short Vowels*

It seems that *u* had a certain tendency to become *e* or *i*, as in *Bredei* or *Bridei* beside *Brude*, or *Drest* beside *Drust*. The forms with *u*, which occur almost exclusively in Irish or Gaelicising sources, may represent the older state of the names, borrowed and stereotyped in Gaelic while they developed still further in Pictish. Before *st*, short *u* seems to give alternatively *ui*, as in *Onuist*, *Unuist*, *Uurguist*, *Druist* and *Druisten*, but the last name is normally *Drostan*. All this may mean that *u* was sometimes advanced and lowered to some sort of *e* or unrounded *ö*-sound, or advanced to a kind of *ü* spelt *ui*; at any rate centralised. It is not likely to be a question of the accent, as it occurs in monosyllables and final and non-final syllables.

(ii) *Celtic Long Vowels*

There seems to be no certain evidence on this from early sources, since the explanation of *Peanfahel* is doubtful and the second element probably Gaelic. If it were really Pictish it would suggest that stressed *ā* remained; however, Scottish Gaelic *pòr* beside Welsh *pawr*, *pori*, might seem to indicate that it became *ō* as in Welsh, if *pòr* was borrowed from Pictish rather than Brittonic (cf. p. 149), which is doubtful. O'Rahilly sees a Pictish cognate of Welsh *blawr* in Scottish Gaelic *blàr*,[2] which would mean that *ā* was unchanged, but the comparison is uncertain.

[1] A convenient collection of Pictish names, with sources, is given by W. Stokes (1890).

[2] T. F. O'Rahilly (1946), 356–7.

(iii) *Celtic Diphthongs*

Original *ei* became *ē* in Common Celtic, and it appears as this in *Deva*, *Devana* in Ptolemy, and perhaps in *Lossio Ueda.* In Brittonic it became *ui* in the second half of the seventh century.[1] The history of the names *Deva* and *Devana*, giving (*Uisge*) *Dé* and *Dea*(*th*)*an* in Gaelic, may mean that it did not do this in Pictish; but if *Uuid* in the king-list, whose three sons died in 635, 641 and 653, is the same as *Ueda*, it may have done so, in the first half of the seventh century. *Deva* and *Devana* might well have been borrowed by Gaelic speakers before then.[2] If *Broichan* is Celtic and has original *oi*, this would seem to have remained in the sixth century; but it evidently gave *ō* later in Pictish, as is seen in the name of king *Onuist* who died in 761, from Celtic **Oinogustus.* Later, presumably around A.D. 800, this *ō* seems to have become *ū*, as with king *Unuist* who died in 834. This did not take place at all in Gaelic, in which the name was *Oengus* at this period[3]; and in British the change to *ū*, which happened there also, did so some centuries earlier.[4] Hence it is a peculiarly Pictish matter here, but the likeness to Brittonic and unlikeness to Gaelic is marked.

(iv) *Vowel Affection*

In Brittonic an *i* in a Celtic final syllable changed the character of an *a*, *o* or *u* in the preceding syllable in a way somewhat analogous to the German umlaut, in the late fifth or early sixth century; and similar changes took place when the *i* was in an old internal syllable, in the seventh to eighth centuries.[5] These things do not seem to have happened in Pictish, so that we have *Alpin* beside Welsh *Elffin*, and *Constantin* beside Old Welsh *Custennhin.* *Elpin* does also occur in Pictish, but this is probably influenced by the Strathclyde Brittonic *Elffin*, from which in any case the name may have been borrowed while it was still at the stage *Alpin* in Brittonic, before the late sixth century. The form *Brun Alban* which occurs in the tract *De Situ Albanie*[6] may contain the Pictish equivalent of Welsh *brynn*, "hill", as Stokes thought,[7] and if so it lacks vowel affection; but no doubt it is a scribal error for *Druim.*[8]

[1] Cf. K. H. Jackson (1953), § 28.

[2] Cf. T. F. O'Rahilly (1946), 383.

[3] Used in the Irish annals and Recension II of the king-list as the Gaelicisation of Pictish *Onuist*; but in rendering it elsewhere as *Hungus* Recension II and other sources only partially Gaelicise *Unuist.*

[4] Cf. K. H. Jackson (1953), § 22.

[5] K. H. Jackson (1953), §§ 155–76.

[6] Chronicles 136, 137.

[7] W. Stokes (1890), 396.

[8] Cf. Marjorie O. Anderson (1949), 40.

(v) *Celtic Semi-Vowels*

Original Celtic *w* gave *f* in Gaelic early in the seventh century, and *gw* in Brittonic in the eighth,[1] but it seems always to have remained in Pictish, spelt *u*. O'Rahilly appears to regard it as giving *v*,[2] but the evidence is not satisfactory, as *-fahel* is probably Gaelic, and *Broichan* is at least as likely to represent **Wroican* as **Vroican*. *Uurguist*, the father of kings *Constantin* and *Unuist* who died in 820 and 834 respectively, and *Uurad* who came to the throne in 839, are Gaelic *Forgus*, Welsh **Gworwst* (whence *Gorwst*, *Gwrwst*), and Gaelicising *Ferad* (in Recension II of the king-list). In the Celtic prefixes **wo-* and **wor-* the *o* often became *u* in Brittonic, giving **wu-* and **wur-*, and the same happened there to *i* in the Celtic element **wiro-* "man", giving **wur*. This is seen in Pictish in *Uurguist*, *Uurad*, *Uuradech*, Pictish kings, and probably (with *wur-* going a stage further to *ur-*) in the *Ur-* prefix in the list of the thirty Brudes.[3] In *Uoret* however in the St Vigeans inscription **wo-* seems to have remained, as it often did in Brittonic. In any case Pictish agrees closely with Brittonic and not with Goedelic here.

(vi) *Lenition, and Loss of Lenited* g

Many Celtic consonants when standing between vowels and in certain other positions became slackened in articulation in the neo-Celtic languages ("lenited", as it is called), so that for instance a *b* became *v*, and so on. Unfortunately the spelling in the early period usually disguises this in most cases; for example in *Artbranan* and *Artcois* it is impossible to assert that the *b* and *c* mean the lenited *v* and *g*, though very likely they do. In other instances apparent lenition may be due to Gaelicisation, as in *Uuradech* for **Uuradec*; the spelling *Uuredeg*, which actually occurs, may betray the true Pictish lenition of *c*. The probability that Pictish had in fact a system of lenition, doubtless applying to all lenitable consonants, seems established by the history of *g*, where it clearly had it. A *g* which originally stood internally between vowels or before *n* or *l* became a spirant in Brittonic in the fifth century and subsequently disappeared, whereas in early Gaelic though it became a spirant it was not lost between vowels, and the result before *n* and *l* was rather different. Pictish goes with Brittonic in this respect, not with Gaelic; so *Onuist*, *Lutrin*, *Maelcon*, *Drosten*

[1] K. H. Jackson (1953), § 49.
[2] T. F. O'Rahilly (1946), 356, 534.
[3] A. O. Anderson's remarks (1950), 86–7, miss this point.

(also *Drostan*) and *Talorgen* or *Talorgan* come respectively from Celtic **Oinogustus*, **Lugutrinos*, *Maglocunos*, *Drustagnos* and **Talorgagnos*. It is noteworthy that *Lutrin* and the alternative forms *Drosten* and *Talorgen* differ from Brittonic, as these would be **Loutrin*, **Drostan* (or **Dristan*) and **Talorgan* in Old Welsh.

(vii) *Non-Lenition of Voiced Stops after* r

In Brittonic, *rb*, *rd*, and *rg* became *rv*, *rδ*, and *rγ* in the fifth century,[1] but the stops evidently remained unaffected in Pictish as in Gaelic. Thus we have the names *Irb* and *Uerb* in the king-list, which the alternative spellings *Erp* and *Uerp* show have *rb*. Again, **carden* as in Adamnan's *Airchartdan* and its modern descendant *Urchardan*, as well as *Kincardine* etc., all have *rd* beside Welsh *rδ* in *cardden*; and the names *Talorg* and *Talorgan* are shown by their alternative spellings *Talorc*, *Talorgg*, *Talorcan*, *Talorggan*, etc., to have *rg*, not *rγ*.

(viii) *Voiceless Stops unaffected when Geminate or after Liquids*

In Brittonic, *pp*, *tt*, *cc* became *ff*, *th*, *ch* in the sixth century.[2] There seems no certain evidence on *pp* and *cc*, but *tt* clearly remains unchanged in the word *pett* by contrast with Welsh *peth*. In much the same way *lp*, *rp*, *rt*, *rc* gave *lff*, *rff*, *rth*, *rch* in Brittonic in the sixth century, but in Pictish they do not change. Hence we have the names *Alpin*, *Gartnait* and *Orc*, and the place-name elements **pert* and **lanerc*. The names *Artbranan*, *Artcois*, *Urpant*, *Urcal*, *Urcint*, *Urcnid*, and *Urcrin* do not prove much, as it could be argued that the *p*, *t*, and *c* are merely scribal in these instances, as often in Old Welsh, and the *Ur-* names are in any case very likely artificial.

(ix) *Celtic Spirants*

The Celtic group *cht* remained in Goedelic, but gave *ith* in Brittonic in the late sixth or early seventh century[3]; in Pictish it appears to have become *it*, not *ith*, and this at least by the early eighth century. As already noted, it is seen in *Nechton*: *Nehton*: *Naiton*.[4] *Nechton*

[1] δ = *th* in English *bathe*, and γ = *g* in South German *tage*; the same as *ch* in Scots *loch* but voiced.

[2] See K. H. Jackson (1953), §§ 145–50.

[3] K. H. Jackson (1953), § 60.

[4] The Lunnasting *Nehhton* is perhaps not quite so early as this would imply, but the change need not have occurred quite so soon in Shetland as in the south.

seems to have become stereotyped in writing, however, under the influence of Gaelic *Nechtan*.

(x) *Celtic Single* s *and Sibilant Groups*

Single *s* disappeared intervocally in British perhaps in the first century A.D., and this is possibly seen in Pictish in Ptolemy's name of the Tay, *Tava*, if it is from older **Tausa*.[1] At the beginning of words it gave *h* in Brittonic in the later sixth century,[2] but it remained in Goedelic; it seems to have remained in Pictish too if *Simul*, the name of a Pict who was imprisoned in 725, has original *s*-. *St* became *s* in Gaelic, and either remains or gave *s* in Brittonic; in Pictish it remains in *Onuist*, *Unuist*, *Uurguist*, *Drust*, *Drostan* etc., and seems never to have become *s*, so that here Pictish agrees better with Brittonic than with Goedelic. *Ks*, that is *x*, gave *ch* in Brittonic at some time between the fourth and sixth centuries [3]; in Gaelic and in Gaulish it became *ss*. As already stated, the *ch* in *Ochil* is very likely due to Brittonic intermediaries, and it may be noted that if this is so the British of this region developed the original *ou* of **ouxelo*- to *ō* and not to *ū* as in Brittonic. On the other hand, *Loxa* giving *Lossie*, and possibly **Loxio* giving *Lossio*, as well as perhaps **Artocoxos* giving *Artcois* (for ? **Artcoss*), may mean that Pictish agreed with Gaulish and Gaelic but not with Brittonic in its treatment of *x*. If this is right, *Argentocoxos* and *Lossio* show that it happened in the first quarter of the third century A.D.

(xi) *Palatalisation*

In Gaelic, and to a much lesser extent in Brittonic for a short period at one stage,[4] a consonant followed by *i* (or in Gaelic also *e*) might be palatalised, which is expressed in Gaelic by writing an *i* before it. It is possible that the same thing happened in Pictish, and that this is seen in *Tarain* from Celtic *Taranis*, in *Uuroid* the genitive of *Uurad*, in *Uipoig namet* if this is related to *Uepogenus*, and perhaps in a few others; the second *e* in *Peanfahel* would be the same, if *-fahel* were Pictish.

[1] K. H. Jackson (1953), 522–3.
[2] Ibid. § 115.
[3] Ibid. § 126.
[4] Ibid. § 158.

(xii) *Loss of Celtic Final Syllables and Syncope of Composition Vowels*

In original Celtic there were case-endings and other final syllables which disappeared both in Brittonic and in Goedelic roughly about A.D. 500. The same thing happened in Pictish, so that there is no trace of them at all in the medieval sources. In much the same way compound nouns and adjectives had a composition vowel *-o-* (or other) joining the two elements; as in *Argento-coxos*; this vanished in Brittonic in the first half of the sixth century and in Gaelic slightly later. It was lost in Pictish too, as in *Artcois, Maelcon, Onuist*; only in Bede's *Meilochon* may we perhaps have a trace of a form written down before Pictish syncope occurred, and in this instance datable to the second half of the sixth century.[1]

(xiii) *Morphology*

There is of course hardly any "grammar" observable in Celtic Pictish. As just noted, *Uuroid* may be genitive of *Uurad*; but nouns in Celtic *-gustus*, which have nominative in *-gus* and genitive in *-guso* in Old Irish, seem to have both nominative and genitive in *-uist* in Pictish, as in *Onuist*.

[1] In Gaelic *Dún Cailden* and *Fortrenn*, from *Calidon-* and *Uerturion-*, the syncope is doubtless Gaelic; these names could well have been borrowed by the middle of the sixth century in Gaelic and then syncopated. Cf. K. H. Jackson (1954), 14.

APPENDIX II

Chapter V, Pictish Art

Introduction:

The studies and discoveries published since those originally listed have made few basic changes, but have continued the process so strongly stimulated by Dr Wainwright, threshing out the innumerable obscurities and divergencies of opinion. Though their nature is mostly evident from their titles, some comments may be useful, roughly in the order of the chapter's sections. Neither the original bibliography nor this supplement cover all the finds since ECM.

The most thorough and constructive revision on Pictish art as a whole, as well as Pictish history, is in Dr Isabel Henderson's well-illustrated *The Picts* (1967). Laing in a useful textbook (1975) has brought together and discussed a very great deal of material, but many of the drawings old and new are misleadingly poor, sometimes with quite inaccurate scales.

Henderson has located the earliest of the incised symbol stones as being round the Moray Firth (1957-58), and considered whether they might be territorial boundary markers rather than tombstones (1971); for the latter there is some new evidence (Close-Brooks 1978-79). Jackson (1971) has shown how in a complex matrilineal society they could commemorate pacts or marriages between lineages. Three successive pairs of symbols have been found on one stone each with an ogam inscription (Stevenson 1958-59). Professor Thomas has pursued animal art far in time and space (1961), but the Scottish examples on which his very early start for the symbols relies, can be challenged (Stevenson 1971). Henderson (1971) would put some as early as the 6th century, while Stevenson's view has hardened to see the whole system as devised about 700 under the influence of the Evangelists' animal symbols and other Christian manuscript sources (1971, 1976). Thomas' interpretations of the individual symbols (1963), is on quite different lines, criticised by Henderson (1971); his identification of the 'comb-case' as a satchel, and three-rings as a cauldron may be accepted more readily than others.

A casting-mould found near Inverness (Small 1972) shows that hanging-bowls with open-work pelta patterns were not just used but made in Pictland. This type, thought to be 5th century (Fowler 1968), may instead be later than the Sutton Hoo burial (now dated c. 630) — so Stevenson (1976), who also suggests in a closer study of the Norrie's Law silver that one of its pins may be earlier than this, without altering the date of the one incised with a symbol (*contra* Thomas 1963 and Fowler 1963); this is all critical for the date of brooches and other ornaments of plain silver which the Picts seem to have favoured.

A date from about 740 proposed for the earliest Anglo-Saxon sculptured crosses (Cramp 1978) suits a rather later date in that century for Pictish cross-slabs (table of conflicting chronologies in Stevenson 1958-59). Henderson has preferred an earlier date (1967, 1978), which would tie up with King Nechtan's known request in 710 for architects from Wearmouth-Jarrow, some of whose work was tentatively identified at Restenneth in Angus, by Douglas Simpson (1963). The sculptors' limited repertoire, including repetitive use of figures taken from the life of David as found in a Mercian manuscript, has been stressed by Henderson in a wider search for sources (1967); the Persian Ahura-Mazda beside a camel has been recognised on Meigle No. 1 by Stevenson (1971). Large-scale patterns may have been used for human figures repeated in places far apart (Shepherd 1977-78). Doubts on the association of the Birsay three-warriors stone with a particular grave (Henderson 1971), are confirmed from site records (Curle forthcoming). Analysis of interlace patterns developed in ECM is being carried further (Walcha 1976, 1978, cf. Lang 1978). Discussion of influences from Pictland on the High Crosses of Iona and from there to Ireland has included the origin of the 'Celtic halo' (Stevenson 1956, cf. Henry 1965). There is a related fragment of free-standing halo-less cross in Angus (Stevenson 1958-59). Arguments for assigning the Book of Kells to Pictland rather than Iona have been put forward (Brown 1972, c.f. Henderson 1980). Sculptured tomb-shrines have been identified as a major class of monument (Radford 1955, Thomas 1971, 1973). The date of that at St Ninian's Isle is relevant to how long Pictish traditions survived under Norse rule (Stevenson 1980; for non-sculptural survivals Ritchie 1976-77), in the centuries when in central areas it was being overlaid by other styles under the Scots (Henderson 1978, Lang 1972-74).

The silver at St Ninian's Isle more than doubled the amount of 8th century metalwork known from Pictland. Pictish brooches can now be recognised (Stevenson 1959, Wilson 1973), confirmed by much important workshop debris from Orkney (Curle 1972-74 and 1981?). The lady on the Hilton of Cadboll stone wears one (Stevenson 1958-59). They devolved from the highly decorated Hunterston- (or 'Tara'-) type, originally devised in an Anglo-Saxon jewellers' tradition strongly influenced by Northumbrian (Lindisfarne) manuscript designs, but in what country is quite uncertain (Stevenson 1974). This uncertainty applies to the bowls and other objects from St Ninian's Isle (Wilson 1973), except that a cast inscription on a 'chape' is read as containing two Pictish names by Professor Jackson[1]. Ecclesiastical use of the items (McRoberts 1965) is not accepted by Wilson. While Picts used types of pin widespread in the British Isles (Stevenson 1955, Laing 1975, Curle 1981), there is an exceptional one with a portrait-head (Close-Brooks 1978-79).

Supplementary Bibliography (1954-1980)

Brown, T.J. 1972. Northumbria and the Book of Kells, *Anglo-Saxon England*, I 219-246.

Bruce-Mitford, R.L.S. 1959. Comments on the bowls and miscellaneous silver, and general conclusions, 257-268 in O'Dell 1959.

Close-Brooks, J. 1974-75. A Pictish pin from Golspie, Sutherland, PSAS 106 208-210.

· 1978-79. Excavations in the Dairy Park, Dunrobin, Golspie, Sutherland, 1977, PSAS 110 forthcoming.

Coutts, H. 1970. *Ancient Monuments of Tayside (Guide)*, Dundee Museum.

Cramp, R. 1978. The Anglian Tradition, 1-32 in Lang 1978.

Cruden, S.H. 1964. *The Early Christian and Pictish Monuments of Scotland*, 2nd ed. (with descriptive catalogue of Meigle and St Vigeans collections), H M S O.

Curle, C.L. 1972-74. An engraved lead disc from the Brough of Birsay, Orkney, PSAS 103 301-307.

1981 *Excavations at the Brough of Birsay, Orkney: The Finds, 1935-74*, Soc. Ant. Scot. Monograph Series, forthcoming.

Finlay, I.F. 1973. *Celtic Art*, Chapters VI-VIII The Christian Era, London.

Fowler, E. 1963. Celtic metalwork of the fifth and sixth centuries A.D., *Arch.J.* CXX 98-160.

1968. Hanging bowls, *Studies in Ancient Europe*, ed. Coles, J.M. and Simpson, D D A, 288-310, Leicester.

Gilbert, J.M. 1975-76. Cross-bows on Pictish stones, PSAS 107 316-317.

Gordon, C.A. 1954-56. Carving techniques on the symbol stones of North-East Scotland, PSAS LXXXVIII 40-46.

1964-66. The Pictish animals observed, PSAS XCVIII 215-224.

Henderson, G. 1972. *Style and Civilisation — Early Medieval*, (Pelican) London.

[1]Antiquity XXXIV, 133, March 1960, p. 38 et seq

Henderson, I. 1957-58. The origin centre of the Pictish symbol stones, PSAS XCI 44-60.

1967. *The Picts*, (Ancient Peoples and Places), London.

1971. North Pictland, also the meaning of the Pictish symbol stones, 37-42 and 53-57, in Meldrum 1971.

1978. Sculpture north of the Forth after the takeover by the Scots, 47-73 in Lang 1978.

1980. Pictish Art and the Book of Kells, *Ireland in Early Medieval Europe*, ed. Whitelock, D., Dumville, D. and McKitterick, R. (Studies in Memory of Kathleen Hughes), Cambridge.

Henderson, I.M. 1972. The Picts of Aberdeenshire and their Monuments. *Arch. J.* 129, 166-174.

Henry, F. 1965. *Irish Art*, I, London.

Jackson, A. 1971. Pictish social structure and symbol-stones: and anthropological assessment, *Scottish Studies* 15 121-140.

Laing, L. 1975. *The Archaeology of Late Celtic Britain and Ireland c. 400-1200 A.D.* London.

Lang, J.T. 1972-74. Hogback monuments in Scotland [incl. Brechin], PSAS 105 206-275.

(ed.) 1978. *Anglo-Saxon and Viking-age Sculpture and its Context*, (*British Archaeological Reports*, 49) Oxford.

McRoberts, D. 1960-61. The ecclesiastical significance of the St Ninian's Isle treasure, PSAS XCIV 301-313.

1965. The ecclesiastical character of the St Ninian's Isle treasure, 224-246 in Small 1965.

National Museum of Antiquities of Scotland 1978. *Sculptured Monuments in Scotland AD 400-1050*, Information Sheet No. 4.

O'Dell, A.C. *et al.* 1959. The St Ninian's Isle silver hoard, *Antiquity* XXXIII 241-268.

1960. *St Ninian's Isle Treasure* — (photographs by Cain, A.), *Aberdeen University Studies* 141, Aberdeen.

Radford, C.A.R. 1955. Two Scottish shrines: Jedburgh and St Andrews, *Arch. J.* CXII 43-60.

Ritchie, A. 1976-77. Excavation of Pictish and Viking-age farmsteads at Buckquoy, Orkney, PSAS 108 174-227.

Robertson, W.N. 1976-77. Fragment of stone carving, St Andrews [from a shrine], PSAS 108 259-61.

Shepherd, A.M. and I.A.G. 1977-78. An incised Pictish figure and a new symbol stone from Barflat, Rhynie, Gordon District, PSAS 109.

Simpson, W.D. 1963. The early Romanesque tower at Restenneth Priory, Angus, *Ant. J.* XLIII 269-283.

Small, A. (ed.) 1965. *The Fourth Viking Congress, York 1961*, (University of Aberdeen) Edinburgh.

et al. 1972. *Interim Report on 1971 Excavations at Craig Phadrig*, Geography Dept., Dundee University, Occasional Papers 1.

(ed.) 1973. *St Ninian's Isle and its Treasure, Aberdeen University Studies* 152, 2 vols., Oxford.

Stevenson, R.B.K. 1951-52. Celtic carved box from Orkney, PSAS LXXXVI 187-190 (see also LXXXVII 195, Kirkness, W.).

1955. Pins and the chronology of Brochs, PPS XXI 197-228.

1956. The chronology and relationships of some Irish and Scottish crosses, JRSAI LXXXVI 84-96.

1958-59. The Inchyra Stone and some other unpublished Early Christian monuments, (appendix, relative chronologies), PSAS XCII 33-55.

1959. The penannular brooches, discussion, 255-257 in O'Dell *et al.* 1959.

1963-64. The Gaulcross hoard of Pictish silver, PSAS XCVIII 206-209.

1971. Sculpture in Scotland in the 6th-9th centuries A.D., *Kolloquium über spätantike und frühmittelalterliche Skulptur, Heidelberg*, II 65-75, Mainz.

1972. Note on mould from Craig Phadrig, 49-51 in Small 1972.

1974. The Hunterston Brooch and its significance, *Medieval Archaeology* XVIII 16-42.

1976. The earlier metalwork of Pictland, 246-251 in Megaw, J.V.S. (ed.) *To Illustrate the Monuments* (Piggott Festschrift), London.

1980. Christian sculpture in Norse Shetland, in Sverri Dahl Festschrift, Torshavn, forthcoming.

Thomas, (A.)C. 1961. The animal art of the Scottish Iron Age and its origins, *Arch. J.* CXVIII 14-64.

1963. The interpretation of the Pictish symbols, *Arch. J.* CXX 31-97.

1971. *The Early Christian Archaeology of North Britain*, (Glasgow University), London.

1973. Sculptured stones and crosses from St Ninian's Isle and Papil, 8-44 in Small 1973.

Walcha, G. 1976. *Bandeflecht-Ornamentik in Schottland*, Kunsthistor—isches Institut der Universität Köln.

1978. Bandgeflecht auf schottischen Reliefsteinen und in insularen Handschriften, *Archiv für Kulturgeschichte* 60 1-52.

Wilson, D.M. 1973. The treasure, 45-148 in Small 1973.

APPENDIX III
Addenda and Corrigenda, Chapter VI

P.138 The "Pictish" Ogam inscription on the bare rock at the top of the hill of Dunadd, the ancient Gaelic capital of Argyll, is of interest here. It is close beside the famous carved boar (itself notably Pictish in style) and the "footprint". This inscription has been known since at least 1953, and was dealt with in detail by the present writer in Antiquity XXXIX (1965), 300-302; but it still passes unnoticed in popular histories of the Gaels in Argyll. It must presumably have been inscribed at the time when the Picts sacked Dunadd in 736, as Mrs. Curle long ago suggested the boar might have been (PSAS. LXXIV, 1939-40, 67: "might be explained as the work of a raiding party of victorious Picts"), though she did not know of the inscription. What it says is of course unknown, though perhaps not beyond conjecture!

P.139 On the name Edarnon/Idarnoin/Ethernan compare Rhys in PSAS. XXXII (1897-98), 397.

P.141 The suggestion has been made that the inscriptions in question were intentionally gibberish. That is, that they were set up in a culture which knew vaguely the Ogam alphabet but not how to apply it to (Celtic) Pictish, by people who paid to have what looked like Ogam epitaphs erected out of a sort of snobbery. But apart from the inherent improbability of this, the inscriptions have, for example, a plausible distribution of vowels and consonants such as could not arise in the circumstances envisaged. Thus, even HCCVVEVV could easily spell some word sounding like English *whew*. Besides, some (e.g. American Indian) languages have extraordinary words which are all consonants, as many as six or seven, without any vowels.

P.143, n.1 I misunderstood Anderson's letter. What he did say, as Mrs Anderson has kindly pointed out to me, was that the MS. reads *de Froichano*; cf. their "Adomnán's Life of Columba", p.84 n.

P.145 Bede's king *Naiton* preserves the original *o* of the second syllable, as in *Nechton* and *Nehhton*; but there is evidence that later, non-Gaelic Celtic sources treated this as *a* (as regularly happened in Gaelic), perhaps under Gaelic church influence; cf. p.164 f. So, Abbot Ceolfrith's letter to the same king as Bede's *Naiton* calls him *Naitan*. Compare the spellings *Nectan* and especially *Nethan* in the Pictish Chronicle; St. *Nechtan* in Cornwall, and St. *Neizhan* in Brittany; and in Scotland, *Cambusnethan* ("Nethan's River-bend") and the fairly recently discovered inscription NEITANO SACERDOS of about 700 AD., at Peebles.

P.146 It is remarkable that in many, perhaps most, Pit- names the second element is clearly Gaelic (though this cannot always be proved, as in the case of Pitarrow, where the second element may well be Pictish *tarw* rather than Gaelic *tarbh*; "bull" in either case). This must mean that the names were formed *as we have them* some time after the Gaelic settlements in Pictland in the middle of the 9th century, whether the original Pictish second elements of old *Pett-* names were translated into Gaelic, or were replaced by a Gaelic name-element, or whether they were names of wholly new foundations of Gaelic date. In this last case, the Gaels must have adopted the unquestionably Pictish *pett* as a name-forming element for their own *new* place-names, no doubt because it expressed some characteristic feature of Pictish land tenure foreign to Gaelic custom but adopted by them when they settled among the Picts. In any case, then, the *Pit-* names remain valid evidence for the extent of the Pictish area about the middle of the 9th century. See further the present writer's "The Gaelic Notes in the Book of Deer" (Cambridge, 1972), pp.114-116. On the distribution of the names see also pp.36-7 above.

P.151, l.31 "Bede's words", i.e. p.133, ll.29-30, above.

P.152, ll.27-9 Of course, efforts have been, and are, made from time to time to show that the language actually *was* Basque — all of them more or less absurd. The most recent known to me is H. Guiter's "La langue des Pictes", in the Boletin de la Real Sociedad Vascongada de los Amigos del País, (San Sebastian, 1968), pp.281-321. Unfortunately M. Guiter is unable to transliterate the Pictish Ogams correctly, and some of his "Basque" renderings hardly inspire confidence, e.g. "The summer was good", at Scoonie.

P.153, n.l. Cf. D. Binchy in M. Dillon, "Early Irish Society" (Dublin, 1954), p.58, "For all practical purposes kinship was, in Irish as in Roman law, agnatic, i.e. reckoned in the male line only, and all the talk about "mother-right" among the Goidels — about survivals of a matriarchal or matrilinear system — are just moonshine". The same may be said of British (Welsh) custom.

P.154, ll.15-18 Some striking parallels may be quoted. The Indo-European Hittites, occupying part of Asia Minor, adopted some of the gods of the pre-Indo-European Hatti among whom they settled and whose name they took for themselves, and they worshipped them in the Hattian language. Again, according to Diodorus Siculus the pre-Greek inhabitants of the island of Samothrace had spoken a non-Greek language which was still preserved when he wrote (mid 1st century BC.) in the religious worship at the famous Greek shrine there; and inscriptions survive there in Greek letters but not in the Greek language.

Perhaps the best-known instance is the way in which Sumerian, the pre-Semitic language of S. Mesopotamia, was adopted by the Semitic Chaldaeans, Babylonians, and Assyrians for literary, religious, diplomatic, legal, and commercial purposes, much as Latin was used in the Middle Ages, and had a wide currency as such in the 3rd century BC., by which time it had pretty well died out as a spoken language. It was still used for magic spells in the later period, when it was less well understood. (I owe this detailed information to the kindness of Mr Jeremy Black.)

Pp.154-158 Compare T.G. Powell in Stuart Piggott, "The Prehistoric Peoples of Scotland" (1962), pp.121 ff., who thought the culture of the builders of the vitrified forts in Scotland represented a Celtic intrusion from the south dating to the 1st century BC, and ultimately of continental Hallstatt origin. He adds, "The Gallo-Brittonic dialect deduced by Jackson as having been spoken within the subsequent Pictish territory may very reasonably be assigned, as he has suggested, to the vitrified fort people." Compare Piggott above, pp.58-63, and Feachem p.70 f.; and Isabel Henderson, "The Picts" (London, 1967), p.20. There is however carbon-dating evidence now that the vitrified forts were being built between about 600 BC. or earlier and about 100 BC; and it is possible that eastern Britain and Scotland were directly influenced in the Hallstatt period by sea from the Rhine and North Sea routes, rather than from France as may have been the case with central southern Britain. (I owe this up-to-date information to Professor Dennis Harding).

I should add that in recent years many archaeologists, though by no means all, have concluded that there were *no* invasions of Britain at all between very early times and shortly before the Roman occupation. How they explain the undoubted fact that P-Celtic was spoken throughout most of Britain well before this *terminus ad quem* is a question not discussed. Fashions are apt to arise and fade away in archaeological thinking, and no doubt this rather striking belief is one of them.

All the same, the archaeological picture of early Scotland, and the background of the builders of the vitrified (better, "timber-laced") forts is somewhat less clear than it appeared to be in 1953, or in 1962 or 1967 for that matter; and the question whether the Pritenic (see p.158 above) of Pictland was merely a northern dialect of the Pritanic/Brittonic spoken further south, or a less closely-related Gallo-Brittonic one, had best be left open at present.

P.161 For the possibility that Pictish long vowels might be shortened in unstressed syllables (Pretonic ones at any rate) in compounds, compare my "Gaelic Notes in the Book of Deer", p.108 f. The early Welsh *mordei*, perhaps "palaces", from *mawr* "big" and *tei* "houses", gives an exact parallel for the etymology of Pictich *mormaer* suggested there. The same development may perhaps be seen in the name of one of the legendary Pictish kings, Necton Morbet ("N. king of the Great World"?). Cf. I. Williams, "Canu Aneirin" (Cardiff, 1938), p.73.

P.164, § vii Add the name *Uurguist*, from **Worgustus*, by contrast with *Unuist*, from **Oinogustus*.

P.165, top. Further instances may be *Abernethy* and *Ythan*; compare W.J. Watson, "The Celtic Place-Names of Scotland" (Edinburgh, 1926), p.211.

REFERENCES AND ABBREVIATIONS

Åberg, N. (1943). *The Occident and the Orient in the Art of the Seventh Century*, Part I. *The British Isles. Kungl. Vitterhets Historie och Antikvitets Akademiens Handlingar*, LVI. i., Stockholm 1943.

AClon. *The Annals of Clonmacnoise*, ed. D. Murphy, Dublin 1896.

Acta Arch. *Acta Archaeologica*, Copenhagen.

Adamnan. *Vita Sancti Columbae*, ed. W. Reeves, Dublin 1857 (2nd. edn. Edinburgh 1874). Also ed. J. T. Fowler, Oxford 1894.

AI. *The Annals of Inisfallen*, reproduced in facsimile by R. I. Best and E. MacNeill, Dublin 1933.

Allen, J. R. See ECM.

Anderson, A. O. (1908). *Scottish Annals from English Chroniclers*, London 1908.

Anderson, A. O. (1922). *Early Sources of Scottish History*, 2 vols., Edinburgh 1922.

Anderson, A. O. (1948). "Ninian and the Southern Picts", SHR XXVII (1948), 25–47.

Anderson, A. O. (1950). "Early Scotland" (review), SHR XXIX (1950), 78–88.

Anderson, J. (1881). *Scotland in Early Christian Times*, 2 vols., Edinburgh 1881.

Anderson, J. (1889). "Notices of some Undescribed Sculptured Stones and Fragments in different parts of Scotland", PSAS XXIII (1888–89), 344–355.

Anderson, J. See also ECM.

Anderson, Marjorie O. [Mrs A. O.] (1949). "The Scottish Materials in a Paris Manuscript", SHR XXVIII (1949), 31–42.

Anderson, Marjorie O. [Mrs A. O.] (1949–50). "The Lists of the Kings", SHR XXVIII (1949), 108–118, XXIX (1950), 13–22.

ANL. *The Archaeological News Letter*, London.

Antiquity. *Antiquity, A Quarterly Review of Archaeology*, Newbury (Gloucester).

AntJ. *The Antiquaries Journal*, London.

Arch. Ael. *Archaeologia Aeliana*, Newcastle upon Tyne.

ArchJ. *The Archaeological Journal*, London.

Ardestie and Carlungie Reports. Excavations at two souterrain sites were carried out during 1949–51. The reports (with notes on other sites) will be published, probably as one volume, under some such title as *The Souterrains of Southern Pictland.*

Arnold, T. See HH and SD.

ASC. *The Anglo-Saxon Chronicle*, ed. Benjamin Thorpe, 2 vols., London 1861.

ATig. *Annals of Tigernach*, ed. Whitley Stokes, RC XVI (1895), XVII (1896), XVIII (1897).

AU. *Annals of Ulster*, vol. I. ed. W. M. Hennessy, Dublin 1887.

Baedae Continuatio. Annals appended to Bede's *Historia Ecclesiastica Gentis Anglorum.* See C. Plummer (1896), I. 361–363.

Bede. *Historia Ecclesiastica Gentis Anglorum*, in *Baedae Opera Historica*, ed. C. Plummer, 2 vols., Oxford 1896.

Beresford, M. W. (1953). "Deserted Villages and the Historian", ANL IV, No. 11 (1953), 161–163.

Bersu, G. (1948a). " 'Fort' at Scotstarvit Covert, Fife", PSAS LXXXII (1947–48), 241–263.

Bersu, G. (1948b). "Rectangular Enclosure on Green Craig, Fife", PSAS LXXXII (1947–48), 264–275.

Best, R. I. See AI.

BG. *C. Iuli Caesaris De Bello Gallico*, ed. T. Rice Holmes, Oxford 1914.

BM (1922). *Guide to the Antiquities of Roman Britain*, British Museum, London 1922.

BM (1947). *The Sutton Hoo Ship Burial, A Provisional Guide*, British Museum, London 1947.

Brown, G. Baldwin (1903–37). *The Arts in Early England*, 6 vols., London 1903–1937.

BSLP. *Bulletin de la Société de Linguistique de Paris*, Paris.

Calder, C. S. T. (1938). "Three Fragments of a Sculptured Cross of Anglian Type now preserved in Abercorn Church, West Lothian", PSAS LXXII (1937–38), 217–223.

Chadwick, H. M. (1949). *Early Scotland*, Cambridge 1949.

Childe, V. G. (1935). *The Prehistory of Scotland*, London 1935.

Childe, V. G. (1938). "The Experimental Production of the Phenomena distinctive of Vitrified Forts", PSAS LXXII (1937–38), 44–55.

Childe, V. G. (1940). *Prehistoric Communities of the British Isles*, London 1940 (3rd. edn. 1949).

Childe, V. G. (1946). *Scotland before the Scots*, London 1946.

Christison, D. (1889). "The Duns and Forts of Lorne, Nether Lochaber, and the Neighbourhood", PSAS XXIII (1888–89), 368–432.

Christison, D. (1900). "The Forts, 'Camps', and other Field-works of Perth, Forfar, and Kincardine", PSAS XXXIV (1899–1900), 43–120.

Christison, D. (1904). "The Forts of Kilmartin, Kilmichael Glassary, and North Knapdale, Argyle", PSAS XXXVIII (1903–04), 205–251.

Christison, D. (1905). "Report on the Society's Excavations of Forts on the Poltalloch Estate, Argyll, in 1904–5", PSAS XXXIX (1904–1905), 292–322.

Chronicles. *Chronicles of the Picts, Chronicles of the Scots and other Early Memorials of Scottish History*, ed. W. F. Skene, Edinburgh 1867.

Clapham, A. W. (1934). "Notes on the Origins of Hiberno-Saxon Art", Antiquity, VIII (1934), 43–57.

Clarke, R. R. (1949). "A Celtic Torc-terminal from North Creake, Norfolk", ArchJ CVI (1949), 59–61.

Colgrave, B. (1940). *Two Lives of St Cuthbert*, ed. B. Colgrave, Cambridge 1940.

Colgrave, B. See also Eddius.

Collingwood, R. G., and Myres, J. N. L. (1937). *Roman Britain and the English Settlements*, Oxford 1936 (2nd. edn. 1937).

Collingwood, W. G. (1927). *Northumbrian Crosses of the Pre-Norman Age*, London 1927.

Colvin, H. M. (1952). "Deserted Villages and the Archaeologist", ANL IV, No. 9 (1952), 129–131.

Coutil, L. (1930). *L'Art Mérovingien et Carolingien*, Bordeaux 1930.

Craw, J. H. (1930). "Excavations at Dunadd and at other sites on the Poltalloch Estates, Argyll", PSAS LXIV (1929–30), 111–127.

Crawford, O. G. S. (1939). "Air Reconnaissance of Roman Scotland", Antiquity XIII (1939), 280–292.

Crawford Essays. *Aspects of Archaeology in Britain and Beyond, Essays presented to O. G. S. Crawford*, ed. W. F. Grimes, London 1951.

CRS. *Cymmrodorian Record Series*, London.

Curle, Cecil L. [Mrs A. T.] (1940). "The Chronology of the Early Christian Monuments of Scotland", PSAS LXXIV (1939–40), 60–116.

Curle, Cecil L. [Mrs A. T.] See also Cecil L. Mowbray.

Davidson, J. M. (1943). "A Pictish Symbol Stone from Golspie, Sutherland", PSAS LXXVII (1942–43), 26–30.

Diack, F. C. (1926a). "Aber and Inver in Scotland", SGS I (1926), 83–98. See also F. C. Diack (1944), 126–134.

Diack, F. C. (1926b). "The Colchester 'Caledonian' of the Third Century A.D.", SGS I (1926), 195–202. See also F. C. Diack (1944), 121–126.

Diack, F. C. (1944). *The Inscriptions of Pictland . . . with Other Writings and Collections*, Aberdeen 1944.

Dickins, B. See Early Cultures.

Dobbs, Margaret E. (1949). "Cé: The Pictish Name of a District in Eastern Scotland", SGS VI (1949), 137–138.

Dunning, G. C. See C. F. C. Hawkes.

Early Cultures. *The Early Cultures of North-west Europe*, ed. Cyril Fox and Bruce Dickins, Cambridge 1950.

ECM. J. Romilly Allen and J. Anderson, *The Early Christian Monuments of Scotland*, Edinburgh 1903.

Eddius. *Vita Wilfridi Episcopi auctore Eddio Stephano*, ed. James Raine in vol. I of *The Historians of the Church of York*, London 1879; and *The Life of Bishop Wilfrid by Eddius Stephanus*, ed. Bertram Colgrave, Cambridge 1927.

Edwards, A. J. H. (1939). "A Massive Double-Linked Silver Chain", PSAS LXXIII (1938–39), 326–327.

Eeles, F. C. (1934). "The Monymusk Reliquary or Brecbennoch of St Columba", PSAS LXVIII (1933–34), 433–438.

EHR. *The English Historical Review*, London.

ESt. *Englische Studien*, Heilbronn (Leipzig).

Feachem, R. W. (1950). "A New Pictish Symbol-Stone in the Lowlands", PSAS LXXXIV (1949–50), 206–208.

Forbes, A. F. See Jocelin.

Förster, M. (1922). "Englisch-Keltisches", ESt LVI (1922), 204–239.

Förster, M. (1941). *Der Flussname Themse und seine Sippe*, München 1941.

Fowler, J. T. See Adamnan.

Fox, C. See Early Cultures.

Fraser, J. (1923). *History and Etymology*, Oxford 1923.

Fraser, J. (1927). "The Question of the Picts", SGS II (1927), 172–201.

Fraser, J. (1942). "Pet(t) in Place Names", SGS V (1942), 67–71.

Gildas. *De Excidio Britanniae Liber Querulus*, MHB 1–16. Also ed. T. Mommsen (MGH XIII. i), Berlin 1894, and H. Williams (CRS III), London 1899.

Golson, J. (1953). "Medieval Deserted Villages", ANL IV, No. 12 (1953), 181–183.

Graham, A. (1947). "Some Observations on the Brochs", PSAS LXXXI (1946–47), 48–99.

Graham, A. (1951). "Archaeological Gleanings from Dark-Age Records", PSAS LXXXV (1950–51), 64–91.

Gresham, C. A. (1942). "The Book of Aneirin", Antiquity XVI (1942), 237–257.

Grierson, P. (1952). "The Dating of the Sutton Hoo Coins", Antiquity XXVI (1952), 83–86.

Grimes, W. F. See Crawford Essays.

Hamilton, J. R. C. (1952). "Recent Excavations at Jarlshof", ANL IV, No. 10 (1952), 159–160.

Hamilton, J. R. C. See also Jarlshof Report.

Hardy, T. D. See MHB.

Haseloff, G. (1951). *Der Tassilokelch*, Munich 1951.

Hawkes, C. F. C. and Dunning, G. C. (1930). "The Belgae of Gaul and Britain", ArchJ LXXXVII (1930), 150–335.

Hencken, H. O'N. (1935). "Ballinderry Crannog No. 1", PRIA XLIII (1935), 103–239.

Hencken, H. O'N. (1942). "Ballinderry Crannog No. 2", PRIA XLVII (1942), 1–76.

Henderson, G. (1898). *Leabhar nan Gleann*, Edinburgh 1898.

Hennessy, W. M. See AU.

Henry, Françoise (1936). "Hanging-Bowls", JRSAI LXVI (1936), 209–246.

Henry, Françoise (1940). *Irish Art in the Early Christian Period*, London 1940.

Henry, Françoise (1952). "A Wooden Hut on Inishkea North, County Mayo", JRSAI LXXXII (1952), 169–171.

Henshall, Audrey S. (1950). "Textiles and Weaving Appliances in Prehistoric Britain", PPS XVI (1950), 130–162.

HH. *Henrici Archidiaconi Huntendunensis Historia Anglorum*, ed. Thomas Arnold, London 1879.

Hinks, R. (1935). *Carolingian Art*, London 1935.

Hodgkin, R. H. (1935). *A History of the Anglo-Saxons*, 2 vols., London 1935 (2nd. edn. 1939, 3rd. edn. 1953).

Hogg, A. H. A. (1943). "Native Settlements of Northumberland", Antiquity XVII (1943), 136–147.

Hogg, A. H. A. (1951). "The Votadini", Crawford Essays, 200–220.

Holder. A. Holder, *Alt-Celtischer Sprachschatz*, 3 vols., Leipzig 1896–1913.

Holmes, T. Rice (1907). *Ancient Britain and the Invasions of Julius Caesar*, Oxford 1907.

Holmes, T. Rice. See also BG.

Howlett, R. See RH(Historia).

Hubert, H. (1934). *The Rise of the Celts*, London 1934.

Jackson, K. H. (1939). "The 'Gododdin' of Aneirin", Antiquity XIII (1939), 25–34.

Jackson, K. H. (1950). "Notes on the Ogam Inscriptions of Southern Britain", Early Cultures, 199–213.

Jackson, K. H. (1951). "Common Gaelic", PBA XXXVII (1951), 71–97.

Jackson, K. H. (1953). *Language and History in Early Britain*, Edinburgh 1953.

Jackson, K. H. (1954). "Two Early Scottish Names", SHR XXXIII (1954), 14–18.

Jarlshof Report. Excavations were carried out at Jarlshof (Shetland) by the Ministry of Works in 1949–52. The report, compiled by J. R. C. Hamilton who supervised the excavations, will probably be published as a separate volume under the title of *Jarlshof*. For reports on earlier excavations at Jarlshof, see PSAS LXVI (1931–32), LXVII (1932–33), LXVIII (1933–34), LXIX (1934–35), LXXII (1937–38).

Jervise, A. (1862). "An Account of the Excavation of the Round or 'Bee-hive' shaped House, and other Underground Chambers, at West Grange of Conan, Forfarshire", PSAS IV (1860–1862), 492–499.

Jocelin. *Vita Kentegerni auctore Jocelino Monacho Furnesensi*, ed. A. F. Forbes, Edinburgh 1874 (*The Historians o* Scotland V, 159–242).

JRSAI. *Journal of the Royal Society of Antiquaries of Ireland*, Dublin.

Kendrick, T. D. (1932). "British Hanging-Bowls", Antiquity VI (1932), 161–184.

Kendrick, T. D. (1938). *Anglo-Saxon Art*, London 1938.

Kendrick, T. D. (1949). *Late Saxon and Viking Art*, London 1949.

Kilbride-Jones, H. E. (1935). "Bronze Terret from Rhynie, and Distribution of the Type", PSAS LXIX (1934–35), 448–454.

Kilbride-Jones, H. E. (1937). "A Bronze Hanging-Bowl from Castle Tioram, Moidart, and a suggested Absolute Chronology for British Hanging-Bowls", PSAS LXXI (1936–37), 206–247.

Laing, S. (1867). "On the Age of the Burgs or 'Brochs' and some other prehistoric remains of Orkney and Caithness", PSAS VII (1866–68), 56–100.

Leeds, E. T. (1933). *Celtic Ornament*, Oxford 1933.

Levison, W. (1940). "An Eighth-century Poem on St Ninian", Antiquity XIV (1940), 280–291.

Lindqvist, S. (1941–42). *Gotlands Bildsteine*, 2 vols., Stockholm 1941–1942.

Loth, J. (1921). "La Première Apparition des Celtes dans L'Ile de Bretagne et en Gaule", RC XXXVIII (1920–21), 259–288.

Macalister, R. A. S. (1928). *The Archaeology of Ireland*, London 1928.

Macalister, R. A. S. (1935). *Ancient Ireland*, London 1935.

Macalister, R. A .S. (1940). "The Inscriptions and Language of the Picts", MacNeill Essays, 184–226.

Macbain, A. (1892). "Ptolemy's Geography of Scotland", TGS XVIII (1891–92), 267–288.

Macbain, A. (1897). "Mr Skene versus Dr Skene", TGS XXI (1896–97), 191–214.

Macbain, A. (1902). W. F. Skene, *The Highlanders of Scotland* (London 1836), ed. A. Macbain, Stirling 1902.

Macdonald, J. (1861). "Historical Notices of 'The Broch', or Burghead, in Moray, with an Account of its Antiquities", PSAS IV (1860–62), 321–369.

MacNeill, E. (1919). *Phases of Irish History*, Dublin 1919.

MacNeill, E. (1933). "The Pretanic Background in Britain and Ireland", JRSAI LXIII (1933), 1–28.

MacNeill, E. (1939). "The Language of the Picts", YCS II (1938–39), 3–45.

MacNeill, E. See also AI.

MacNeill Essays. *Essays and Studies presented to Professor Eoin MacNeill*, ed. John Ryan, Dublin 1940.

Mahr, A. (1937). "New Aspects and Problems in Irish Prehistory", PPS III (1937), 262–436.

Mahr, A. and Raftery, J. (1932–41). *Christian Art in Ancient Ireland*, 2 vols., Dublin 1932–1941.

Marshall, D. W. H. (1929). *The Sudreys in Early Viking Times*, Glasgow 1929.

Marstrander, C. (1932). "Okklusiver og Substrater", NTS V (1932), 258–314.

MGH. *Monumenta Germaniae Historica, Auctores Antiquissimi*, Berlin.

MHB. *Monumenta Historica Britannica*, ed. T. D. Hardy, London 1848.

Mitchell, A. (1874). "Vacation Notes in Cromar, Burghead, and Strathspey", PSAS x (1872–74), 645–670.

Moar, P. (1944). "Newly discovered Sculptured Stones from Papil, Shetland", PSAS LXXVIII (1943–44), 91–99.

Mowbray, Cecil L. (1936). "Eastern Influences on Carvings at St Andrews and Nigg, Scotland", Antiquity x (1936), 428–440.

Mowbray, Cecil L. See also Cecil L. Curle.

Murphy, D. See AClon.

Myres, J. N. L. See R. G. Collingwood.

Nash-Williams, V. E. (1950). *The Early Christian Monuments of Wales*, Cardiff 1950.

Nennius. *Historia Britonum*, MHB 47–82. Also ed. T. Mommsen (MGH XIII. i), Berlin 1894, and F. Lot, Paris 1934.

Nicholson, E. W. B. (1896). *The Vernacular Inscriptions of the Ancient Kingdom of Alban*, London 1896.

Nicholson, E. W. B. (1904). *Keltic Researches*, London 1904.

Nordenfalk, C. (1947). "Before the Book of Durrow", Acta Arch. XVIII (1947), 141–174.

NTS. *Norsk Tidsskrift for Sprogvidenskap*, Oslo.

OE. Old English.

ON. Old Norse.

O'Rahilly, T. F. (1935). "The Goedels and their Predecessors", PBA XXI (1935), 323–372.

O'Rahilly, T. F. (1946). *Early Irish History and Mythology*, Dublin 1946.

Ordnance Survey (1938). *Ordnance Survey Map of Britain in the Dark Ages, North Sheet*, Southampton 1938.

Payne, F. G. (1948). "The Plough in Early Britain", ArchJ CIV (1948), 82–111.

PBA. *Proceedings of the British Academy*, London.

Petersen, J. (1940). *British Antiquities of the Viking Period found in Norway* (*Viking Antiquities in Great Britain and Ireland*, ed. Haakon Shetelig, v, Oslo 1940).

Piggott, Cecily M. [Mrs S.] (1948). "A Late Bronze Age Burial from Orrock near Burntisland", PSAS LXXXII (1947–48), 306–308.

Piggott, Cecily M. [Mrs S.] (1949). "The Iron Age Settlement at Hayhope Knowe, Roxburghshire. Excavations 1949", PSAS LXXXIII (1948–49), 45–67.

Piggott, Cecily M. [Mrs S.] (1950). "The Excavations at Bonchester Hill, 1950", PSAS LXXXIV (1949–50), 113–137.

Piggott, S. (1949). *British Prehistory*, Oxford 1949.

Piggott, S. (1950). "Swords and Scabbards of the British Early Iron Age", PPS XVI (1950), 1–28.

Piggott, S. (1951). "Excavations in the Broch and Hill-fort of Torwoodlee, Selkirkshire, 1950", PSAS LXXXV (1950–51), 92–117.

Piggot, S. (1952). "Excavations at Castle Law, Glencorse, and at Craig's Quarry, Dirleton", 1948–50", PSAS LXXXVI (1951–52), 191–196.

Piggott, S. (1954). *Neolithic Cultures of the British Isles*, Cambridge 1954.

Plummer, C. (1896). See Bede.

Pokorny, J. (1933). *A History of Ireland*, Dublin 1933.

Pokorny, J. (1938). *Zur Urgeschichte der Kelten und Illyrier*, Halle 1938.

Pokorny, J. (1940). "Eriu and the Coming of the Goidels", MacNeill Essays, 237–243.

Pokorny, J. (1953). *Keltologie*, in *Wissenschaftliche Forschungsberichte, Geisteswissenschaftliche Reihe, herausgegeben von Professor Dr Karl Hönn*, Berne 1953.

PPS. *Proceedings of the Prehistoric Society*, New Series, Cambridge.

PRIA. *Proceedings of the Royal Irish Academy*, Dublin.

PSAS. *Proceedings of the Society of Antiquaries of Scotland*, Edinburgh.

Radford, C. A. R. (1942). "The Early Christian Monuments of Scotland", Antiquity XVI (1942), 1–18.

Raftery, J. (1940). "A Suggested Chronology for the Irish Iron Age", MacNeill Essays, 272–281.

Raftery, J. See also A. Mahr.

Raine, J. See Eddius, RD, RH(Annotatio), RH(Historia).

RC. *Revue Celtique*, Paris.

RCAMS. The Royal Commission on the Ancient and Historical Monuments of Scotland, Reports I–XIV (1909–53).

RD. *Reginaldi Monachi Dunelmensis Libellus De Amirandis Beati Cuthberti Virtutibus*, ed. James Raine, Surtees I (1935).

Reeves, W. See Adamnan.

RH(Annotatio). *Quaedam Brevis Annotatio Ricardi Prioris Hagustaldensis Ecclesiae De Antiquo et Moderno Statu ejusdem Ecclesiae et De Pontificibus ejusdem Ecclesiae*, ed. James Raine, Surtees XLIV (1863), 1–62.

RH(Historia). *Historia Ricardi Haugustaldensis De Gestis Regis Stephani et De Bello Standardii*, ed. James Raine, Surtees XLIV

(1863), 63–106. Also ed. Richard Howlett (London 1886) in *Chronicles of the Reigns of Stephen, Henry II, and Richard*, III, 139–178.

Rhys, J. (1892). "The Inscriptions and Language of the Northern Picts", PSAS XXVI (1891–92), 263–351.

Rhys, J. (1893). "The Inscriptions and Language of the Northern Picts (Addenda and Corrigenda)", PSAS XXVII (1892–93), 411–412.

Rhys, J. (1898). "A Revised Account of the Inscriptions of the Northern Picts", PSAS XXXII (1897–98), 324–398.

Richardson, J. S. (1907). "An Undescribed Sculptured Stone with Symbols in the Island of Raasay", PSAS XLI (1906–07), 435–436.

Ryan, J. See MacNeill Essays.

Scott, W. L. (1947). "The Problem of the Brochs", PPS XIII (1947), 1–36.

Scott, W. L. (1948). "Gallo-British Colonies. The Aisled Round-House Culture in the North", PPS XIV (1948), 46–125.

Scott, W. L. (1951). "The Colonisation of Scotland in the Second Millenium B.C.", PPS XVII (1951), 16–82.

SD. *Symeonis Monachi Opera Omnia*, ed. Thomas Arnold, 2 vols., London 1882–1885.

SGS. *Scottish Gaelic Studies, Issued from the Celtic Department of the University of Aberdeen*, London.

Shetelig, H. (1948). "The Norse Style of Ornamentation in the Viking Settlements", Acta Arch. XIX (1948), 69–113.

Shetelig, H. See also J. Petersen.

SHR. *The Scottish Historical Review*, Edinburgh.

Simpson, W. D. (1927). *The Historical Saint Columba*, Aberdeen 1927 (2nd. edn. 1927).

Simpson, W. D. (1935). *The Celtic Church in Scotland*, Aberdeen 1935.

Simpson, W. D. (1943). *The Province of Mar*, Aberdeen 1943.

Skene, W. F. (1836). *The Highlanders of Scotland*, London 1836 (2nd. edn. A. Macbain, Stirling 1902).

Skene, W. F. (1876–80). *Celtic Scotland*, 3 vols., Edinburgh 1876–1880 (2nd. edn. 1886–1890).

Skene, W. F. See also Chronicles.

Sprockhoff, E. (1941). "Niedersaschens Bedeutung für die Bronzezeit Westeuropas", *Bericht der Römisch-Germanischen Kommission* XXXI (1941), 1–138, Berlin.

Stenton, F. M. (1943). *Anglo-Saxon England*, Oxford 1943 (2nd. edn. 1947).

Stevenson, R. B. K. (1944). "Some Relics from Kildalton, Islay", PSAS LXXVIII (1943–44), 120–125.

Stevenson, R. B. K. (1949a). "Braidwood Fort, Midlothian", PSAS LXXXIII (1948–49), 1–11.

Stevenson, R. B. K. (1949b). "The Nuclear Fort of Dalmahoy, Midlothian, and other Dark Age Capitals", PSAS LXXXIII (1948–49), 186–198.

Stokes, W. (1890). "On the Linguistic Value of the Irish Annals", TPS (1888–90), 365–433.

Stokes, W. See also ATig.

Stuart, J. (1856–67). *Sculptured Stones of Scotland*, 2 vols., Aberdeen 1856 (vol. I) and Edinburgh 1867 (vol. II).

Surtees. *The Publications of the Surtees Society*, London.

TGS. *Transactions of the Gaelic Society of Inverness*, Inverness.

Thorpe, B. See ASC.

Thurneysen, R. (1884). *Keltoromanisches*, Halle 1884.

TPS. *Transactions of the Philological Society*, London.

Ure, D. (1793). *The History of Rutherglen and East-Kilbride*, Glasgow 1793.

Varley, W. J. (1948). "The Hill-Forts of the Welsh Marches", ArchJ CV (1948), 41–66.

Vendryes, J. (1924). "Remarques sur les graffites de la Graufesenque", BSLP XXV (1924), 34–43.

Vendryes, J. (1940). "Prydain et Britanni", MacNeill Essays, 160–166.

Waddell, J. J. (1932). "Cross-slabs recently discovered at Fowlis Wester and Millport", PSAS LXVI (1931–32), 409–412.

Wainwright, F. T. (1948a). "Nechtanesmere", Antiquity XXII (1948), 82–97.

Wainwright, F. T. (1948b). "Ingimund's Invasion", EHR LXIII (1948), 145–169.

Wainwright, F. T. (1949). "Problems and Policies", Antiquity XXIII (1949), 73–82.

Wainwright, F. T. (1951). "A Symbol Stone at Kinblethmont, Angus", PSAS LXXXV (1950–51), 180–182.

Wainwright, F. T. (1953a). "A Souterrain Identified in Angus", AntJ XXXIII (1953), 65–71.

Wainwright, F. T. (1953b). "Souterrains in Scotland", Antiquity XXVII (1953), 219-232.

Wainwright, F. T. See also Ardestie and Carlungie Reports.

Watson, W. J. (1913). "The Circular Forts of North Perthshire", PSAS XLVII (1912–13), 30–60.

Watson, W. J. (1915). "Circular Forts in Lorn and North Perthshire; with a Note on the Excavation of one at Borenich, Loch Tummel", PSAS XLIX (1914–15), 17–32.

Watson, W. J. (1926). *The History of the Celtic Place-names of Scotland*, Edinburgh 1926.

Werner, J. (1951). "Ein Langobardischer Schild von Ischl", *Bayerische Vorgeschichtsblätter* XVIII (1951), 45–58, München.

Wheeler, R. E. M. (1952). "Earthwork since Hadrian Allcroft", ArchJ CVI Supplement (1952), 62–82.

Williams, I. (1938). *Canu Aneirin*, Cardiff 1938.

Wilson, D. (1851). *The Archaeology and Prehistoric Annals of Scotland*, Edinburgh 1851 (2nd. edn., *Prehistoric Annals of Scotland*, 2 vols., London and Cambridge 1863).

YCS. *Yorkshire Celtic Studies*, Leeds.

Young, H. W. (1890). "The Ancient Bath at Burghead", PSAS XXIV (1889–90), 147–156.

Young, H. W. (1891). "Notes on the Ramparts of Burghead as revealed by recent Excavations", PSAS XXV (1890–91), 435–447.

Young, H. W. (1893). "Notes on Further Excavations at Burghead", PSAS XXVII (1892–93), 86–91.

Zimmer, H. (1898). "Matriarchy among the Picts", in G. Henderson (1898), 1–42.

INDEX

Printed by John G Eccles Printers Ltd, Inverness